THE POLITICS OF
MILITARY OCCUPATION

Peter M. R. Stirk

EDINBURGH
University Press

© Peter M. R. Stirk, 2009, 2012

First published in hardback in 2009 by
Edinburgh University Press Ltd
22 George Square, Edinburgh EH8 9LF

www.euppublishing.com

This paperback edition 2012

Typeset in Sabon
by Servis Filmsetting Ltd, Stockport, Cheshire, and
printed and bound in Great Britain by
CPI Group (UK) Ltd, Croydon CR0 4YY

A CIP record for this book is available from the British Library

ISBN 978 0 7486 4484 1 (paperback)

Contents

Acknowledgements

I am grateful to Durham University for Research Leave in 2007 that enabled me to begin writing this book and to The Leverhulme Trust for the award of a Research Fellowship in 2008 that enabled me to complete it.

Introduction

Military occupation has been a recurrent feature of recent history and is recognised as a distinct phenomenon in international law, most notably in the Hague Regulations of 1907 which remain in force today. It is a phenomenon which excites great passion especially because of the savagery which often accompanies it. In this respect the paintings and drawings of Francisco de Goya symbolise the cruelties of military occupation in a way analogous to Picasso's synthesis of the horrors of modern warfare in his depiction of the destruction of Guernica. Yet despite the relative legal continuity of definition and the passions excited by the experience of particular occupations reflection upon the phenomenon has been discontinuous and fragmentary. Each occupation has invoked its own outpouring of commentary and memoir, either lamenting the shortcomings of occupation policies and the unanticipated difficulties encountered by military occupiers or the suffering inflicted upon the inhabitants of occupied territory, or celebrating the real or supposed successes and restraint of the occupiers. Occupation, or the prospect of it, has sometimes induced reflection upon earlier occupations, usually in the hope of drawing useful lessons for the impending occupation.[1] More recently, the opening of government archives or the desire to redress the victor's image of military occupation and to recapture the experience of occupation from the viewpoint of the defeated populations subject to military occupation has induced further reflection.[2] Much of this, however, has concerned itself with particular instances of occupation.

Systematic and comparative studies of military occupation remain however rare. This is true even in the field of international law where one might have expected more continuity.[3] It may be that part at least of the reason for this curious neglect lies in the nature of military occupation. It is usually regarded as a product of warfare but is to varying degrees distinct from the conduct of hostilities. As such it has frequently been resented, disparaged, and even feared, by military officers for whom it has been an unwanted burden for which they have not been trained. It is supposedly regulated by international law and yet it frequently entails activities, such as the administration of justice within a territory, the imposition and collection of taxes, the regulation of public health, and even the holding of elections, which are usually regarded as falling within the remit of the domestic authority of a state. By the same token, although it might be said to be a form of government, it is the government of the inhabitants of one state by the armed forces, and other agents, of another state or coalition of states. It involves the claim to exercise authority, and not merely power, yet it is an authority of a distinctive and peculiar kind for it is exercised under the circumstance of the 'authority of the legitimate power having in fact passed into the hands of the occupant'.[4]

A second reason for the lack of systematic study may be the fact that the concept of military occupation, as distinct from conquest, for example, emerged only slowly during the nineteenth century. Even approximately one century after the Hague Regulations of 1907 sought to stabilise understanding of the phenomenon, conflation of the two categories can easily be found in academic studies of military occupation.[5] Nor is it only conquest and occupation that can fuse in the minds of occupiers and observers. The boundary between occupation and empire or occupation and intervention can also appear to be a fluid one. The difficulty in distinguishing between occupation and intervention may have been compounded by the fact that both concepts are products of the upheavals brought about by the French Revolution and the Napoleonic wars, though intervention is undoubtedly the more elastic term, never receiving the kind of international legal definition given to occupation.[6] Similarly, military occupation has been so closely construed as a product of warfare that it has been held to be incompatible with the notion of military occupation in the absence of violent resistance by the inhabitants of occupied territory. Yet, on the eve of the First World War, a French author devoted a substantial volume to military occupations beyond the realm of war. It was, he noted, the first study of its kind.[7] These difficulties of definition and distinction are not primarily the product of carelessness but rather of the fact that military occupation is a disputed normative concept. It is a moral status with an attendant set of obligations imposed upon occupiers, those subject to military occupation and other parties. Occupiers and others frequently violate those obligations, even in their own eyes. That, however, is no more an obstacle to holding that military occupation is a moral status than is deviant behaviour from any other norm.

The fact that military occupation is a normative concept, and one of relatively recent historical provenance, suggests a third reason for the lack of systematic and comparative study. Precisely because of the savagery depicted by Goya and amplified in the twentieth century beyond what Goya could have imagined, military occupation has come to be seen as an inherently disreputable activity. Occupation, as Paul Bremer, Administrator of the Coalition Provisional Authority in Iraq, said is 'an ugly word'.[8] Military occupiers have preferred, therefore, to describe themselves as something else. They have preferred to see themselves as liberators or allies upholding natural or international law rather than as the oppressors, enemies and tyrants that they associate with military occupation. Such evasion undoubtedly became more common after the Second World War.[9] However, it will be suggested below that it has a pedigree as long as that of the concept of military occupation. It is notable also that there is an increasing tendency to question such evasive strategies, even where they are apparently most plausible, that is in the case of certain activities authorised by the United Nations.[10] Nevertheless, the accumulated antipathy to military occupation as a practice, quite understandable in the light of the conduct of many occupiers, is probably the third reason for the lack of comparative and systematic study of military occupation.

None of these obstacles is trivial. All pose significant problems for those who wish to understand the phenomenon of military occupation and, arguably even more so, for those engaged in or subject to military occupation. Any attempt at understanding military occupation also involves a choice about what approach or perspective to adopt. Here, there is no sole approach or perspective that recommends itself to the exclusion of all others. It is evident from the comments made above that the approach adopted in this text is in part at least normative. It is not necessary to adopt a normative approach. It is possible to explicitly disavow such an approach and to enquire, for example, into the conditions which account for the 'success' or 'failure' of military occupations in terms of 'whether the occupying power accomplished its goals and at what cost'.[11] A related approach is summarised in the title *Does Conquest Pay?*[12]

Assuming that a normative approach is adopted there are still choices to be made. It is clearly possible to approach military occupation in terms of existing international law or in terms of what one believes should become international law. Indeed, if one sets aside historical studies of specific occupations or occupiers, this is the most

3

common approach to the phenomenon. It can lead to defence of the practice of military occupation, either in general or in particular cases, or to a condemnation of the practices of at least some, and often most, military occupiers. The dilemma of whether the law of occupation should serve to buttress the activities of military occupiers or to constrain them was indeed present in the minds of those who first sought to codify the law of military occupation, as will be shown below. It has been much more common recently, however, for exposition of the law of occupation to issue in condemnation of occupiers. It is also possible to reach a similar conclusion by deploying normative arguments that explicitly seek to legitimate resistance to military occupiers.[13]

The approach adopted in this text draws heavily upon normative legal arguments, but does so from a specific perspective. In the first place it seeks to use such arguments in order to elucidate how military occupiers have understood their status and role. This is important because uncertainty and confusion about the nature of military occupation are recurrent features of the practice of military occupation. That uncertainty is compounded by the fact that occupiers frequently believe that they are faced with unprecedented problems for which they have been ill-prepared and for whose management they have inadequate resources. In the second place it seeks to use such arguments in a way that does not deviate so far from the practice of at least some military occupiers as to be incomprehensible to them or set standards that they must inevitably fail to meet.[14] In the third place it seeks to set such arguments in the context of military occupation as a political phenomenon, that is, above all else, as a form of government. That military occupation entailed military government was once a widely accepted assumption.[15] The term fell into neglect as part of the process that culminated in the evasion of the label of military occupation. The disrepute was already evident in a comment recalled by F. S. V. Donnison from discussion about the impending military government of Burma in the Second World War: 'Surely we don't speak of military *government*? We have civil *government* but only military *administration*'. As Donnison observed the distinction was a 'dangerous misconception'.[16] It was dangerous precisely because it sought to deny the reality of military government.

The following chapters seek to unfold the implications of this basic claim that military occupation is a political phenomenon and above all a form of government. This text makes no pretensions to be a history of military occupation. Too many instances of the genre find no mention or highly selective discussion in order to illustrate specific points. Some understanding of the evolving practice of military occupation is necessary and Chapter 1 is devoted to this task. It is important because military occupation is often presented in terms of trajectories, from a concern with relations between states and state elites to a concern with protection of human rights, or from a willingness to tolerate and even preserve the institutions of occupied territories to a commitment to regime transformation, that are partial truths. The practice of military occupation is neither a static recurrence of age-old verities nor a linear progression either in terms of a reduction of the harshness of military occupation or an increasing transgression of once-recognised limits.

Chapter 2 is devoted to the problem of defining military occupation. This might seem a simple task, and some accounts of military occupation presume that it is.[17] It is not. The concept of military occupation only gained clarity slowly, in distinction from the concept of conquest, and was subsequently muddied by the attempts of occupiers to evade that status. The definition of military occupation is important because it potentially gives greater clarity about the moral status of military occupiers as well as the range of instances covered by the term. It tells us little, however, about the contours of military government itself.

Discussion of that issue is divided into two separate chapters, Chapter 3 on forms of military government, that is government instituted by military officers through a military chain of command, and Chapter 4 on the role of civilian governors in military occupations. This separation may seem to revive the 'dangerous misconception' against which Donnison warned, but it does not. In both cases the authority of the government rests upon the presence of military forces. It is nevertheless the case that at various times civilian agencies and actors distinct from the military chain of command have been deployed breaking the apparently monolithic unity of the occupier. It is also the case that these agencies and actors create distinctive difficulties for the occupation regime, not necessarily to the benefit of the inhabitants of occupied territory.

Chapter 5 takes up a theme that is essential to any form of government, namely the political obligation of the inhabitants to the government. Yet if the term military government in the context of occupation has fallen into neglect and disrepute, the concept of obligation has been so entirely repressed as to appear to have left little trace. This was not always the case. Obligation was regarded as central, yet also as problematic. This chapter seeks to explain why discussion of obligation disappeared from the agenda, save in lapidary references in military manuals, and suggests how obligation might be plausibly understood to exist. It does not presume or imply that obligation is owed to the occupation regime regardless of the nature and policies of the occupation regime.

No such neglect has befallen the theme of Chapter 6, namely the concept of sovereignty. Indeed, if anything, the concept of sovereignty is now made to do too much work. From the recognition that the occupier is not the sovereign power which formed the core of the emerging concept of military occupation, statesmen and observers have moved on to presume that sovereignty must persist somewhere untarnished by the fact of military occupation. This chapter suggests that this is to fundamentally underestimate the fragility of polities subject to military occupation. Ironically, the attempt to mitigate the impact of military occupation by insisting upon the persistence of sovereignty or its rapid return to the occupied masks rather than mitigates the threat to the community from which such insistence seeks to protect it.

The theme of Chapter 7, justice, has also seen no diminution of interest and discussion. Justice, the rule of law, is often seen as the potential constraint upon the tyrannical and arbitrary behaviour of the occupier. Yet, as indicated above, it was clear from the outset that law in the shape of the law of military occupation could buttress as well as constrain the status of the occupier. Justice under conditions of military occupation is inevitably the victor's justice and will to some degree inevitably carry the pejorative taint suggested by that term. This chapter seeks to elaborate the Janus face of justice under military occupation and warns against expecting too much from appeals to the rule of law or to human rights as a barrier to the potential caprice of occupiers. Here too, expecting too much from the language of human rights may serve to mask the distinctive status of the occupier and that of those subject to occupation, to the benefit of the former rather than the latter.

Chapter 8 deals with one of the most pressing contemporary concerns with military occupation, namely regime transformation or 'imposed constitutionalism'.[18] It is contentious because Article 43 of the Hague Regulations has been understood as embodying an injunction to conserve the existing constitutional order, save where it is necessarily suspended by virtue of the fact of occupation and the dictates of military necessity. It is also contentious because the imposition of a constitutional order is seen as inconsistent with the principle of self-determination. It is suggested, however, that in some circumstances regime transformation may be the only way in which to bring military occupation to an end short of even less-desirable outcomes. This is, of course, no guarantee that occupiers will engage in such a project, still less that they will succeed in any meaningful sense.

The Conclusion offers some final reflections on the difficulties inherent in trying to understand military occupation as a political phenomenon and the nature of the challenges it poses to those engaged in it.

Notes

1. A prime example is Ernst Fraenkel [1944], 'Military occupation and the rule of law', in Ernst Fraenkel, *Gesammelte Schriften*, vol. 3 (Baden-Baden: Nomos, 1999), pp. 139–347, which was commissioned by the Carnegie Endowment for International Peace.
2. See for example John Dower, *Embracing Defeat* (London: Penguin, 1999); Giles McDonogh, *After the Reich* (London: Murray, 2007); Norman Naimark, *The Russians in Germany* (Cambridge, MA: Harvard University Press, 1995).
3. Eyal Benevenisti's *The International Law of Occupation* (Princeton, NJ: Princeton University Press, 2004), first published in 1993, has been a notable exception in recent decades. More recently, David M. Edelstein, *Occupational Hazards. Success and Failure in Military Occupation* (Ithaca, NY: Cornell University Press, 2008), is a welcome exception to what he notes is a surprising neglect, ibid. pp. 15–16. There are older studies, usually concerned with the development of the law of military occupation, such as Gerhard von Glahn, *The Occupation of Enemy Territory* (Minneapolis, MN: University of Minnesota Press, 1957); Doris Apel Graber, *The Development of the Law of Belligerent Occupation 1863–1914* (New York, NY: AMS, 1949); and Ernst Feilchenfeld's *The International Economic Law of Belligerent Occupation* (Washington, DC: Carnegie, 1942).
4. Article 43 of the Regulations Respecting the Laws and Customs of War on Land Annexed to the International Convention Concerning the Laws and Customs of War on Land signed at the Hague on 18 October 1907. Further reference to these Regulations will simply specify the article number, Hague Regulations, 1907.
5. A striking example is Eric Carlton, *Occupation. The Policies and Practices of Military Conquerors* (London: Routledge, 1992) which stretches from the practices of the ancient Assyrians through to the Iraqi

occupation of Kuwait in 1990 to 1991 and confounds conquest, colonialism and occupation. There is also an evident lack of discrimination in the title of Peter Liberman, *Does Conquest Pay? The Exploitation of Occupied Industrial Societies* (Princeton, NJ: Princeton University Press, 1996).

6. This, of course, does not mean that definitions of intervention are wanting. See the definition of intervention in the classic study by R. J. Vincent, *Nonintervention and International Order* (Princeton, NJ: Princeton University Press, 1974), p. 13, as 'that activity undertaken by a state, a group of states, or an international organization which interferes coercively in the domestic affairs of another state. It is a discrete event having a beginning and an end, and it is aimed at the authority structure of the target state. It is not necessarily lawful or unlawful, but it does break a conventional pattern of international relations'.

7. Raymond Robin, *Des Occupations Militaries en Dehors des Occupations de Guerre* (Washington: Carnegie, [1913] 1942). This is a partial translation of the much longer French text of 1913.

8. Quoted in Ivo H. Daalder and James M. Lindsay, *America Unbound* (Washington, DC: Brookings Institution Press, 2003), p. 154.

9. Benvenisti, *The International Law of Occupation*, pp. 149–50.

10. See Gregory H. Fox's advocacy of the term 'humanitarian occupation' where 'others use terms such as "international territorial administration", "internationalized territory" and "neo-trusteeship"'. *Humanitarian Occupation* (Cambridge: Cambridge University Press, 2008), p. 3.

11. See Edelstein, *Occupational Hazards*, p. 7. For the explicit disavowal of a normative approach, see p. 17. This does not make Edelstein an advocate of military occupation. He says it 'should be an option of last resort', p. 169.

12. Liberman, *Does Conquest Pay?*

13. See Karma Nabulsi, *Traditions of War* (Oxford: Oxford University Press, 1999).

14. In that sense, it aspires to follow Michael Walzer's strategy in his *Just and Unjust Wars* (Harmondsworth: Penguin, 1980). It does not share his view that the lawyers have constructed a world divorced from the moral world inhabited by occupiers, at least not in a systematic way. Without wishing to dismiss the tension between the law and practice of occupation, it is worth emphasising that the military officers and lawyers close to them have played a crucial role in the formulation of the law of military occupation.

15. See, for example, William E. Birkhimer, *Military Government and Martial Law* (Kansas, MO: Hudson, 1914).

16. F. S. V. Donnison, *Civil Affairs and Military Government. Central Organization and Planning* (London: HMSO, 1966), p. 19.

17. See the problematic definition in Edelstein, *Occupational Hazards*: 'To be an occupation, the intervening power must take control of the occupied territory and exercise sovereignty over that territory for a significant length of time', p. 4.
18. The latter phrase is that of Noah Feldman, 'Imposed constitutionalism', *Connecticut Law Review*, 37 (2005), pp. 857–89.

Chapter 1

The Evolving Practice and Meaning of Military Occupation

Tracing the evolving practice and meaning of military occupation immediately encounters problems of definition and chronology. Both are compounded by the fact that military occupation is an unusual and problematic political phenomenon because it breaks through many distinctions by which political life is normally organised and understood, as it also breaks through analogous legal distinctions.[1] Under conditions of military occupation the distinctions between the international and the domestic, between war and peace (or at least active armed conflict and its cessation), between violence and the exercise of political authority, become fluid and uncertain. Given these peculiarities, as well as the diversity of conditions in which military occupation has taken place, it is not surprising that doubt has been expressed about the definition and utility of the concept of military occupation and the numerous other qualifications of the term occupation, though others have suggested, for example, that despite the variety of forms, the 'core meaning is obvious enough'.[2] As will be demonstrated below, the core meaning has often been in dispute. More importantly, there has been uncertainty about the core meaning not only in the minds of commentators or even the draftsmen of military manuals and legal conventions, but also in the minds of occupiers and occupied populations. As General von Voigts-Rhetz, one of the German delegates to the Brussels Conference of 1874 which paved the way for the subsequent Hague Peace Conferences, pointed out, that could have disastrous consequences for occupied populations.[3]

There is somewhat less uncertainty about how to date the phenomenon, though still significant divergence. Some accounts simply take the Hague Regulations of 1907 as the starting point, though usually noting that these were the culmination of earlier commentary and codification.[4] There is something to be said for this given the striking resilience of those Regulations in the face of the divergent practices

10

of occupiers.[5] An alternative is to trace back that earlier tradition of commentary and codification which typically leads to the Lieber Code of 1863, that is, to the General Orders number 100 issued to the Union armies in the American Civil War.[6] While such landmark codes provide neat chronological precision and link periodisation with such analytical clarity as the codes possess, they remain a retrospective attempt to clarify the practice of military occupation, as well as being a normative claim to bind the future practice of military occupation and to avoid what were seen as the errors and vices of earlier practice.

A better guide is provided by the basic conceptual distinction between conquest and occupation that is most widely accepted as fundamental to the emergence of military occupation as a distinctive form of military government and temporary authority. According to a French publicist, 'before the nineteenth century, publicists and statesmen adopted the opinion that the taking possession of the territory of one belligerent by another, conferred on the latter the power of freely disposing of it'. In his own day, he continued, such confusion was generally avoided.[7] The distinction was insisted upon as early as 1819 in Jean Louis Klüber's *Droit des Gens Moderne de l'Europe* and complaint about the confusion of the two was evident as early as 1844.[8] By the end of the century, the importance of the distinction was widely noted by Englishmen such as Robert Phillimore, Latin Americans such as Carlos Calvo and Italians such as Pasquale Fiore.[9] The consensus was of progress from an earlier age, before the nineteenth century, when the brute fact of the assertion of authority by military force amounted to the assertion of sovereignty, to one in which temporary assertion of authority (military occupation) was distinguished from the permanent assertion of authority (conquest) which typically took place only by virtue of confirmation in a treaty of peace.

This is indeed consistent with the emergence of increasingly detailed commentaries, military manuals and conventions dealing with military occupation as a distinct phenomenon. The picture which this sequential transition suggests is however misleading. It is misleading because it exaggerates the dominance of the norms and practice of conquest. Conquest was indeed recognised in a way that it is not now since the Kellogg–Briand Pact, the proclamation of the Stimson Doctrine and other international agreements and declarations, whether unilateral or multilateral. It is, however, important to be precise about what was involved in the acceptance of conquest in earlier periods. For much of the medieval and early modern period of European history, conquest was so bound up with just war theory that brute conquest alone was rarely seen as sufficient, especially if this amounted to less than conquest of the whole country. At the time of the Thirty Years War, mere conquest was regarded by the French as a very inferior type of claim, while the Spanish held brute conquest, even when supplemented by the passage of time, to be a threat to stability.[10] Examples drawn from the sixteenth and seventeenth centuries that appear to confirm the contrary often turn out to be more equivocal than they seem to be at first glance.[11]

Nor was the concept of unrestrained sovereignty sufficiently well formulated to facilitate the idea that one sovereignty could be displaced by another in its entirety by nothing more than brute conquest. Yet it is precisely this that is often suggested, or implied, by referring to a period in which conquest was an accepted part of international relations. Hence, when Irénée Lameire searched the archives of France and surrounding territories, which he believed to offer the most promising source of evidence of an immediate displacement of sovereignty brought about solely by conquest, he found little before the sixteenth century, and the late sixteenth century at that. Even later, he found much evidence of what he termed the 'precariousness', as well as simple uncertainty, about changes in sovereign title. It is true, however, that he found more evidence as the eighteenth century unfolded.[12]

The irony of this is that, as Lameire himself noted, at the end of the eighteenth century, in revolutionary France, we have the first principled declaration of the renunciation of conquest as a means of foreign policy. This renunciation played a role in discrediting the sheer possession of power as sufficient title to hold territory, though that presumption in favour of sheer possession was, as already indicated, something of recent provenance and far from unaffected by other considerations in most cases. So too did the conquests made by revolutionary and Napoleonic armies; the conquests were justified in the name of liberation. As one revolutionary put it as early as 1791: 'This is a crusade for the freedom of all . . . Each soldier will speak thus to his enemy: Brother, I do not come to slay you. I come to free you from the yoke under which you are groaning'.[13] The reality was that French armies treated the territory they occupied as enemy territory from which they expected to live.

Foreshadowing the later involvement of civilian agencies in military occupations 'representatives on mission' dispatched by the revolutionary Convention organised the exploitation of occupied territory, in some cases under the appropriately named 'agencies of commerce and extraction'.[14] Sometimes these representatives, like the later army commissaries and intendant-generals, clashed with the generals of the armies but rarely succeeded in controlling their excesses.[15] Operating on the basis of a right of conquest that more clearly resembled the right misleadingly ascribed by publicists to an earlier age, Napoleon redrew the political map of much of Europe – though as one historian has observed in respect of Italy these structures never 'lost this aspect of impermanence, of improvisation'.[16] That was, of course, emphasised by the publicists who celebrated the triumph over the French revolutionaries and their heir, Napoleon Bonaparte. Thus, Arnold von Heeren, under the subtitle 'Restoration of the political system of Europe', wrote that 'our European princes are legitimate rulers, not because they happen to be in possession of power, for this would apply with equal force to a usurper, but because they are so in point of law, owing to their right of succession'.[17] Mere possession of power, a longstanding problem in the shape of the usurper, had taken on new form in the shape of a military occupier, albeit one who asserted a right to transform political institutions and society on a hitherto unknown scale.

This was not the only problem to be bequeathed by the revolutionary and Napoleonic era. The most striking was that of the partisans or guerrillas who operated in Spain after Napoleon's defeat of traditional Spanish armies. Openly described as 'land pirates' by the junta that called for their formation, their resistance was condemned as banditry by Marshall Soult, with execution the penalty for their resistance.[18] The result was a vicious conflict which also turned Spaniard against Spaniard but whose chief legacy was its, albeit disputed, part in Napoleon's downfall and the clash between the authority proclaimed by the occupier and the right of resistance proclaimed by the Spanish partisans.

These were, to be sure, not the only models and experiences of military occupation in this era. France's enemies had been occupiers as well. The Duke of Wellington's much-quoted retrospective gloss offered a different model of military occupation:

> I have governed a large portion of the population of a country by my own will. But then, what did I do? I declared that the country should be governed according to its own national law . . . I governed the country strictly by the laws of the country; and I governed it with such moderation, I must say, that political servants and judges, who at first fled, or

had been expelled, afterwards consented to act under my direction. The judges sat in the courts of law, conducting their judicial business, and administered the law under my direction.[19]

This ignored the chaos and disorder following on from the flight of these officials, as well as Wellington's sometimes very close involvement in the details of government. However, it was to be an aspiration of some military occupiers, if only because it promised to relieve them of the burdens of government, especially, as was almost invariably the case, when the resources and personnel at their disposal were insufficient to take over the full range of government activities.[20] The Allied military occupation of France imposed by the Treaty of Paris, confined as it was to certain frontier districts, entailed even less activity but it stood as guarantor of 'the re-establishment of order and tranquillity'.[21]

Although such 'pacific' occupations, as some later designated them, were quite common, it was military operations that were to bring more clarity to the nature of military occupation. As American armies prepared to invade Mexican territory in 1846, Secretary of War Marcy advised Brigadier-General Stephen Kearny that he should 'establish temporary civil government', although the clear intent of the enterprise was annexation. He added that 'it is foreseen that what relates to civil government will be a difficult and unpleasant part of your duty, and much must necessarily be left to your discretion'.[22] The difficulties of implementing military government was to be a recurrent theme, as was the discretion left to military commanders who were not necessarily well prepared for the task. General Scott, who occupied Mexico as part of the same war the following year, had however studied the record of Napoleon's disastrous occupation of Spain. Conscious that attacks on the Catholic religion and its institutions had embittered that conflict, Scott was determined to avoid a repetition of such events and took elaborate precautions to reassure Mexico's Catholics of his respect for their religion.[23] That also involved strict measures to maintain discipline among his own soldiers, a lack of which exposed the absence of any specific provision for punishing crimes committed by Americans outside the territorial borders of the United States. He rectified this through his General Orders number 287, which provided for military commissions to try certain types of case.[24] He preferred, however, to leave the administration of justice between Mexicans to Mexican courts. As American military commanders struggled with varying success to implement military government, Colonel Mason discovered a problem which was only later resolved, at least to the satisfaction of the Supreme Court, namely that whilst the war with Mexico lasted he understood that his authority derived from the laws of war. After the Treaty of Guadaloupe-Hidalgo ending the war with Mexico but before the admission of the new state to the Union, it was not clear what the source of authority of the Union's military governors was.[25]

Further complications arose in the American Civil War. Indeed, a later commentator lamented the fact that much of American law on military occupation stemmed from this rebellion.[26] From the viewpoint of the Union forces, the Confederate states were in revolt and Union leaders were inevitably influence by the sentiment that, as one military governor put it, 'treason must be made odious'.[27] Yet it seemed impossible to treat the Confederates as traitors or outlaws as Soult had declared the Spanish partisans to be. The alternative seemed to be to treat them as belligerents and the governments established in reclaimed Confederate territory as military governments, as if they were in foreign territory. The difficulty in reconciling the two views was reflected in the Lieber Code which allowed for treating them as belligerents on the grounds of humanity while claiming this 'does in no way whatever imply a partial or complete acknowledgement of their government . . . or of them, as an independent or sovereign power'.[28] By the time Lieber's code was promulgated, military occupation and military governments were facts created by the success of Union armies. It was also already clear that there were tensions between advocates of government by military commanders and government by civilians, even if the latter had been given commissions to enhance their status. Speaking for the former, General Grant declared: 'Please advise the President not to attempt to doctor up a State Government for Georgia by the appointment of citizens in any capacity whatever'.[29]

As with the revolutionary and Napoleonic armies of France, military occupation became linked to imposed constitutions. 'Imposed constitutionalism', though often regarded as a recent phenomenon, was not only a feature of those wars but also of the Civil War, extending by virtue of Presidential authority and, when this was deemed insufficient, by virtue of the Reconstruction Acts of 1867, well into the post-war period.[30] Uncertainty about the requisite authority to justify such government, as well as the passage of a third act to deflect attempts to challenge the remit of military government, indicate the difficulties experienced in dealing not just with the fact that military occupation per se breaks through normal distinctions and practices but also with adapting rudimentary customs designed for inter-state war to conditions of civil war.

Despite these complications, the Lieber Code promulgated during that war undoubtedly exercised considerable influence on subsequent publicists and codifiers. By the time the latter gathered in Brussels in 1874 they had a more recent experience to reflect upon, namely the Franco-Prussian war of 1870–1. Although, as always, the protagonists disagreed sharply about the events of the occupation and even more so about their legality, there was no doubt that Prussian rule was severe. Such severity, noted Spaight, was 'undoubtedly successful', though he questioned its prudence because, but for the short duration of the war, 'France might have proved to the Germans what Spain proved to the French sixty years before – a country one could defeat but never subdue'.[31] The severity included the use of forced guides and forced labour, the taking of hostages and the burning and pillage of the village of L'Isle Adam on the grounds that the resistance shown by its inhabitants took place in already occupied territory; a status denied by French publicists. In general, however, there was no dispute, with the exception of clear German intent to annex Alsace-Lorraine, that this was a matter of military occupation. What was prominent and contentious was the position of French citizens in occupied territory caught between the injunctions of German occupation authorities and countervailing instructions still being issued by a French government, especially when a Republic was proclaimed in place of the French Empire, whose emperor was in German captivity.[32]

It was inevitable that these issues concerned the delegates who met at Brussels in 1874 and that the definition of occupation, the right to resort to a *levée en masse,* and the extent of the authority of the occupier should occasion dispute. There was no dispute that military occupation and conquest were two different things and agreement was reached without much difficulty on the principle that the occupier 'will maintain the laws which were in force in the country in time of peace, and will only modify, suspend, or replace them by others if necessity obliges him to do so'.[33] It has been held that given the envisaged brevity of occupation and low level of state involvement in the economy this was, at the time, a plausible assumption, but that the subsequent expansion of the state rendered it problematic. While there is some truth in this, occupiers and publicists did not necessarily share this view. Germans in France had struggled in vain with the complexities of the French taxation system in the absence of many French tax officials.[34] The general point was well put before the First World War by Spaight: 'In all civilized countries there exists a vast and complex organism whose function is the performance of all those duties for the sake of which all State Government is established. That organism is, *anglice*, the "Civil Service"'.[35] It was less the absence of a complex organism and rather the existence of it that tempted the delegates at Brussels to presume that the proposed restraint was relatively unproblematic. Where it did not exist, as in Bulgaria when the Russians occupied that territory in 1877–8, the occupier established a 'new social and political *régime*'.[36]

There was more respect for existing laws in the Japanese occupations in connection with the Russo-Japanese war of 1904–5, though this was eased by the fact that much of the occupied territory was in fact neutral Chinese territory.[37] There was even respect for Transvaal law in the Boer war despite the fact that the British had proclaimed the annexation of the Orange Free State and the Transvaal. The fact that they announced the annexations before even achieving effective military occupation of the territories was widely criticised, even in the House of Commons where James Bryce denounced this 'monstrous proclamation ... based on a paper annexation ... which purported to treat the inhabitants of the two Republics as rebels – rebels, forsooth, on the basis of a paper annexation'.[38] The clarity of formal codification still clearly left scope for considerable variation in practice. Nor did such clarity extend to providing detailed guidance for military governors. As Lord Milner, Governor of the Cape Colony lamented: 'Unfortunately there are no British regulations defining the powers and duties of a Military Governor'.[39]

A different kind of occupation took place at roughly the same time as a result of the Spanish-American war that broke out in 1898. Cuba, Puerto Rico and the Philippines were amongst the territories occupied by American forces. Cuba presented a peculiar problem because it was not envisaged for annexation, the fate of Puerto Rico, or transformation into a colony, the fate of the Philippines, but nor did the Americans abandon their occupation upon termination of the war with Spain. In justification of the position of American occupying forces, Charles Magoon suggested

> if the doctrine is correct that a military government is a substitute, *ad interim*, for sovereignty, and further, that the purposes for which the military forces of the United States were sent to Cuba are uncompleted, it would seem to follow that said military government may properly

exercise the rights of a belligerent without regard to the fact that the war has ended.[40]

This was not the first time that American forces had remained in occupation, engaged in the transformation of a political regime. That had already happened in the reconstruction of the southern states at the end of the Civil War, and indeed earlier in the occupation of California and New Mexico at the end of the American-Mexican war of 1846–8.[41] In these cases the territory was, or was intended to become, part of the United States. That was not the case in Cuba.

Despite these and numerous other military occupations, the First World War found military occupiers unprepared for the task of government. It was not, as is sometimes mistakenly asserted, the first time that military occupiers failed to respect existing laws and institutions. Yet that requirement was now firmly enshrined in Article 43 of the Hague Conventions:

> The authority of the legitimate power having in fact passed into the hands of the occupant, the later shall take all the measures in his power to restore and ensure, as far as possible, public order and civil life, while respecting, unless absolutely prevented, the laws in force in the country.[42]

The occupied had, of course, an interest in restrictive interpretations of this provision, or at least exiled governments and those loyal to them did. When occupiers themselves became subject to military occupation they too discovered the virtues of such restrictive interpretations, regardless of their earlier arguments and practice. During the war, and in much subsequent argument, Belgium's fate formed the focus of attention. The centrality of Belgium in the propaganda battle between the two alliances, violation of Belgian neutrality having been cited by Britain as the reason for its entry into the war, the prolonged nature of the occupation, and the vigour of Belgian arguments, all contributed to this focus. Yet military occupation was a fact elsewhere, across swathes of Eastern Europe and into the Middle East and Africa. Reporting on the occupation of Lemberg in the eastern parts of the Austro-Hungarian Empire, Sigmund Cybichowski noted that occupiers, in this case the Russians, were all too tempted to abandon the constraints of military occupation in favour of the old doctrines of conquest as soon as their confidence in ultimate victory grew.[43] Visions of a post-war order played a role in the West as well. For Belgium, this would probably have meant control of its ports and infrastructure and the subordination of its military forces to Germany, leaving behind the shell of a nominally independent state, or possibly separate states for the Walloon and Flemish popula-tions.[44] Yet the practice of military occupation was driven as much, or more, by the exigencies of war as by these visions. Here, recalled a member of the German occupation authorities, Ludwig von Köhler, the Germans found 'a situation which was tantamount to the disso-lution of the constitutional order'. The fleeing government had even taken the plates used for printing banknotes. In general, 'the whole Belgian state machinery was not only at a standstill but was com-pletely incapable of functioning'.[45] The German response turned into what von Köhler described as 'over organisation', though it might be better described as a proliferation of ill-coordinated authorities, with repeated clashes between German military authorities and German civilian authorities.[46]

German practice was also driven by the nature of the war. As one German openly pointed out to the Belgians, faced with an economic blockade intended to reduce Germany by starvation, it was inevitable that the Germans would exploit the resources of Belgium in order to strengthen their own war machine and to alleviate hardship in their own country.[47] This was undoubtedly influenced by the specific circumstance of the English blockade of German shipping and the emergence of total war. It is also true that German policy, especially in respect of the deportation of Belgian workers to Germany, from the perspective of the immediate post-war years appeared 'to be without precedent in modern wars'.[48] The deportation of labour on this scale was unprecedented but the notion that war and occupation were economic conflicts was not. As an American commentator reflected, economic considerations had a significant place in the Lieber Code 'for – as has been well said – "cotton was the principal support of the rebellion"'.[49]

The tension between political strategies and military strategies, between governing and the strictly defined conduct of combat, between those who specialised in the former, whatever their title, and those who specialised in the latter, confronted the British in Mesopotamia where the Chief Political Officer, Percy Cox, clashed with Lieutenant-General Stanley Maude. Indeed the latter protested that 'there should be no Political Officer'.[50] In Mesopotamia the situation was complicated by the fact that Ottoman officials, includ-ing judges, fled before British armies, leaving the latter in a position where they had no experience to rely on in interpreting Turkish law, which they found inadequate in so far as they understood it. The result was the administration of justice on the basis of the Indian civil and criminal codes in Basra but recourse to modified Egyptian and Sudanese codes in Baghdad.[51] There was no possibility here for Wellington's confident reliance on established systems or even the acrimonious clashes between Germans and French judges, and subsequently Germans and Belgian and French judges in the Franco-Prussian war and the First World War. Indeed, in Palestine, the Chief Judicial Officer of the military occupation noted that the courts took over tasks that would 'normally', that is within the domestic jurisdiction of a country at peace, have been exercised by the executive branch of government.[52]

As on several previous occasions, the termination of war did not entail the termination of occupation. Amidst the chaos of the disintegration of empires and civil war that accompanied the end of the war, numerous military occupations took place, often of a fleeting nature. It was, however, the Allied occupation of the Rhineland that attracted most attention because of its protracted nature, scheduled to last for fifteen years though it lasted only ten, and its prominence in the propaganda battle between the victors and the vanquished. The view that it represented the 'first important exception' to the annexation of conquered territory at the end of a war is misguided.[53] The phenomenon of military occupation beyond the framework of belligerency was common in the nineteenth century.[54] The occupation of the Rhineland itself was novel in one sense. According to Ernst Fraenkel 'it represented the exercise of power politics against a conquered enemy, and at the same time, in applying Wilsonian principles to the field of military occupation, it reflected an almost unlimited belief in the force of law'.[55] It was consistent with this ambiguity that the military character of the occupation was diluted, not least in the designation of the staff responsible for administration as the Civil Affairs Branch.[56] This opened room for dispute about whether it really amounted to military occupation at all and, if it did, how this kind of military occupation differed from other kinds. Nor was this solely a matter of the desire for analytic clarity. As one commentator has observed, the appointment of Lieutenant-General Charles as Military Governor of the British zone 'in the circumstances, proved misleading both to the Germans and to the British Corps Commanders since the Military Governor commanded no troops and could issue no orders to the Corps Commanders'.[57]

The occupations during the Second World War were remarkable for their extent and in many instances for their brutality. As Lauterpacht put it, Germany 'became guilty, particularly with regard

to the territories occupied in Eastern Europe, of unprecedented violations of all the laws of belligerent occupation'.[58] The fact that these
crimes were committed in occupied territories judged to have been the
result of illegal wars of aggression added to the problem of making
sense of what happened in terms of laws of occupation formulated at
the end of the nineteenth and the beginning of the twentieth century.
Yet the temptation to dismiss them for fear of lending any credence
to the authority of such an occupier had to be balanced against the
fear that the established standards for the behaviour of the occupier
vis-à-vis the occupied populations would fall by the wayside at the
same time.[59] The alternative of taking a war of aggression as a taint
on every act committed by the aggressor was little more attractive.
As the United States Military Tribunal argued,

> If we should adopt the view that by reason of the fact that the war was
> a criminal act of aggression every act which would have been legal in a
> defensive war was illegal in this one, we would be forced to the conclusion
> that every soldier who marched into occupied territory or who fought in
> the homeland was a criminal and a murderer.[60]

Although violations of the laws of military occupation inevitably
became the focus of much attention, the extent of the violation varied
across occupied Europe in part at least in connection with the form of
occupation. The different forms occupation took attracted attention
even during the war and has remained resistant to classification.[61]
One striking feature which cut across the division suggested by the
level of barbarity was the deployment of Nazi *Gauleiter* as Reich
Commissars in Norway, the Netherlands and in two areas of the
Soviet Union (Ostland and Ukraine). Those appointments signified
the priority to be given to political strategies: to a process of self-
Nazification and incorporation into a Greater German Reich in the
two former cases and to a massive programme of population transfers
in the latter two cases. These were some striking examples of a more
general phenomenon, namely the penetration of Nazi party agencies
and Himmler's security apparatus into the occupation regimes. These
jostled for position, even competing with each other through proxy
collaborationist factions, adding to the more usual tensions between
military authorities and command structures and civilian or quasi-
civilian agencies.

The phenomenon of collaboration was, of course, not new,
especially from the viewpoint of those hostile to the occupier. The
phenomenon and the animosities associated with it were evident

during Napoleon's occupation of Spain. During the Second World War, however, the phenomenon gained an enhanced profile by virtue of the complicity of the collaborationist parties and militias in the crimes of the occupier. Many officials in various capacities, especially police officials, were tainted in the same way. Yet such complicity, as well as acts of officials that were not so tainted, were essential to the maintenance of the occupation regimes. As in previous occupations, the shortage of manpower was a major consideration in the organisation and politics of military occupation.

Many of these considerations applied in the Far East. In Japanese military occupations a strategy of promoting collaboration was even more widespread, especially as the war turned against Japan.[62] The endemic brutality of Japanese occupation was aggravated by lack of preparation for occupation, though this was more severe in some case than others.[63] Conflict within the Japanese administrations between military and civilian elements, with the former showing undisguised contempt for the latter, contributed to the uncertainty that beset Japanese occupation strategy, leaving only the ruthless exploitation of resources for the Japanese war economy as a guideline.[64]

As the war turned against the Axis powers the British, Americans and Russians became military occupiers in their turn, occupying the retaken territory of their allies as well as enemy territory. Yet when General Wavell, contemplating military occupation of Italian East Africa, sought guidance from the War Office in London in December 1940, the response revealed considerable confusion and even basic misunderstanding of British military occupations twenty years earlier.[65] As larger-scale occupations became more imminent, Britain and America sought to train civilians and military officers for the task of military government. In both countries, previous experience played some role. In America, for example, a report by Colonel Hunt on military occupation of the Rhineland spurred preparation for a School for Military Government, though the reality of the training was less impressive than the scale of the activity.[66] Nor did the assumptions behind strategies for military occupation always prove well founded. Reliance upon Vichy officials in North Africa led to embarrassment when those officials, who did not share the American view that they were being liberated rather than occupied, continued to implement the Vichy regime's anti-Semitic legislation.[67]

Consideration of the sentiments of those about to be subjected to military occupation, as well as more general antipathy to military rule in democracies, led to a preference for the designation 'civil affairs' when referring to the organisations intended to undertake the task of governing. Terms like civil government or civil administration were hardly new but the predominant view had been, as the American *Rules of Land Warfare* of 1914 put it, that 'it is immaterial whether the government established . . . be called a military or a civil government. Its character is the same and the source of its authority is the same'.[68] Although that view was still present, and agreements with some exiled governments acknowledged that the commanders of allied forces would exercise 'supreme responsibility and authority', the general climate was clearly changing, at least in respect of retaken allied territory.[69]

The position in respect of enemy territory was different. Especially in the case of Germany, the effective subjugation of the country and the proclamation of supreme authority by General Dwight Eisenhower led to the assertion of something much more than military occupation as it had been understood, including the express assertion that the Hague Regulations were not applicable. In the words of a later court ruling,

> the Control Council and the Zone and Sector Commanders in their respective spheres are neither mere *de facto* authorities set up by a belligerent occupant with limited powers nor are they ruling the occupied territory adversely to any existing German Government, for there is no other German Government; but they are, for the time being, the supreme organs of Government in Germany.[70]

This sounded like the old doctrine of conquest, though the Allies had formally renounced any intent to annex Germany. That in turn raised the question of whether this supreme authority amounted to sovereignty and, if it did, whether the German state had ceased to exist as a legal entity.[71]

In the Soviet sector, the authorities did in fact behave as if older doctrines of conquest, indeed the more severe versions of them, were applicable. The Soviet Union had already invoked the doctrine of subjugation, along with a host of other arguments, in justification of its invasion of Poland in 1939.[72] The reality of occupation in the Soviet zone bore more resemblance to the pillage practised in early modern European and the worst excesses of Napoleonic warfare than it did to anything in the Hague Regulations, save that Russia too held to the agreement not to annex Germany.[73] In Germany, as in other parts of Europe occupied by Soviet forces, with the exception of Austria, strategy was ultimately guided by Stalin's view that 'this war is not as in the past; whoever occupies a territory also imposes on it his own social system'.[74]

The same logic was followed by the occupiers of the western zones of Germany and by the Americans in Japan and, with much more equivocal results, South Korea. In the latter case, the strategy, devised for Japan, of using existing authorities and structures had the unfortunate consequence of entailing reliance on Japanese occupiers and their allies, at least in the first instance.[75] That was not the only instance in which the personnel of the defeated occupier would be initially employed by the victors. Even without this complication there seemed something paradoxical even in Germany and Japan in using hierarchical and authoritarian structures, that is, military forces, in order to promote the development of democratic polities.[76]

The practice of regime transformation was not sanctioned by the Fourth Geneva Convention of 1949, which, in response to the practices of the Axis powers, concentrated on seeking to strengthen the rights of individuals in war and occupation. Indeed, the leading commentary by Jean Pictet on the Convention noted that such transformations are prohibited. The equivocation that followed was, however, indicative of the unresolved problem, for Pictet added that the Convention 'does not expressly prohibit the Occupying Power from modifying the institutions or government of the occupied territory. Certain changes might conceivably be necessary and even an improvement'.[77]

Despite the equivocation and the unusually extensive powers that the victors arrogated, the increasing disrepute into which the practice of military occupation fell meant that in the post-war period the tendency was to avoid openly acknowledging that military occupation had taken place at all. Nor was this restricted to those engaged in occupation. Thus, in the United Nations General Assembly debate in response to the occupation of Budapest by Soviet forces and British, French and Israeli action in Egypt in 1956, the Indian representative expressed support for United Nations' intervention in Egypt on the assumption that this 'would be a temporary force, for the emergency, and not a lasting occupation force'.[78] Similarly, he insisted that 'Hungary was a sovereign state and a Member of the UN, not an occupied territory'.[79]

Such evasion was evident also in the response of the Arab League to the occupation of Palestinian territory by Jordan in 1948: 'such measures should be looked upon as temporary and devoid of any character of the occupation or partition of Palestine'.[80] Yet the appointment of a Military Governor and his proclamations bore close resemblance to the reality of occupation as did similar actions by Egypt in the Gaza Strip.[81] It was, however, to be the Israeli occupation of the West Bank and Gaza that was the focus of attention. Those occupations were unusual in the post-war world because of Israel's relatively open admission of the applicability of occupation law, or at least part of it. They were perceived to be unusual because of the length of the occupation, though prolonged occupations had taken place in the nineteenth century.[82] They were also perceived to be unusual because of the uncertainty about the precise status of the territories that Israel had occupied, though such uncertainty was far from entirely novel. Finally, they were unusual because of the express extension of the jurisdiction of the Israeli Supreme Court to cover acts taken by the occupation authorities. One thing was clear. It was an instance of military government, organised initially on the basis of an extension of Israel's Internal Territorial Defence Regions before separating out as a distinct structure.[83]

For the most part, however, the pattern was one foreseen by an acute observer in the 1920s: 'It can easily be seen how facile and easy is the next step – to secure a *pronunciamento* from some kind of local tools, and on the strength of that to pose as allies and no longer as invaders'.[84] That was an accurate description of the Soviet invasion and subsequent occupation of Afghanistan in 1979.[85] The American citation of an invitation from the Governor General in Grenada in 1983 was little more plausible. On other occasions, where such evasions were even less plausible, other excuses were found. In Panama in 1989, the United States denied the reality of occupation by claiming that 'the increase in U.S. military forces in Panama did not displace the authority of the legitimate government in Panama'.[86] That existing government structures persisted sufficient to exempt the occupier from the charge of having displaced the authority of the legitimate government had been argued as early as the Russo-Japanese war of 1904–5 in respect of neutral Chinese territory occupied in that conflict.[87] Yet that had not led to the outright denial of the fact of occupation by the Japanese.

Towards the end of the twentieth century, a 'new interventionism' emerged as the United Nations authorised or respectively sanctioned the deployment of military force in Bosnia-Herzegovina, East Timor and Kosovo. For the most part the language used by those involved, as well as observers, to describe such situations was that of intervention and international territorial administration. Where explicit reference was made to military occupation it was often done either with the intent of discrediting the forces involved or to discard the applicability of the term. United Nations' authorisation, it was claimed, sufficed to distinguish these cases from those of military occupation.[88] Even where it was conceded that something of relevance might be learned from military occupation stress often fell on the limitations of what might be learned.[89] Were it not for the general discredit into which the idea of military occupation had fallen, this would have been surprising. The extent of governmental authority, backed by military force, was so extensive that it more readily conjured up analogies with imperial rule of colonial territory.[90] In Kosovo, Regulation No. 1 of 25 July 1999 proclaimed that 'all legislative and executive authority with respect to Kosovo, including the administration of the judiciary, is vested in UNMIK and is exercised by the SRSG'.[91] It was indeed a striking assertion of untrammelled authority.

That such developments might be at least similar to military occupation did not escape comment.[92] More importantly, the Australian army conceded that 'a UN-mandated force can be in at least *de facto* occupation of the area of operations', even if it did want to concede the obligation to abide by the law of occupation in such cases.[93] On the other hand, a former Commander of the Kosovo Force lamented the 'misperception induced by the "politically incorrect" word "occupation"' and the associated preference for the '"Liberation Syndrome"', that is, for the need for those engaged in military occupation to perceive themselves as liberators and not occupiers.[94]

Nowhere was this syndrome more evident than in the 2003 invasion of Iraq. According to General Tommy Franks, 'this has been about liberation not occupation'.[95] As the reality of occupation set in the Administrator of the Coalition Provisional Authority (CPA), Paul Bremer, summed up the ambivalence that characterised attitudes in the crucial early phases of the occupation: 'Occupation is an ugly word, not one Americans feel comfortable with, but it is a fact'.[96] The lack of preparation for occupation that recurs throughout the record of the practice of occupation was so striking in the case of Iraq that soon it was being lamented from all sides. Lack of preparation followed inevitably from the initial reluctance to admit the reality of the practice, though that reality was soon recognised in the Security Council Resolution that sanctioned a transformation of Iraqi society and politics that seemed to make a mockery of the occupation law that it simultaneously called upon the CPA to uphold.[97] That reality included confusion and a lack of coordination between the civilian-led CPA and the military forces.[98]

Conflict between civilian and military leaders, the confusion of liberation and occupation, the transformation of society under conditions of occupation and lack of clarity about what occupation entails, or should entail, recall the practices of revolutionary and Napoleonic France. Yet a static picture of repetition and recurrence is no more satisfactory than linear progression from restraint in transforming society under conditions of occupation to regime transformation as a goal of occupation. Even the idea of a transition from an understanding of occupation law as a pact between elites to one focused on the (human) rights of those subject to occupation conceals as well as reveals. It conceals the extent to which the rights of those subject to the authority of military occupiers were a matter of concern as soon as any coherent understanding of military occupation emerged. It reveals an undeniable shift in emphasis embodied in the Fourth Geneva Convention. It simultaneously reveals and distracts attention from the understanding of military occupation as a form of government, albeit of a peculiar kind. The following chapters are devoted to an attempt to clarify the nature of that form of government.

Notes

1. As recognised by Carl Schmitt, *The Nomos of the Earth* (New York, NY: Telos, 2003), p. 209.
2. Adam Roberts, 'What is a military occupation?', *British Yearbook of International Law*, 55 (1984), p. 249.
3. *Correspondence Respecting the Brussels Conference on the Rules of Military Warfare* (London: House of Commons, 1875), p. 237.
4. See Eyal Benvenisti, *The International Law of Occupation* (Princeton, NJ: Princeton University Press, 2004), pp. 7–8.
5. For an early comment on this, see Ernst H. Feilchenfeld, *The International Economic Law of Belligerent Occupation* (Washington, DC: Carnegie, 1942), p. 27.
6. Hence the title of Doris A. Graber, *The Development of the Law of Belligerent Occupation 1863–1914* (New York, NY: AMS Press, 1949).
7. Henri Bonfils, *Droit International Public* (Paris: Rousseau, 1894), p. 642.
8. Jean Louis Klüber, *Droit des Gens Moderne de l'Europe* (Stuttgart: Gotta, 1819), p. 402; August Wilhelm Heffter [1844], *Das Europäische Völkerrecht der Gegenwart*, ed. Heinz Geffecken (Berlin: Müller, 1888), p. 288.
9. Robert Phillimore, *Commentaries upon International Law*, vol. 3, part

2 (London: Butterworths, 1885), p. 814; Charles [Carlos] Calvo, *Le Droit International*, vol. 4 (Paris: Guillaumin, 1888), p. 385; Pasquale Fiore, *Le Droit International Codifié* (Paris: Pedone, 1911), p. 686.

10. Andreas Osiander, *The States System of Europe, 1640–1990* (Oxford: Clarendon Press, 1994), p. 50.

11. Thomas Baty, 'The relations of invaders to insurgents', *Yale Law Journal*, 36 (1927), pp. 966–72.

12. Irénée Lameire, *Théorie et Practique de la Conquête dans l'Ancien Droit* (Paris: Rousseau, 1902).

13. Quoted in John Herz, *Political Realism and Political Idealism* (Chicago, IL: University of Chicago Press, 1951), p. 81.

14. Michael Rapport, 'Belgium under French occupation', *French History*, 16 (2002), pp. 63–7.

15. Stuart Woolf, *Napoleon's Integration of Europe* (London: Routledge, 1991), p. 55.

16. Geoffrey Bruun, *Europe and the French Imperium 1799–1814* (New York, NY: Harper & Row, 1938), p. 110.

17. Arnold Hermann Ludwig von Heeren [1830], *A Manual of the History of the Political System of Europe* (London: Bohn, 1873), p. 477.

18. John Lawrence Tone, *The Fatal Knot* (Chapel Hill, NC: University of North Carolina Press, 1994), pp. 71, 203.

19. J. Gurwood (ed.), *The Speeches of the Duke of Wellington in Parliament*, vol. 2 (London: Murray, 1854), pp. 723–4.

20. See A. R. Wellesley (ed.), *Supplementary Despatches, Correspondence and Memoranda of Field Marshall Arthur Duke of Wellington*, vol. 9 (London: Murray, 1862), pp. 7–8, 37–8.

21. 'Treaty of Paris', in Michael Hurst (ed.), *Key Treaties for the Great Powers*, vol. 1 (Newton Abbot: David & Charles, 1972), p. 132.

22. Quoted in Ralph Gabriel, 'American experience of military government', *American Political Science Review*, 37 (1943), p. 419.

23. See David Glazier, 'Ignorance is not bliss', *Rutgers Law Review*, 58 (2005), pp. 139–42.

24. Reprinted in William E. Birkhimer, *Military Government and Martial Law* (Kansas, MO: Hudson, 1914), pp. 581–3.

25. See 'Cross et. al. *v.* Harrison', *US Reports*, 57 (1853), pp. 164–202 and H. W. Halleck, *International Law* (San Francisco, CA: Bancroft, 1861), pp. 784–7.

26. Morris G. Shanker, 'The law of belligerent occupation in American courts', *Michigan Law Review*, 50 (1952), p. 1078.

27. Peter Maslowski, *Treason Must be Made Odious* (Millwood, NY: KTO, 1978), p. 80.

28. Article 152, Lieber Code.

29. Robert J. Futtrell, 'Federal military government in the south, 1861–1865', *Military Affairs*, 15 (1951), p. 184.

30. For the term 'imposed constitutionalism' see Noah Feldman, 'Imposed constitutionalism', *Connecticut Law Journal*, 37 (2005), pp. 857–89.
31. J. M. Spaight, *War Rights on Land* (London: Macmillan, 1911), p. 324.
32. For an example, see Graber, *The Development of the Law of Belligerent Occupation*, p. 272.
33. *Correspondence Respecting the Brussels Conference*, p. 239.
34. Graber, *The Development of the Law of Belligerent Occupation*, p. 270
35. Spaight, *War Rights on Land*, p. 360.
36. Ibid. p. 357.
37. War Office, *Manual of Military Law* (London: HMSO, 1914), p. 289, noting that 'the legitimate power of the state had not passed *de facto* into the hands of the Japanese'.
38. Spaight, *War Rights on Land*, p. 331.
39. Quoted in F. S. V. Donnison, *Civil Affairs and Military Government. Central Organization and Planning* (London: HMSO, 1966), p. 9.
40. Charles E. Magoon, *Report on the Law of Civil Government in Territory Subject to Military Occupation by the Forces of the United States* (Washington, DC: War Department, 1903), p. 33.
41. On the latter see Myra K. Saunders, 'California legal history', *Law Library Journal*, 88 (1996), pp. 488–522.
42. This is the translation suggested in Edmund Schwenk, 'Legislative power of the military occupant under Article 43, Hague Regulations', *Yale Law Journal*, 54 (1945), p. 393. The inaccuracy of the standard English translation was noted earlier by John Westlake, *International Law, Part 2: War* (Cambridge: Cambridge University Press, 1907), p. 84. The significance of the translation of the authoritative French text is discussed later.
43. Sigmund Cybichowski, 'Die Besetzung Lembergs im Kriege 1914/15', *Niemeyers Zeitschrfit für Internationales Recht*, 26 (1916), p. 429.
44. For the details, see Fritz Fischer, *Germany's Aims in the First World War* (London: Chatto & Windus, 1967).
45. Ludwig von Köhler, *The Administration of the Occupied Territories*, vol. 1 Belgium (Washington, DC: Carnegie, 1942), p. 13.
46. Ibid. pp. 45, 201.
47. Feilchenfeld, *The International Economic Law of Belligerent Occupation*, p. 43.
48. James Wilford Garner, *International Law and the World War*, vol. 2 (London: Longmans, 1920), p. 183.
49. Elbridge Colby, 'Occupation under the laws of war', *Columbia Law Review*, 26 (1926), p. 164.
50. Quoted in Donnison, *Civil Affairs and Military Government Central Organization and Planning*, p. 14.

51. Alwyn V. Freeman, 'War crimes by enemy nationals administering justice in occupied territory', *American Journal of International Law*, 41 (1947), p. 594.

52. Norman Bentwich, 'The legal administration of Palestine under the British military occupation', *British Yearbook of International Law*, 1 (1920–1), p. 147.

53. For the error, see Allan Gerson, 'War, conquered territory and military occupation in the contemporary international legal system', *Harvard International Law Journal*, 18 (1977), p. 531.

54. Raymond Robin, *Des Occupations Militaries en Dehors des Occupations de Guerre* (Washington, DC: Carnegie, 1942).

55. Ernst Fraenkel [1944], 'Military occupation and the rule of law', in Ernst Fraenkel, *Gesammelte Schriften*, vol. 3 (Baden-Baden: Nomos, 1999), p. 149.

56. Donnison, *Civil Affairs and Military Government. Central Organization and Planning*, p. 25.

57. Ibid. p. 17.

58. L. Oppenheim, *International Law*, 7th edn, vol. 2, ed. H. Lauterpacht (London: Longmans, 1952), pp. 448–9.

59. Thus, Felice Morgenstein, 'Validity of the acts of the belligerent occupant', *British Yearbook of International Law*, 28 (1951), p. 321.

60. 'In *re* Altstötter and Others', *Annual Digest*, 14 (1947), p. 288.

61. For an early attempt, see Franz Neumann, *Behemoth* (London: Gollancz, 1942), pp. 145–8. For a later attempt, see Czeslaw Madajczyk, 'Die Besatzungssyteme der Achsenmächte', *Studia Historicae Oeconomicae*, 14 (1980), pp. 105–22.

62. Hitler explicitly rejected imitation of the Japanese; Madajczyk, 'Die Besatzungssyteme der Achsenmächte', pp. 108–9.

63. Yoji Akashi, 'Japanese military administration in Malaya', *Asian Studies*, 7 (1969), p. 85.

64. For a general survey, see Nicolas Tarling, *A Sudden Rampage* (London: Hurst, 2001).

65. Donnison, *Civil Affairs and Military Government. Central Organization and Planning*, pp. 1–2, 21–4.

66. See John Brown Mason, 'Lessons of wartime military government training', *Annals of the American Academy of Political and Social Science*, 267 (1950), p. 183; Harold Zink, 'A political scientists looks at military government in the European theatre of operations', *American Political Science Review*, 40 (1946), pp. 1098–100.

67. Donnison, *Civil Affairs and Military Government. Central Organization and Planning*, p. 63; Benvenisti, *The International Law of Occupation*, pp. 81–2.

68. War Department, *Rules of Land Warfare* (Washington, DC: War Department, 1917), p. 108.

69. See the agreement with Norway in F. S. V. Donnison, *Civil Affairs and Military Government. North-West Europe 1944–1946* (London: HMSO, 1961), p. 469.
70. 'Dalldorf and Others', *Annual Digest*, 16 (1949), p. 438.
71. See later, Chapter 6.
72. George Ginsburgs, 'A case study in the Soviet use of international force: Eastern Poland in 1939', *American Journal of International Law*, 52 (1958), pp. 69–84.
73. On the reality of occupation, see Norman M. Naimark, *The Russians in Germany* (Cambridge, MA: Harvard University Press, 1995).
74. Milovan Djilas, *Conversations with Stalin* (New York, NY: Harcourt, 1962), p. 114.
75. Park Chan-Pyo, 'The American military government and the framework for democracy in South Korea', in Bonnie B. C. Oh (ed.), *Korea Under the American Military Government, 1945–1948* (Westport, CT: Praeger, 2002), pp. 126–8.
76. Carl J. Friedrich, 'Military government as a step towards self-rule', *The Public Opinion Quarterly*, 7 (1943), pp. 527–41. For a critical view of this in the context of the occupation of Japan, see Ralph J. D. Braibanti, 'The role of administration in the occupation of Japan', *Annals of the American Academy of Political and Social Science*, 267 (1950), pp. 154–63.
77. Jean S. Pictet, *Commentary: Fourth Geneva Convention* (Geneva: ICRC, 1958), p. 274.
78. 'General Assembly', *International Organization*, 11 (1957), p. 81.
79. Ibid. p. 84.
80. Quoted in Allan Gerson, 'Trustee-occupant: the legal status of Israel's presence in the West Bank', *Harvard International Law Journal*, 14 (1973), p. 38.
81. Meir Shamgar, 'The observance of international law in the administered territories', *Israel Yearbook on Human Rights*, 1 (1972), p. 264.
82. See the French occupation of the Papal States from 1849 to 1870, Robin, *Des Occupations Militaries*, p. 25.
83. Meir Shamgar, 'Legal concepts and problems of the Israeli military government – the initial stage', in Meir Shamgar (ed.), *Military Government in the Territories Administered by Israel 1967–1980* (Jerusalem: Hebrew University, 1982), pp. 23–4.
84. Baty, 'The relations of invaders to insurgents', p. 984.
85. See Michael Reisman and James Silk, 'Which law applies to the Afghan conflict?', *American Journal of International Law*, 82 (1988), pp. 459–86.
86. Quoted in Benvenisti, *The International Law of Occupation*, p. 172.
87. Nagao Ariga, *La Guerre Russo-Japonaise* (Paris: Pedone, 1908), p. 423.

88. Richard Caplan, *International Governance of War-Torn Territories* (Oxford: Oxford University Press, 2005), pp. 3–4.
89. Simon Chesterman, *You, the People* (Oxford: Oxford University Press, 2004), pp. 44–7.
90. See for example, Gerald Kraus and Felix Martin, 'The travails of the European Raj', *Journal of Democracy*, 14 (2003), pp. 60–74.
91. Quoted in Alexandros Yannis, 'The UN as government in Kosovo', *Global Governance*, 10 (2004), p. 69. Yannis invokes comparisons with protectorates, p. 80.
92. See especially Stephen R. Ratner, 'Foreign occupation and international territorial administration: the challenges of convergence', *European Journal of International Law*, 16 (2005), pp. 695–719.
93. Michael J. Kelly *et al.*, 'Legal aspects of Australia's involvement in the international force for East Timor', *International Review of the Red Cross*, 83, no. 841 (2001), p. 115.
94. Fabio Mini, 'Liberation and occupation: a commander's perspective', *Israel Yearbook on Human Rights*, 35 (2005), pp. 82–4.
95. Quoted in Jordan J. Paust, 'The US as occupying power over portions of Iraq and relevant responsibilities under the laws of war', *ASIL Insights* (April 2003).
96. Quoted in Ivo H. Daalder and James M. Lindsay, *America Unbound* (Washington, DC: Brookings Institution Press, 2003), p. 154.
97. S/RES/1483 (2003).
98. Christopher M. Schnaubelt, 'After the fight: interagency operations', *Parameters*, 20 (Winter 2005–6), pp. 47–61.

Chapter 2

Defining Occupation

The definition of military occupation has been disputed in terms of the core meaning ascribed to it and even in terms of the appropriateness of the term itself, with some commentators preferring the term 'belligerent occupation', in continuation of the Roman idea of *occupatio bellica*. Where such preference has been expressed, it has been acknowledged that there are other types of military occupation.[1] That same preference and concession is repeated in the British *Manual of the Law of Armed Conflict*, according to which 'classically, this [belligerent occupation] refers to the occupation of enemy territory, that is, when a belligerent in an armed conflict is in control of some of the adversary's territory and is directly responsible for administering that territory'.[2] This manual includes occupation of neutral territory during wartime in belligerent occupation, but excludes liberation of allied territory, international administration of territory under such organisations as the United Nations and the presence of armed forces in another state in accordance with some treaty or agreement.[3] Obviously, the core meaning ascribed to occupation will affect the extent of the range of types of occupation, with belligerent occupation suggesting a narrower range than the more expansive term military occupation. Yet the two issues, of the core meaning and the range of types of occupation, have not received the same consistency of attention. The first systematic study of military occupation beyond war, by Raymond Robin, was not published until 1913.[4] In part at least, this neglect may have been encouraged by the tendency to treat certain occupations under the heading of intervention. Thus, in the 1880s, Calvo treated intervention separately from occupation.[5] Even after Robin's work, a leading French author, Paul Fauchille, continued this practice, despite favourable reference to Robin and explicit acknowledgement of 'occupations of intervention'.[6] Robin himself suggested that in these occupations, and even more so those intended to establish a protectorate or to lead to annexation, 'the true character of the occupation is perverted'.[7]

This is not the only possible source of confusion, as can be seen from the Duke of Wellington's reference to martial law: 'I contend that martial law is neither more nor less than the will of the general who commands the army . . . Now I have, in another country, carried out martial law'.[8] The confusion, as later writers were to observe, was that the term martial law was used to cover no less than three distinct forms of law. As John Westlake explained, the law governing the relations between occupiers and occupied populations, which he still referred to as martial law, had to be distinguished from the martial law proclaimed by governments in states of emergency or cases of rebellion and from 'the military laws issued by governments for the discipline and conduct of their own armies'.[9] Although the latter have some bearing upon the relations between occupying forces and the occupied, it was the fact that those military laws governing general discipline were insufficient to regulate the relations between occupier and occupied that had induced General Scott to take some of the earliest steps in codifying the law of military occupation. Ironically, it was in a situation of further confusion, namely the American Civil War in which perceived rebels were treated as belligerents, that some clarity was brought to the distinctions. Chief Justice Chase of the Supreme Court distinguished between the 'military law' providing for discipline in the army, 'martial law proper' covering cases such as rebellion and states of emergency, and 'military government' covering military occupation.[10] In view of the fact that this was a minority opinion it is perhaps not surprising that Birkhimer still complained at the end of the century that these distinctions 'were, by most authorities, hopelessly confounded'.[11] For Birkhimer, the distinctions – especially that between military government and martial law, or as Chase put it, martial law proper – were important because the wide discretion of the military commander was likely to be resented even more by citizens subject to the military authority of their own armed forces.

It is not necessary to concur with Birkhimer that in cases of military occupation the commander should have 'no responsibility other than [to] his military superiors' in order to recognise the analytical clarity as well as the potential practical implications of the distinctions. Separating out military government from martial law has the additional advantage of avoiding the interpretation of military occupation through the lens of the regulations of the armed forces engaged in the occupation.[12] Likewise, it helps to resist the temptation to which Carl Schmitt succumbed to be fascinated by the 'striking parallels' between the role of the commander in military occupation and the executive in states of emergencies;[13] the temptation is easy to see. Both involve the wide exercise of discretion and often invoke considerations of necessity. Both are regarded as temporary states of affairs. Yet such analogies gloss over the inescapable fact that the military commander of an occupation force represents an alien power. That is clear in the repeated insistence that the military commander must give priority to interests, typically the safety of his own forces and usually other considerations such as the prosecution of a war, that are far from being the same as those of occupied populations. The point was well put by Birkhimer when he noted that military government is a form of government in which 'that primary element of stability – a confidence grounded in the mutual interests of the people and their rulers self imposed for the benefit of all – is here wanting'.[14]

Yet maintaining this distinction is not always easy, as American experience demonstrates. The problem during the Civil War was that the Union held that the Confederate states were in rebellion and yet decided to treat Confederate forces as if they were legitimate belligerents without conceding any legitimacy to the governments of the Confederate states. That, in turn, meant accounting for the obedience shown by citizens of those states to the governments of them. The solution to which Union courts resorted was to treat that obedience as if it was obedience to de facto governments of the kind established by occupying powers. They did so because, as one court judgement put it,

> the preservation of order, the maintenance of police regulations, the prosecution of crimes, the protection of property, the enforcement of contracts, the celebration of marriages, the settlement of estates, the transfer and descent of property, were, during the war, under the control of the local governments constituting the so-called Confederate States.[15]

In effect, these 'de facto governments' were treated as if they were the military governments of an occupying power to which the inhabitants owed no allegiance; hence the need to explain the obedience shown to them. Yet, the inhabitants of the Confederate states clearly believed that they owed allegiance to those states and Union practice, in continuing what amounted to military government under the Reconstructions Acts, contained implicit recognition of that fact. Such inconsistencies are, perhaps, inevitable in circumstances like those of the American Civil War. Nevertheless, the response of American courts and commentators to that war and the nature of military government did help to separate out military government as a distinct form of government. The open acknowledgement that this was *military* government also had the advantage of avoiding the evasions to which later occupiers were tempted to resort, increasingly so as the practice of military occupation fell into disrepute.

The dilemma that citizens subject to such government were potentially placed in was also revealed. Living under a de facto government, they faced the prospect of returning to the authority of the ousted regime. Even before the American experience of the difficulties of dealing with the edicts and laws of de facto government, it had been recognised that citizens subject to such authority could not reasonably be exposed to a kind of double jeopardy, subject to having transactions and commitments entered into under the authority of a de facto government arbitrarily invalidated by the subsequent decisions of restored authorities.[16] From the perspective of the nineteenth century, it seemed that the obstacle to such risks lay in obsolete conceptions of sovereignty. Thus, noting the albeit exceptional attempts to override transactions undertaken under the authority of a de facto government in the wake of the defeat of Napoleonic France, Robert Phillimore commented:

> The discreditable exception of these German States arose, no doubt, in some measure from the habit which their rulers still retained of considering the power which they as sovereigns possessed, as equivalent to that of a father over his children and of treating the whole country as their patrimony.[17]

Yet, more modern conceptions of sovereignty created their own obstacles to defining the position of the occupying power. This was already evident in the discussions at the Brussels Conference of 1874 and the Hague Peace Conference of 1899 which informed the adoption of the Hague Regulations of 1907. In 1899, Auguste Beernaert, a Belgian representative, worried about the general implications of a treaty defining the status of an occupying power and 'put the question whether it is wise "in advance of war and for the case of war, expressly to legalise rights of a victor over the vanquished, and thus organise a *régime* of defeat"'.[18] In Brussels, another Belgian, the Baron Lambermont, had raised a similar concern from the perspective of his country's constitution: 'One of the Articles of the Constitution lays down that: "All power emanates from the nation". Has the executive power, *i.e.* the ordinary legislative power, the right to declare that another power may exercise authority in the country?'[19] Lambermont did not press his point yet it lies at the heart of a major obstacle to defining the position of an occupying power. From the modern perspective of sovereignty as something inherent in the nation or people the very recognition of the position of an occupying power must appear paradoxical. It was consistent with this basic insight that Belgian courts in the wake of the First World War ruled that none of the measures taken by German occupation authorities had any validity, despite the fact that during the war they had acted upon the diametrically opposed principle.[20] Both the lack of consistency of the Belgian courts and the strained argument of jurists expose the difficulty. Thus Charles de Visscher quoted a court judgement that since 'Belgian sovereignty emanates from the nation' and mere occupation does not amount to annexation there could be no question of the occupying power being sovereign.[21] Similar sentiments were expressed in Oppenheim's declaration that 'there is not an atom of sovereignty in the occupant', though he based his statement on the assumption that sovereignty persisted in the hands of the legitimate government rather than the more-modern Belgian claim on behalf of the nation.[22] De Visscher's conclusion was that 'there is not, therefore, a transmission of power in a juridical sense . . . but solely a transfer of the factual authority which serves as the *material* base of the *exercise* of the legitimate sovereignty'.[23]

Both Oppenheim and de Visscher sought to bolster their position by invoking the then dominant conception that international law applied only between states and was 'in no way a law between States and individuals'.[24] That is no longer a plausible position, especially after the provisions of the Fourth Geneva Convention and the provisions of numerous human rights agreements. Yet it was already implausible in the emergence of military occupation as a distinct phenomenon, for military occupation brings about a direct relationship between the forces of one state and the inhabitants of another without the mediation provided by the sovereign or state of those inhabitants.

The vigour with which Oppenheim and de Visscher denied this was due not only to the influence of prevalent conceptions of international law but also to their opposition to a doctrine advanced by German publicists, which strains credibility in another direction. Thus, according to Christian Meurer, occupation creates a 'juridical community' [*Rechtsgemeinschaft*] between the occupying power and the inhabitants of occupied territory.[25] It is, however, less Meurer's insistence that the relationship can be construed in terms of law that is problematic but rather his suggestion that some kind of community is created by this relationship. It is problematic because it conjures up the presumption of mutual interest that Birkhimer described as the foundation of 'that primary element of stability' found in normal government and that is conspicuously lacking in military occupation.[26]

It was awareness of this precariousness of the relationship established by military occupation that lay behind the problematic nature of other attempts to understand the position of the occupying power. Here, the language of Article 43 of the Hague Resolutions, largely reflecting the formula agreed at Brussels, played an unintended role. In Brussels, the agreed formula was 'the authority of the legitimate power being suspended and having in fact passed into the hands of the occupant . . .'.[27] In the 1899 Hague Conference, however, the words 'and being suspended' were deleted at the suggestion of Beernaert, with little discussion.[28] Whilst the reasons for doing this are not clear, it is not difficult to discern suspicion of anything that might detract from the persistence of the claim to sovereignty by the ousted authorities.

This led to the curious doctrine that if, as the formula of 1899 and 1907 had it, the 'authority of the legitimate power' had passed into the hands of the occupier, then it was literally the authority of the invaded state that the occupying forces exercised. It was precisely this that the German Governor General of Belgium claimed to exercise during the First World War when he established a Flemish University in Ghent 'in the name of the King of the Belgians'. As one German critic pointed out, the King of the Belgians wanted nothing to do with such a creation and was adamantly opposed to it.[29] Nor is this the only objection to the formula. Occupying powers have not invariably recognised the displaced power as the legitimate one. The Union forces in the American Civil War clearly did not regard the de facto governments of the Confederate states as legitimate. The Allied forces during the Second World War clearly did not regard the government of Nazi Germany as legitimate but saw it as a criminal enterprise they intended to punish. After the Spanish-American war the United States regarded Spanish authority over Cuba as so firmly and finally displaced as to no longer be a plausible legitimate power in this sense, whilst simultaneously declining to assume that title itself.

Ultimately, all these formulations along with the debates they spawned arise from the ambivalence of the position of the occupier. Failure to accord the occupier any authority, including the authority to approve or prohibit engagements and transactions by members of the occupied population, threatens to paralyse life in a society under occupation or to render such engagements and transactions highly precarious even where they are otherwise unobjectionable. On the other hand, there has been a clear reluctance to endow the occupier with anything that might be interpreted as an authority equivalent to that of a legitimate power. That either by intent or by circumstance occupying forces might be tempted to assume such authority is too frequently the case for such concerns to be set aside lightly. Thus, as Ernst Fraenkel suggested in the wake of the Second World War, 'in the absence of a sovereign government of Korea the Commander of the United States armed forces in Korea exercised . . . vicariously the authority of a sovereign government of South Korea'. He added that international law 'does not contain any specific provisions on the exercise of a de facto sovereign right of a military occupant in a country without a government of its own'.[30] He might more usefully have concluded that the occupier does not exercise sovereignty no matter how extensive the powers that the occupier assumes.

As indicated above, the invocation of the sovereignty inherent in the nation, rather than the sovereignty embodied in the ousted authorities, has not mitigated this problem either.[31] In some respects, it has aggravated it. That can be seen from consideration of the question of whether or not the inhabitants of occupied territory are under any obligation to obey occupying authorities. The question has been complicated by the habit, analogous to the conflation of martial law and military government, of linking certain forms of disobedience to actions described within domestic law as rebellion and treason. War rebellion and war treason were listed in the Lieber Code as activities for which the penalty should be death.[32] Such provisions appeared in British and American military manuals until after the Second World War, although there is a lapidary remnant of them in the British *Manual of the Law of Armed Conflict*: 'a *levée en masse* is not possible after effective occupation'.[33] In general, however, as Richard Baxter put it, revision of military codes and the 1949 Geneva Conventions seemed to 'constitute a suitable occasion for the abandonment of the principles of a duty of obedience imposed by international law, of war treason, and of war rebellion'.[34] Others treated the language of war treason and war rebellion as a matter of 'legal aesthetics', arguing that

> to speak of a 'legal duty of obedience' appears but a shorthand way of saying that reviewing decision-makers [that is, courts] have refrained from imposing criminal responsibility upon members of occupation

forces for responding to certain acts of inhabitants by inflicting certain deprivations upon such inhabitants.[35]

Both positions are problematic. Baxter was right to condemn the language of war treason and war rebellion because of the conflation of the condition of military occupation with the condition created by acts undertaken by members of a political community against their own community. Yet it does not follow from this that all and any notion of obligation towards an occupying power should be cast aside. More importantly, the attempt to conjure away the language of obligation, leaving only an impunity to act on the part of the occupier, reduces the authority ascribed to the occupier to a fiction, while simultaneously impairing the duty of the occupant towards protected persons.[36] As one author put it, 'the correlation of protection and obedience is more than a legal formula'.[37] It is so because government without authority is impossible, especially amidst the uncertainties accompanying military occupation. There is a final reason for not casting aside any and all notions of obligation along with the untenable language of war treason and war rebellion. This is that the inhabitants of occupied territory are potentially under threat not just from predatory occupiers but also from vengeful ousted authorities upon their return or from fellow citizens during the occupation. That applies especially to officials who may even be obliged by their own state to remain at their posts in the event of military occupation, as in the case of Belgian officials in 1940.[38]

There is then a prima facie case for retaining the idea of such an obligation, though the reasons for being suspicious of it are strong ones. The general case was expressed with vigour by de Lansberge for the Netherlands in 1874:

> Every clause . . . which has a tendency in any manner whatsoever to detach citizens from the sacred duty of defending their country by every means in their power, or which, instead of limiting the power of the enemy would establish as a right facts brought about solely by the employment of force, facts to which necessity may compel a nation to submit, but which cannot be consented to beforehand, – every clause of this nature would be condemned by public opinion.[39]

The fact that subsequent experience suggested that occupiers would assume more or less unlimited powers over those subject to them only enhanced these sentiments.[40] Some recognition of this is evident in the provisions of the Geneva Convention, giving increased status and protection to partisans, though reaching agreement on these provisions even in the light of the recent experience of the Second World War was difficult.[41]

No such revision was made in the most problematic clause of the Hague Regulations, namely that the occupier 'shall take all the measures in his power to restore and ensure, as far as possible, public order and civil life, while respecting, unless absolutely prevented, the laws in force in the country'.[42] The reference to 'public order and civil life' is clearly more expansive than the usual translation of the French text as 'public order and safety' and was intended to have an expansive meaning by those who formulated it at the Brussels Conference. They intended the term '*vie publique*' to include 'social functions, ordinary transactions, which make up an every-day life'.[43] It is this that stops Article 43 being little more than a clause intended to protect the interests of ousted governments rather than one designed to promote the interests of occupied populations.[44] It is, however, the restrictive element of the clause, 'while respecting, unless absolutely prevented, the laws in force in the country', that has attracted the most attention because of the repeated and manifest violation of this restriction in occupations driven by ideological considerations or occupations which have been prolonged.

More recent occupations, however, have led to the suggestion of the emergence of a 'de facto modern law of occupation' in place of the rigid constraints of the nineteenth century, though others have denied the emergence of any such new law.[45] In fact, the earlier constraint was not necessarily as rigid as is supposed. Thus, Johann C. Bluntschli, one of the German negotiators at Brussels, noted that in the case of 'wars of liberation' it was in the interest of the occupying power 'also to introduce provisional new orders through which the hitherto repressed inhabitants of occupied territory can be endowed with improved rights and their sympathies won over'.[46] Citing the wars of the French Revolution, the American Civil War and the Russo-Turkish war of 1877–8, he showed no objection to such cases. Lieber, writing for Union armies in the Civil War, understandably made clear that certain laws of the Confederate states were not to be respected, appealing not to military necessity but to natural law: 'Slavery, complicating and confounding the ideas of property (that is, of a thing), and of personality (that is, of humanity), exists according to municipal or local law only. The law of nature has never acknowledged it'.[47] Nor did other commentators always apply a rigid constraint. An Italian asserted only that it is 'forbidden for the occupant to completely change the civil legislation of an occupied country without reason'.[48]

The presumption behind the restrictive reading of the clause was that, with a limited number of exceptions, the laws in force in the country were consistent with and constitutive of 'social functions, ordinary transactions, which make up an every-day life'. What was potentially lacking in cases of invasion was the authority to uphold those laws and permit them to operate. It is, of course, easy to see both why the constraint hardened and why, in some cases, it had to be overridden. In the case of German occupation of Belgium in the First World War, which had a significant impact in such matters, not only did the Germans resort to 'savage exploitation' of the economy[49], but the German occupation authorities sought to promote a separate Flemish identity, calling into question Flemish loyalty to the Belgian state. The endemic resort to such strategies, and worse, during the Second World War reinforced the desire to assert constraints on occupiers at the same time as the barbarous nature of the regimes that resorted to them were taken as justification for radical change in much the same way that Bluntschli and Lieber justified them. The constraints embodied in Article 43 only make sense on the basis of the assumption made by those who formulated the article and they were clearly aware that there were exceptions to this assumption. It is the restoration of conditions akin to the 'social functions, ordinary transactions, which make up an every-day life' that is decisive and not an absolute constraint upon the power of an occupier to legislate, or even a constraint to be breeched only by the dictates of military necessity.

The alternatives to recognition of some such criterion are not evidently more attractive, once it is accepted that simple reiteration of the constraints embodied in Article 43 can only generate an understanding of military occupation that will persistently fail to correspond to the practice and will do so to the detriment of the obligation 'to restore and ensure, as far as possible, public order and civil life'. It is possible to attempt to revive the ancient doctrine of *debellatio*, that is, the complete subjugation of a country followed by its annexation. This seems to do justice to instances such as Germany after 1945 or Iraq after 2003 in the sense that both countries had been completely defeated, the sovereign authorities destroyed and dispersed and any notion of a legitimate sovereign government waiting in the wings was obviously irrelevant. It was for this reason that Hans Kelsen revived the doctrine in 1945.[50] Kelsen drew the logical conclusion from this doctrine: 'Germany has ceased to exist as a state in the sense of international law'.[51] The difficulty was that the Allies had explicitly renounced any intention of annexing Germany, just as they exhibited no intention of annexing Iraq, or, as Kelsen noted, as the United States had renounced any intention of annexing Cuba. The declared status of the latter was, he claimed, a political definition not a legal one.[52] Yet Kelsen's recommendations for a legal solution made no more sense of the reality of Allied occupation and subsequent developments than did later attempts to apply a modified version of the doctrine of *debellatio* to the case of Iraq.[53] In the case of Iraq, this led to an explanation of the various restrictions supposedly binding the occupiers of Iraq by invoking the restrictions over title to property in Anglo-American property law.[54] Resort had been made to similar analogies in the case of Germany.[55] The problem with such strategies is that neither Germany in 1945 nor Iraq in 2003 was a piece of property, and that to treat them on such an analogy is to implicitly subscribe to the patrimonial theory of sovereignty that Phillimore had condemned in the nineteenth century.

In part, at least, what such analogies were meant to resolve is the apparent paradox of an assumption of power, with clear intent to transform a regime, without the intent to annex the territory. Yet it is not the extent to which the occupier transforms the regime that distinguishes the phenomenon of military occupation. It is rather the explicit acknowledgement of the temporary nature of military government that identifies it as a form of military occupation. It is this temporary status that also distinguishes the phenomenon of military occupation from rule over colonies, for in the latter sovereignty was typically asserted and intended to be permanent.[56] There are, of course, instances where the history of empire and military occupation overlap; though even there, in, for example, the case of the prolonged British occupation of Egypt, the difference between the two was seen to have considerable significance so far as the allegiance of Egyptian citizens was concerned.[57]

It is not, however, true that the temporary nature of this occupation is defined by the brevity of the occupation or invalidated by prolonged occupation. As the concept of occupation crystallised, prolonged occupation was a recognised, if infrequent, occurrence. It was also acknowledged that prolonged occupation would require the occupying power to pay more attention to the needs of the inhabitants.[58] It has, however, been argued that prolonged occupation should be understood differently from short occupations or even that prolongation turns military occupation into a distinctive type of, illegal, occupation.[59] The focus for the latter claim was provided by the assertion of a Justice of the Supreme Court of Israel, Meir Shamgar, with respect to the occupations that arose from the 1967 war: that 'the right of military administration over the territory and its inhabitants had no time-limit, because it reflected a factual situation and pending an alternative political or military solution this system of government could, from the legal point of view, continue indefinitely'.[60] Against this, it has been claimed that the temporary nature of military occupation must imply that it has a 'definite end' and hence cannot continue 'indefinitely'. In the absence of any agreement on what temporal duration that might set, save for the specification that certain provisions of the Geneva Convention were to cease to apply 'one year after the general close of military operations',[61] it is then suggested that recourse be had to the notion of 'reasonable time' as embodied for example in commercial codes.[62] As with the resort to analogies from private law in order to try to find a solution to the problems created by the peculiar nature of the supreme authority asserted by the Allies after 1945, resort to such analogies here obscures the nature of the phenomenon. The significance of the temporary nature of military occupation is that it brings about no change of allegiance. Military government remains an alien government whether of short or long duration, though prolonged occupation may encourage the occupying power to change military occupation into something else, namely annexation.[63]

It is, however, true that prolonged occupation perpetuates the burden of being subject to an alien jurisdiction and that annexation has, in the past, sometimes entailed a reduction of the authority of the military.[64] Indeed, the prospect of having to extend rights of citizenship has sometimes acted as a brake on annexationist inclinations and preference for an extension of occupation, as in the case of Cuba in the wake of the Spanish-American war.[65] The perpetuation of occupation carries with it the persistence of a threat to the integrity of the occupied state. That inevitably follows if one takes the integrity of territorially based jurisdiction as definitive of the modern state.[66] The threat posed by military occupation has nothing to do with the acceptance by many modern states of a hierarchy of jurisdiction allowing appeal to bodies such as the European Court of Justice and associated Community law. That is compatible with and can be reinforcing of the integrity of the jurisdiction of the individual state. The threat under military occupation comes from a quite different concept of jurisdiction. As Elbridge Colby put it, 'military law is non-territorial and is personal in effect. It is applicable to persons subject thereto, wherever they may be, provided only they be officers or soldiers in the army, or civilians connected therewith'.[67] To this is added such jurisdiction over the inhabitants of occupied territories as the occupying power asserts. Although this may entail the introduction of new codes and procedures, as happened in Mesopotamia after the First World War or Kosovo, occupiers have often preferred to leave as much as possible to indigenous jurisdictions, even allowing them to continue to pronounce justice in the name of the ousted sovereign. Whatever the precise extent of the penetration of the judicial system, military occupation threatens the legal integrity that binds together the community subject to it.

Military occupation, then, may be provisionally defined as a form of government imposed by force or threat thereof that establishes a type of mutual obligation between the occupier and the occupied, but without bringing about any change in allegiance. It is a form of authority that can, in principle, exclude other forms of authority, including authorities to whom those subject to military government believe themselves to owe allegiance. It remains distinct from the condition of *debellatio*. It has no set duration and prolonged occupation cannot by itself turn it into annexation. It poses a threat to the integrity of the community subject to occupation and does so by its very nature, independently of any perverse aims that the occupier may, or may not, pursue. Yet, without ceasing to be itself a threat, the occupier can be the only effective guardian of that community.

The question remains of how widely has this form of government been employed? The question can appear to be one of mere semantics. Thus, in 1941, Arnold McNair preferred the term 'belligerent occupation', claiming that it 'is clearly better than "military occupation", which can occur in time of peace . . . or in pursuance of an agreement for an armistice"'.[68] Beyond the fact that most of the occupations in 1941 had clearly not taken place at a time of peace, it is not clear why preference should be given to the more restrictive term. That the more restrictive term was problematic, even by 1941, was evident in the fact that the Czech lands had been occupied by German forces in 1939 without any armed resistance – a fact that was recognised in common Article 2 of the Geneva Conventions of 1949 applying its provisions to 'all cases of partial or total occupation of the territory of a High Contracting Party, even if the said occupation meets with no armed resistance'.[69] It is tempting also to cite the case of Austria in 1938, especially as the Allies subsequently decided to treat Austria as a 'liberated' country. Yet the status of Austria as an occupied country was always dubious, for the *Anschluss* which it brought about had, at times, enjoyed such support amongst Austrians[70] that the peacemakers at the end of the First World War thought it prudent to expressly bind Austria to preserve its own independence.[71] The crucial argument for not assimilating the position of Austria after 1938 to that of the Czech lands after 1939 was well put by Adam Roberts: 'to the extent that there was not the sharp conflict of allegiance characteristic of most occupations there would have been little point in such a categorization'.[72]

The supposition that belligerent occupation is fundamentally different arises in part from the view that occupation is, as Halleck suggested, 'one of the incidents of war . . . [which] . . . flows directly from the right to conquer'.[73] Yet, leaving aside the fact that no such right is now recognised, and that such a right had been questioned in principle at the time that a distinct concept of occupation began to emerge, occupation without the intent to conquer was well known before Halleck asserted the linkage between occupation and conquest. That was evident in the Treaty of Paris of November 1815 where the Allied powers justified their 'military occupation' of parts of France in terms of 'maintaining inviolate the Royal authority', asserting that this occupation 'shall in no way prejudice the Sovereignty of His Most Christian Majesty'.[74]

Despite such professions, the reality was that the Allied powers were uncertain of the stability of the regime and were determined to maintain the ability and authority to ensure it, in their interest as well as in the interest of France, as they perceived it. Their position resembled that of the Allies who proclaimed an Occupation Statute in May 1949 in respect of western Germany, which stated that they 'reserve the right . . . to resume, in whole or in part, the exercise of full authority' in the event of serious disturbances.[75]

That the threat of the deployment of force, the assertion of authority to use it and the lack of allegiance by those potentially subject to it, can be found in both sets of circumstances, does not mean that there are no differences between the two cases. Indeed Robin insisted upon the importance of the distinction between belligerent occupations and 'military occupation apart from war'. In part the distinction matters, he argued, because belligerent occupations exhibit a certain unity of purpose, namely 'to establish the superiority of the stronger power', whereas military occupation apart from war 'is decidedly variable as to its purpose and its methods of operation are necessarily diverse'.[76] The crucial difference, he continued, is that the former is 'a mere fact to which necessity attaches certain juridical consequences', it 'rests only on a *de facto* situation', whereas the latter 'results from an agreement with the occupied state', it 'rests on a right, a right granted by the sovereign of the occupied state'.[77]

Although Robin tended to emphasise the greater restrictions on occupation by agreement or convention, the possibility that the enhanced, juridical rather than merely de facto, status of the occupant might entail more extensive powers was emphasised by L. Cavaré. Enjoying a juridical status implies, he claimed, greater legislative authority.[78] Moreover, he continued, the presumption that such agreements should be interpreted in favour of restricting the powers of the occupant rests on an unwarranted assimilation of such cases to conditions of belligerent occupation, where a restrictive interpretation is consistent with the interest of the occupier in avoiding overburdening the occupation forces. He added that 'non conventional occupations', that is occupations usually designated as interventions, appear to resemble belligerent occupation, but he warned that this is not necessarily the case: here the occupier plays 'the role of an international police [force], which intervenes with a view to the realisation of a certain end.'[79] In fact, Robin noted that while occupations apart from war typically assigned responsibility for policing to the authorities of the occupied state, the occupier might expressly be given the power to assume policing functions, as in the case of American forces in Manila in 1898. More generally, drawing on examples from the time of the revolutionary and Napoleonic wars, he argued that conventions governing occupation forces could assign extensive powers to the latter. In the instance of American occupation of Cuba, he conceded that 'the occupant encountered no legal *limitation*'. [80]

Not only did such variation exist in the extent of power ascribed to the occupying forces but a country subject to occupation could undergo different phases of occupation, multilateral and unilateral, belligerent and conventional, as, Robin recalled, had Mexico in the years 1862–7. That situation was further complicated by the fact that Emperor Maximilian, dependent as he was upon the occupying forces to maintain himself against domestic opposition, sought, ultimately unsuccessfully, to prolong the occupation.[81] By the time that Cavaré wrote about pacific occupation, he had before him a contemporary example that caused much dispute, namely the Allied occupation of the Rhineland. Initially undertaken in the name of the armistice agreement, this too changed its character as it came to be regulated through the Rhineland Agreement of June 1919. Even the earlier phase had been designated by German authors as a form of 'mixed occupation' (*Mischbesetzung*), that is, one which 'grew from martial ground' but which by virtue of the armistice had changed, 'approximating considerably pacific occupation'.[82] The point behind this designation became clear with the assertion that the occupier could not claim any more rights than he could assert in the more familiar condition of belligerent occupation.[83] Not surprisingly, French authorities and commentators tended to argue for a more expansive interpretation of the occupiers' rights.[84] Sometimes, German authors too sought to emphasise at least the extent of the rights claimed by the occupier, if only to discredit them by highlighting the extent of the humiliation to which Germany was subject.[85] Significant though these disagreements were, they took place largely within the common assumption that some form of military occupation was at stake. They are disagreements about the proper range of an occupier's powers which, although related to disagreements about the status of the occupier, do not impinge on the definition given above.

As already indicated, uncertainty about the fact of military occupation during the Second World War concerned primarily the nature of the 'supreme authority' asserted by the Allied military commanders over the defeated Axis states. Significant though this is for understanding the nature of sovereignty under conditions of military occupation, in one key respect it does not affect the core definition of military occupation suggested above.[86] Whatever the extent of Allied authority, there was no claim that this amounted to a claim to allegiance or to the extinction of the nationality of those subject to occupation.[87] The distinction between belligerent occupation and 'post-surrender occupation', introduced in order to account for discrepancy between the extent of the transformation of society that the occupier engages in, makes no difference in this respect.[88] Belligerent occupation, post-surrender occupation and occupations beyond war remain military occupations and pose no serious challenge to the core definition of military occupation.

The major challenge for any definition of occupation comes rather from those instances of 'international territorial administration' associated with the United Nations. According to one approach, despite a 'strong family resemblance', the simple fact of United Nations' authorisation suffices to distinguish such cases from military occupation, though supplementary factors are added, such as greater 'constraints' imposed in United Nations' operations and the consent of the parties, 'even if only grudging consent'.[89] Yet the source of authorisation has no inherent effect on the relationship between the occupied and the occupiers.[90] The latter remain alien to the former, claiming no allegiance but expecting and enforcing obedience. Whether consent has been extracted grudgingly or even willingly, as in the Norwegian consent to the exercise of 'supreme authority' in Norwegian territory at the end of the Second World War, makes no difference. The greater constraints that United Nations' operations are subject to are difficult to discern in the wide-ranging grant of powers in the case of Kosovo. Indeed, acknowledgement of the position of American and British forces as occupying powers was grudgingly given in order to attempt to restrict the remit of their occupation of Iraq for fear that United Nations' authorisation without the ascription of such a status would legitimise a wider remit, albeit in vain.[91]

Alternatively, it has been suggested that military occupation and United Nations' 'governance' follow distinct logics, in that the former 'presumes a pre-existing fully functioning state' and seeks the restoration of the status quo whereas the latter presumes some form of state failure and is oriented toward reconstruction.[92] Yet, state failure was explicitly invoked in the American invasion and occupation of Cuba in 1898 and there were expectations of finding a functioning state, albeit no intent of a return to the status quo, in the American assumptions about the occupation of Iraq.[93] There is no inherent logic derivable from the status of a military occupier that can ensure that the administrative structure of a state subject to occupation will retain sufficient resilience to continue to function. Moreover, it could equally well be suggested, as Roberts has, that 'international peace-keeping forces . . . could theoretically find themselves in the role of occupant if, for example, the government which had invited them in collapsed totally, without any successor, and the force stayed on to maintain order'.[94]

Acknowledged military occupiers as well as United Nations' operations have shown a preference for working with existing structures and have found themselves drawn into more direct government when those structures failed. Both have also failed to respond to the challenges posed when such failure took place. Yet so persistent is the presumption that military occupation is, or should be, something other than a form of government that *The Kosovo Report* noted that 'KFOR discovered early on that its mission involved more than just the military occupation of a liberated province'.[95] The presumption behind these two supposedly distinct logics is that military occupation is less than military government, especially government intent upon regime transformation. The practice of military occupiers as well as the acknowledgement of occupiers of their role too frequently belies the distinction for it to be tenable.

This does not mean that international territorial administration is an empty category all of whose cases can be subsumed under military occupation. There is a recognisable distinction between the authority exercised by virtue of the existence of KFOR in Kosovo and the authority exercised by virtue of the Treaty of Versailles through the High Commissioner, appointed by the League of Nations, over the Free City of Danzig from 1919 to 1939.[96] On the other hand, the provision that Upper Silesia 'shall be occupied by troops belonging to the Allied and Associated Powers' is unequivocal despite the limited purpose of the occupation, namely the supervision of a plebiscite.[97] The case of the Columbian town and district of Leticia after the withdrawal of Peruvian irregular forces, which had briefly occupied the area, was somewhat equivocal. There, a League of Nations Commission administered the territory from 1933 to 1934, but was supported by Columbian soldiers.[98] Yet such cases as Danzig and Leticia are not the real problem, which is rather the systematic rejection of the concept of occupation in cases of United Nations' operations, or the neglect of the concept of military occupation in assessment of such operations.

Both rejection and neglect are, however, increasingly being challenged, especially in the context of the application of international humanitarian law, of which the law of occupation forms a part, to these operations. Even where this application is accepted, however, the limitations are as notable as the acknowledgement:

> It is significant in this respect that the 'UN Secretary-General's Bulletin on the Observance by United Nations Forces of IHL [international humanitarian law]', which refers to many rules of IHL to be respected by UN forces when engaged in armed conflicts, does not mention one single rule of IHL of belligerent occupation.[99]

Similarly, in the American army, the partial recognition that the laws of war apply to 'Military Operations Other Than War' is limited by a persistent failure to specify which laws of war apply.[100] Alternatively, one finds recognition of military occupation and denial of it in the same operation. Thus, while Australian forces recognised the application of international humanitarian law, including the law of occupation, in their involvement in Somalia, this recognition was rejected by the commanders of the Unified Task Force, in part at least in order to restrict their responsibility but also on the grounds that this was a humanitarian mission.[101]

Commentators who are in general critical of the reluctance to acknowledge the fact of occupation also often exhibit an inclination to restrict the use of the concept. So, for example, Sylvain Vité argues for Security Council recognition of occupation law at the beginning of operations but its subsequent replacement by a different set of regulations.[102] Similarly, Marco Sassòli opposes the argument that United Nations' authorisation suffices to set aside occupation law on the grounds that this is to confound *jus ad bellum* arguments with the application of *jus in bello* and to allow a condition – military occupation – that should be recognised as a fact to be glossed over by a Security Council resolution. Yet, at the same time Sassòli repeats the old objection that only belligerent occupation strictly construed is at issue, and hence the consent of a state rules out the occurrence of military occupation.[103] Nor does the objection that those subject to such operations are not regarded as enemies exclude the possibility of military occupation. Military occupation of allied territory, as in the occupation of France by the Allied powers, or neutral territory, as in Japanese occupation of Chinese territory in the Russo-Japanese war, or even military occupation of a state's own colony upon recapture from an enemy, as in the case of Burma during the Second World War, are familiar enough.[104]

Ironically, one of the greatest obstacles to recognising the continuity between earlier, openly acknowledged occupations, and those undertaken under the aegis of the United Nations is precisely what makes some of the latter such striking examples of military occupation, namely the extent of the government functions undertaken by them. Since this range of functions is inconsistent with the requirement to respect existing laws, it is held that occupation law, understood in the sense of Article 43 of the Hague Regulations, clearly cannot justify such activity. From this it is concluded that they are not instances of military occupation. Yet, as indicated above, the restrictive sense of Article 43 has never been consistently respected and there are arguments that it should not always be respected. Even were this not the case, the conclusion which is drawn amounts to allowing the phenomenon – a political relationship between alien armed forces and the population of an occupied territory – to be defined by how that relationship should be conducted rather than the fact that it exists at all, whereas it is the latter that is at the heart of the definition of military occupation even in Article 43 of the Hague Regulations.

That the conclusion is misguided is suggested also by the similarity between the powers arrogated in some openly avowed military occupations and operations that are held to be different. Thus, in 1945 General Eisenhower proclaimed: 'supreme legislative, judicial and executive authority and powers within the occupied territory are vested in me as Supreme Commander of the Allied Forces and as Military Governor, and the Military Government is established to exercise these powers under my direction'.[105] Almost sixty years later, in language similar to that used in Kosovo in 1999, Ambassador Bremer, the Administrator of the Coalition Provisional Authority (CPA), proclaimed:

> The CPA is vested with all executive, legislative and judicial authority necessary to achieve its objectives, to be exercised under relevant U.N. Security Council resolutions, including Resolution 1483(2003), and the laws and usages of war. This authority shall be exercised by the CPA Administrator.[106]

In all three cases, the fusion of executive, judicial and legislative power is similar. The most striking difference is that Eisenhower spoke as supreme commander and that neither Paul Bremer in Iraq nor Bernard Kouchner in Kosovo could do so.

The assumption of unified governmental power vis-à-vis the population of the occupied territory does not mean that all governmental functions will be carried out by the personnel of the occupying powers, whether military or civilian. Indeed Eisenhower's proclamation also specified that 'all officials are charged with the duty of remaining at their posts until further orders'.[107] No indication is given in the suggested core definition of military occupation offered above as to how that unified power is used. Nor need an indication be given, though the issue is more important than the authorisation or not of military occupation by the United Nations, for that would detract attention from the unity underlying the diverse practice of military occupation. Yet it is important. Much depends on whether occupation is guided by a celebration of that unified power, indulged in by Werner Best when he proclaimed in 1941 that 'all the hitherto attempted limitation of the concept of "administration" [Verwaltung] must be superseded and that the "administration" must be understood again as the comprehensive "rule" [Walten] over all public affairs of the individual realms'.[108] An alternative aspiration was set out a few years later in a question raised by Ernst Fraenkel, reflecting on the experience of the occupation of the Rhineland while looking forward to the occupation of Germany:

In a modern constitutional state, the powers of the government are subject to certain definite limitations – whether by a system of checks and balances, by the requirements of natural law as incorporated in specific bills of rights, or by constitutional prohibitions. Can comparable restrictions be imposed on a military occupation?[109]

In practice, the reality of military government presents enormous obstacles to both aspirations not only because definitions of military occupation, like all occupation law, have little to say about how military occupation is organised, that is, about what kind of government it is. They also present obstacles because armed forces are neither designed for nor structured with a view to governing and because the incorporation of civilian elements into occupation authorities brings with it problems of its own, not the least of which is the relationship with the military forces they are supposed to aid.

Nor does the core meaning of military occupation give any precise indication of when military occupations end. Even the simplest and apparently most self-evident criterion, the withdrawal of all military forces, is not reliable for occupying forces may leave behind forces stationed in bases which, although posing some threat to the juridical integrity of the territory, may, or may not, constitute a continuation of occupation.[110] Treaties may mark the end of occupation but they may also provide for prolonged or new occupations, as did the Treaty of Paris in 1815. The more recent phenomenon of 'peace agreements' are even weaker guides.[111] The establishment of new governments in occupied territories to replace discredited regimes destroyed by the occupiers is no more sure an indicator of the end of occupation. The promulgation of an Occupation Statute in 1949 in connection with the creation of the Federal Republic of Germany was an open acknowledgement of that. The proclamation of an end of occupation and the assumption of sovereignty on 28 June 2004 by an Iraqi government was an attempt to slough off the unwanted status of an occupier, though whether this was anything more than a sham is doubtful.[112]

It will be suggested below that military occupation has to be considered not as a fixed condition, requiring the deployment of a quantifiable force, or even involving the assumption of a specified number of functions and offices, but as a continuum. There is no more inherent analytic difficulty in this than there is in making similar assumptions about the concept of sovereignty, discussion of which had been bedevilled by the assumption that it entails *summum imperium, summa potestas*.[113] That assumption, inherent in and glorified by Best's approach to military government, will prove, on closer inspection, to be as problematic as Fraenkel's aspiration.

Behind these difficulties lies an even more basic issue. One of the enduring characteristics during the practice and debate around the phenomenon of military occupation is that it is defined by a factual situation. The authority of the occupier has been defined as a de facto authority. The obligation, if any, owed by inhabitants of occupied territories to occupiers has been defined as a de facto obligation. Yet authority, obligation and sovereignty are not facts but norms. They have a material foundation but are not themselves something material. It is these norms, whether expressed in positive international law or not, which constitute the political relationship between the occupier and the inhabitants of occupied territory and define military occupation as a form of government. Before turning to those concepts it is advisable however to consider the nature of military occupation as a form of government in more detail.

Notes

1. Arnold D. McNair, 'Municipal effects of belligerent occupation', *The Law Quarterly Review*, 57 (1941), p. 33.
2. UK Ministry of Defence, *The Manual of the Law of Armed Conflict* (Oxford: Oxford University Press, 2004), p. 274.
3. Ibid. pp. 274–5. A separate, albeit brief, chapter is devoted to Peace Support Operations, pp. 377–81.
4. Raymond Robin, *Des Occupations Militaries en Dehors des Occupations de Guerre* (Washington, DC: Carnegie, 1942).
5. Charles Calvo, *Le Droit International*, vol. 1 (Paris: Pedone, 1887), pp. 268–355, *Le Droit International*, vol. 4 (Paris: Pedone, 1888), pp. 236–383.
6. Paul Fauchille, *Traité de Droit International Public*, vol. 2 (Paris: Rousseau, 1921), pp. 221–2. See also T. Funck-Brentano and Albert Sorel, *Précis de Droit des Gens* (Paris: Plon, 1900), p. 217.
7. Robin, *Des Occupations Militarires*, p. 14.
8. J. Gurwood (ed.), *The Speeches of the Duke of Wellington in Parliament*, vol. 2 (London: Murray, 1854), p. 723.
9. John Westlake, *International Law, Part 2: War* (Cambridge: Cambridge University Press, 1907), p. 88. For an account of the origins of the confusion in England see W. S. Holdsworth, 'Martial law historically considered', *Law Quarterly Review*, 18 (1902), pp. 117–32.
10. 'Ex parte Milligan', *US Reports*, 71 (1866), pp. 142–3.
11. Birkhimer [1892], 'Preface', 1st edn, *Military Government and*

Martial Law (Washington, DC: Chapman, 1892), p. v. See also William Winthrop, *Military Law and Precedents* (Washington, DC: Government Printing Office, 1920), p. 799.

12. As was rejected by the US Military Tribunal at Nuremberg, Gerhard von Glahn, 'Taxation under belligerent occupation', in Emma Playfair (ed.), *International Law and the Administration of Occupied Territories* (Oxford: Clarendon Press, 1992), p. 355.

13. Carl Schmitt, *The Nomos of the Earth* (New York, NY: Telos, 2003), p. 207. See also Nehal Bhuta, 'The antinomies of transformative occupation', *The European Journal of International Law*, 16 (2005), pp. 727–8.

14. William E. Birkhimer, *Military Government and Martial Law* (Kansas City, MO: Hudson, 1914), p. 66.

15. 'Baldy *v.* Hunter' *US Reports*, 171 (1897), p. 389.

16. See Robert Phillimore, *Commentaries upon International Law*, vol. 3, part 2 (London: Butterworths, 1885), pp. 841–52.

17. Ibid. p. 851.

18. *The Proceedings of the Hague Peace Conferences. The Conference of 1899* (New York, NY: Oxford University Press, 1920), p. 52.

19. *Correspondence Respecting the Brussels Conference on the Rules of Military Warfare* (London: House of Commons, 1875), p. 239.

20. For a summary see Eyal Benevnisti, *The International Law of Occupation* (Princeton, NJ: Princeton University Press, 2004), pp. 44–6, 192–5.

21. Charles de Visscher, 'L'occupation de guerre', *Law Quarterly Review*, 34 (1918), p. 72.

22. L. Oppenheim, 'The legal relations between an occupying power and the inhabitants', *Law Quarterly Review*, 33 (1917), p. 364.

23. de Visscher, 'L'occupation de guerre', p. 74.

24. Oppenheim, 'The legal relations between an occupying power and the inhabitants', p. 367.

25. Christian Meurer, 'Die völkerrechtliche Stellung der vom Feind besetzten Gebiete', *Archiv des öffentlichen Rechts*, 33 (1915), p. 369.

26. Birkhimer, *Military Government and Martial Law*, p. 60.

27. The comparable articles of the landmark codes are tabulated in Doris A. Graber, *The Development of the Law of Belligerent Occupation 1863–1914* (New York, NY: AMS Press, 1949), p. 304.

28. Ibid. p. 61.

29. Edgar Loening, 'Das Subjekt der Staatsgewalt im besetzten feindlichen Gebiete', *Niemeyers Zeitschrift für Internationales Recht*, 28 (1920), p. 304.

30. Ernst Fraenkel [1948], 'Structure of the United Army military government in Korea', in Ernst Fraenkel, *Gesammelte Schriften*, vol. 3 (Baden-Baden: Nomos, 1999), p. 427.

31. This is overlooked by Benvenisti, *The International Law of Occupation*, p. 95.
32. See Articles 85 and 92 of the Lieber Code.
33. UK Ministry of Defence, *The Manual of the Law of Armed Conflict*, p. 279.
34. Richard Baxter, 'The duty of obedience to the belligerent occupant', *British Yearbook of International Law*, 27 (1950), p. 266.
35. Myres S. McDougal and Florentino P. Feliciano, *The International Law of War* (New Haven, CT: New Haven Press, 1994), p. 794.
36. It also falls foul of Grotius's observation: 'As to *Permission*, it is not properly speaking an Action of the Law, but a meer [sic] Inaction, unless it obliges every other Person not to hinder the doing of that which the Law permits any one to do', Hugo Grotius, *The Rights of War and Peace*, vol. 1 (Indianapolis, IN: Liberty Fund, 2005), pp. 148–9.
37. L. Oppenheim, *International Law*, 7th edn, vol. 2, ed. H. Lauterpacht (London: Longmans, 1952), p. 425.
38. Those who fled were held to be 'deserters'. Nico Wouters, 'Municipal government during the occupation (1940–5)', *European History Quarterly*, 36 (2006), pp. 224–5.
39. *Correspondence Respecting the Brussels Conference*, p. 235.
40. See Elbridge Colby's warning, 'Occupation under the laws of war', *Columbia Law Review*, 26 (1926), p. 165.
41. See Jean Pictet, 'the discussions regarding this provision were the most lively of all and it might well have been that no agreement could have been reached', *Commentary: Third Geneva Convention* (Geneva: ICRC, 1960), p. 53.
42. Edmund Schwenk, 'Legislative power of the military occupant under Article 43, Hague Regulations', *Yale Law Journal*, 54 (1945), p. 393.
43. *Correspondence Respecting the Brussels Conference*, p. 239.
44. For the common assumption that it was predominantly designed in the interest of ousted governments, see Benevenisti, *The International Law of Occupation*, pp. 26–9, which then becomes an assertion that this was its exclusive purpose. See for example Brett McGurk, 'Revisiting the law of nation building', *Virginia Journal of International Law*, 45 (2005), p. 458.
45. Grant T. Harris, 'The era of multilateral occupation', *Berkeley Journal of International Law*, 24 (2006), p. 68; Leslie C. Green, 'Is there a "new" law of intervention and occupation?', *Israel Yearbook on Human Rights*, 35 (2005), p. 68.
46. Johann C. Bluntschli, *Das moderne Völkerrecht der civilisirten Staten* (Nördlingen: Beck, 1878), p. 307.
47. Article 42.

48. Pasquale Fiore, *Le Droit International Codifié* (Paris: Pedone, 1911), p. 689.
49. For the phrase see the comments of General Voigts-Rhetz, *Correspondence Respecting the Brussels Conference*, p. 251.
50. Hans Kelsen, 'The legal status of Germany according to the Declaration of Berlin', *American Journal of International Law*, 39 (1945), pp. 518–26.
51. Ibid. p. 519.
52. Ibid. p. 522.
53. For a useful survey of the inconclusive debates about Germany's status see Josef L. Kunz, 'The status of occupied Germany under international law', *Western Political Quarterly*, 3 (1950), pp. 538–65.
54. See Melissa Patterson, 'Who's got the title? Or the remnants of debellatio in post-invasion Iraq', *Harvard International Law Journal*, 47 (2006), p. 484.
55. R. Y. Jennings, 'Government in commission', *British Yearbook of International Law*, 23 (1946), p. 137.
56. On this see J. Fisch, 'Africa as *terra nullius*: the Berlin Conference and International Law', in Stig Förster *et al.* (eds), *Bismarck, Europe and Africa* (Oxford: Oxford University Press, 1988), pp. 347–75.
57. See Thomas Baty, 'The relations of invaders to insurgents', *Yale Law Journal*, 36 (1927), pp. 973–7.
58. See Edgar Loening, 'L'administration du Gouvernement-Général de l'Alsace durant la guerre de 1870–1871', *Revue de Droit International et de Législation Comparée*, 4 (1872), p. 634.
59. For the latter see Orna Ben-Naftali *et al.*, 'Illegal occupation: framing the occupied Palestinian territory', *Berkeley Journal of International Law*, 23 (2005), pp. 551–614.
60. Meir Shamgar, 'Legal concepts and problems of the Israeli military government', in Meir Shamgar (ed.), *Military Government in the Territories Administered by Israel 1967–1980* (Jerusalem: Hebrew University Press, 1982), p. 43.
61. This provision was effectively withdrawn in the Additional Protocol I of 1977. On this, see Adam Roberts, 'Prolonged military occupation', *American Journal of International Law*, 84 (1990), pp. 55–7.
62. Ben-Naftali *et al.*, 'Illegal occupation', p. 599.
63. As Ben-Naftali rightly emphasises; see Orna Ben-Naftali, 'A la recherché du temps perdue', *Israel Law Review*, 38 (2005), pp. 224–5.
64. As noted by Irénée Lameire, *Théorie et Practique de la Conquête dans l'Ancien Droit* (Paris: Rousseau, 1902), p. 46.
65. On the complex issue of acquisition of territory by the United States, see Gary Lawson and Guy Siedman, *The Constitution of Empire* (Hew Haven, CT: Yale University Press, 2004).
66. See John H. Herz, *International Politics in the Atomic Age* (New York, NY: Columbia University Press, 1959), pp. 49–61.

67. Colby, 'Occupation under the laws of war', p. 918.
68. McNair, 'Municipal effects of belligerent occupation', p. 33.
69. Article 2.
70. For the early phase see Lajo Kerekes, 'Zur Aussenpolitik Otto Bauers 1981/1919. Die Alternative zwishcen Anschlusspolitik und Donaukonföderation', *Vierteljahreshefte für Zeitgeschichte*, 22 (1974), pp. 118–45.
71. See *The Treaty of Versailles and After* (New York, NY: Greenwood, 1968), pp. 198–202.
72. Adam Roberts, 'What is a military occupation?', *British Yearbook of International Law*, 55 (1984), p. 276.
73. H. W. Halleck, *International Law* (San Francisco, CA: Bancroft, 1861), p. 776.
74. 'Treaty of Paris', in Hurst (ed.), *Key Treaties for the Great Powers*, vol. 1, pp. 128, 132.
75. W. Benz (ed.), *Deutschland Seit 1945* (Munich: DVA, 1990), p. 201.
76. Robin, *Des Occupations Militaires*, pp. 10–11.
77. Ibid. p. 135.
78. L. Cavaré, 'Quelques notions générales sur l'occupation pacifique', *Revue Générale du Droit International Public*, 31 (1924), pp. 342, 347, 352.
79. Ibid. p. 360.
80. Robin, *Des Occupations Militaires*, p. 236.
81. Ibid. pp. 27–40, 230.
82. See Karl Strupp, 'Das Waffenstillstandsabkommen zwischen Deutschland und der Entente vom 11 November 1918 im Lichte des Völkerrechts', *Zeitschrift für Völkerrecht*, 11 (1920), p. 266.
83. Ibid. p. 267.
84. On the disputes, see Fraenkel, 'Military occupation and the rule of law', pp. 282–99.
85. See the case of Carl Schmitt discussed in Peter Stirk, *Carl Schmitt, Crown Jurist of the Third Reich* (Lampeter: Mellen, 2005), pp. 91–114.
86. The issue of sovereignty is dealt with later, Chapter 6.
87. See the case of 'Rex *v*. Bottrill, ex parte Kuechenmeister', as discussed in Jennings, 'Government in commission', pp. 119–20.
88. On the distinction, see Roberts, 'What is military occupation?', pp. 267–71; Allan Gerson, 'War, conquered territory and military occupation in the contemporary international legal system', *Harvard International Law Journal*, 18 (1977), pp. 530–2.
89. Richard Caplan, *International Governance of War-Torn Territories* (Oxford: Oxford University Press, 2005), pp. 3–4.
90. See the remarks of Jean-Philippe Lavoyer: 'Once a situation exists that factually amounts to an occupation, the law of occupation applies. In

this respect it makes no difference whether an occupation has received Security Council approval, what its aim is, or whether it is labelled an "invasion", "liberation", "administration" or "occupation"'. 'Jus in bello: occupation law and the war in Iraq', *American Society of International Law Proceedings*, 98 (2004), p. 121.

91. See Harris, 'Era of multilateral cooperation', pp. 59–60.

92. Michael Ottolenghi, 'The Stars and Stripes in Al-Fordos Square: the implications for the international law of belligerent occupation', *Fordham Law Review*, 72 (2004), p. 2182.

93. On the latter, see Toby Dodge, *Inventing Iraq* (New York, NY: Columbia University Press, 2003), pp. 161–4.

94. Roberts, 'What is military occupation?', p. 289.

95. The Independent International Commission on Kosovo, *The Kosovo Report* (Oxford: Oxford University Press, 2000), p. 105.

96. On the latter, see *The Treaty of Versailles and After*, pp. 253–62 and the comments in Ralph Wilde, 'From Danzig to East Timor and beyond', *American Journal of International Law*, 95 (2001), pp. 583–606.

97. See the Annex to Article 88, *The Treaty of Versailles and After*, p. 216.

98. Simon Chesterman, *You, the People* (Oxford: Oxford University Press, 2004), pp. 24–5.

99. See Marco Sassòli, 'Legislation and maintenance of public order and civil life by occupying powers', *European Journal of International Law*, 16 (2005), p. 687.

100. For examples of the ensuing uncertainty see Timothy P. Bulman, 'A dangerous guessing game disguised as enlightened policy', *Military Law Review*, 159 (1999), pp. 152–82.

101. Sylvain Vité, 'L'applicabilité du droit international de l'occupation militaire aux activités des organisations internationales', *International Review of the Red Cross*, 853 (2004), p. 21; F. M. Lorenz, 'Law and anarchy in Somalia', *Parameters*, 23, 4 (1993), p. 35.

102. Vité, 'L'applicabilité du droit international de l'occupation militaire', p. 34; despite recognising the problems of Article 43 of the Hague Regulations, p. 17.

103. Sassòli, 'Legislation and maintenance of public order and civil life', pp. 688–90.

104. For the case of Burma, see F. S. V. Donnison, *British Military Administration in the Far East 1943–1946* (London: HMSO, 1956), pp. 33–50.

105. Quoted in F. S. V. Donnison, *Civil Affairs and Military Government. North-West Europe 1944–1946* (London: HMSO, 1961), p. 477.

106. CPA/REG/16 May 3003/01.

107. Quoted in Donnison, *Civil Affairs and Military Government. North-West Europe*, p. 477.

108. Werner Best, 'Grundfragen einer deutschen Grossraum-Verwaltung', in *Festgabe für Heinrich Himmler* (Darmstadt: Wittich, 1941), p. 35.
109. Fraenkel, 'Military occupation and the rule of law', p. 298.
110. On the different threats, see Herz, *International Politics in the Atomic Age*, pp. 118–26 and Paul H. Douglas, 'The American occupation of Haiti I', *Political Science Quarterly*, 42 (1927), pp. 228–58, especially pp. 228–9.
111. On these, see Christine Bell, 'Peace agreements: their nature and legal status', *American Journal of International Law*, 100 (2006), pp. 373–412.
112. For the suggestion that it was not, see Adam Roberts, 'The end of occupation: Iraq 2004', *International and Comparative Law Quarterly*, 54 (2005), pp. 27–48, especially p. 46.
113. For criticism of the assumption, see Georg Jellinek [1882], *Die Lehre von den Staatenverbindungen* (Goldbach: Keip, 1996), p. 95.

Chapter 3

Forms of Military Government

Military government readily appears archaic and not merely because of the increasing preference for such terms as civil administration and international territorial administration to refer to what are in fact instances of military occupation. It appears archaic because of the increasing reality of the involvement of civilians and civilian agencies in military occupation. It appears archaic because the isolation of the occupier from the occupied inherent in the definition of military occupation gives it a caste-like character that is at odds with a world in which it is common to speak of global 'governance' or 'multi-level governance' where the term governance, especially in the English language, has an elasticity not always easily reproduced in other languages.[1] Its ultimate reliance upon coercion further distances it from the emphasis upon persuasion, 'interstate cooperation and transnational networks' often associated with the language of governance, even if those who employ such language often readily acknowledge that the institutions of this governance can become dysfunctional or oppressive.[2] Despite its conceptual separation from conquest it seems to resemble the form of government depicted by Franz Oppenheimer when he sought to locate the origins of the state in conquest:

> The State, completely in its genesis, essentially and almost completely during the first stages of its existence, is a social institution, forced by a victorious group of men on a defeated group, with the sole purpose of regulating the dominion of the victorious group over the vanquished, and securing itself against revolt from within and attacks from abroad.[3]

This analogy seems even more plausible in those instances where the occupying forces attain a degree of autonomy that seems to make them look like a state within a state vis-à-vis the power that they represent.[4]

Yet the caste-like autonomy of military government is, in varying degrees, an illusion precisely because it is the agent of a foreign power and because it is dependent, as are all forms of government, upon the behaviour of those subject to it. Its purpose is never solely its own though it may have, or acquire, interests that seem to demand autonomy; most evidently in the sense of the dictates of military necessity and the protection of its own members, but not only in this sense. Its relationship to the population of occupied territory is almost always complicated by the fact that the societies over which it rules are either divided before the occupation takes place or are divided by the fact of occupation. Here, the injunction to respect existing laws may well turn out to suggest a degree of neutrality which is unattainable. Respecting existing laws may mean frustrating the desire for change by at least part of the population and has indeed been consciously used for this purpose.[5]

The caste-like character of military government is misleading because, despite the coherence that can be achieved by virtue of a unified chain of command within purely military administrations, conflicts of interest arise within military structures and are often aggravated by the varying skills and functions of elements of the occupying forces. Not even the geographical extent and contours of military government can be taken for granted. That was recognised by the provision in Article 42 of the Hague Regulations that 'territory is considered occupied when it is actually placed under the authority of the hostile army. The occupation extends only to the territory where such authority has been established and can be exercised'.[6] This provision was formulated in order to exclude paper occupations but it reflects a more fundamental fact, namely, that by virtue of its nature as the extension of control by a foreign power, by virtue of the violation of the territorial integrity of a state, military occupation embodies an alien principle to that on which the modern state and its government rests. No better illustration of that can be found than in the fact that military government in the American Civil War is typically discussed under the heading of towns such as New Orleans and Nashville. Military government was pre-eminently municipal government because beyond these municipal centres control fluctuated with the movement of the contesting armies.[7]

In the light of such considerations, it may seem obvious to respond to the complexity of military government in the same way as some have responded to the problem of defining military occupation, namely by establishing a typology. For millennia, political science has responded to the diversity of government by seeking to classify it. Why should this not be the appropriate response to the diversity of military government? It is striking however that there has been little attempt to do this. Even where the diversity stands out in the case of a single occupying power, namely German occupation regimes in Europe during the Second World War, such a strategy has been limited and intermittent. Moreover, such classifications as have been suggested have been held together only by subdivisions based on heterogeneous criteria. Thus Hans Umbreit's category of 'civil administrations' includes

> states whose 'protection' the German Reich had assumed, under a Reich plenipotentiary: Denmark . . . states with a 'Germanic' population . . . under Reich commissioners: Norway; the Netherlands . . . future German settlement areas whose 'colonization' was already planned and begun during the war: Protectorate Bohemia and Moravia; Government-General; Reich commissariats for 'Eastland' and the 'Ukraine'.[8]

Here we have a category subdivided according to firstly a legal concept, the assumption of a protectorate, secondly, a natural fact, or rather a presumed one rejected by most of those to whom it was applied, namely the supposedly 'Germanic' nature of Norway and the Netherlands, and thirdly, a purpose or intent whose implementation was limited by the exigencies of the war. The classification is further weakened by the fact that it provides only a snapshot at a given time, namely the end of 1941. The fact that this diversity can be found within the occupation regimes under the control of a single, and distinctive, power, the totalitarian state of Nazi Germany, only raises further concern about the proliferation of types to which any search for a typology is likely to lead.

The alternative adopted here is to consider military government under conditions of military occupation in terms of a normatively laden understanding of its potential to maintain its own coherence, and hence its ability to function as a government, and its potential to maintain in being the society over which it presides. The factors which affect this potential, including the nature of the state of which the occupying force is an agent, the structure of the occupying forces, the purpose of both the state and the occupying forces, and the reaction and resilience of the society subject to occupation, are themselves so diverse and varied in their impact as to make any meaningful correlation with such potential tenuous at best. Nevertheless, military government can function in a symbiotic relationship with indigenous structures or with structures modified or created by military government. That precarious relationship can face numerous threats, most drastically where military government wilfully destroys indigenous structures without the intent of creating anything to replace them but also from lack of resources available to the occupier or from challenges by other agencies representing the occupying power.

The fragility of military government was evident from the start in the predatory nature of the occupations carried out by the armies of revolutionary France, especially since in these occupations the 'central role . . . the pivot around which all else revolves, is the army'.[9] These armies were unusually large, relying in part upon sheer weight of numbers to overcome the more professional armies of their opponents. As such they could not be maintained by the bankrupt state of revolutionary France. The outcome in the Rhineland was recalled by Marshall Soult:

> We had no kind of financial resources whatsoever . . . We had no kind of administrative organization to deal with requisitions . . . One can imagine all the disorder which then ensued, for the commanding officers had other things to worry about than taking care of administration – they were incapable of doing it anyway. At the same time, one can imagine the distress of the army; it could exist only by plundering.[10]

To plunder as a necessity was added plunder as a reward for unpaid French soldiers. and as a punishment for those who rebelled.

For all the reforms introduced under revolutionary and Napoleonic rule, the introduction of new codes, the extension of the French system of departments to annexed territory or their imitation by satellite states, and the deployment of specialist administrators to train the Bavarian army or to organise a gendarmerie in Belgium, the army remained the backbone of French system in Europe.[11] Napoleon's attempt to transform the provisional reality of military occupation into something more permanent was vitiated by the fact that he did so by creating a network of fiefdoms linked to him by familial relationship or friendship. As one later observer noted this

> attempt to revive the forms of old Europe for the new Europe, came from the man who had reduced the old world to ruins. Vassalage appeared to Bonaparte as the appropriate form to maintain in dependence some small principalities bestowed by him on relatives and favourites.[12]

The fragility of these structures was evident when, after having appointed his brother Joseph as King of Spain, he contemplated annexing Catalonia and much of northern Spain but placed these areas under the control of his generals. Spain demonstrated Napoleon's 'ultimate inability to find a definitive solution to the mechanics of

occupation' and provided the prime example of a 'simplified, exasper-
ated and appropriately belligerent means of resolving the issue'.[13]

While Napoleon, preceded in this by the armies of the French
Revolution, sought to change forms of government even prior to
annexation, the Americans in California and New Mexico, though
intent on annexation, established a more limited form of military
government. Nevertheless, this included a 'governor, secretary, marshall, district attorney, treasurer, auditor and three Supreme Court
judges'.[14] In California, the appointment of a customs collector
showed more confidence in military government's authority in this
area, which had not been evident in the brief British occupation of
Michigan in 1812.[15] Even so, Governor Mason could still write to the
War Department:

> I am fully aware that, in taking these steps, I have no further authority
> than that the existing government must necessarily continue until some
> other is organized to take its place, for I have been left without any defi-
> nite instructions in reference to the existing state of affairs.[16]

There was hesitancy too in the attitude of the military government
towards existing institutions and laws. Although both had come
under pressure from increasing American immigration, which turned
into a flood after the discovery of gold in California in 1848, the military government preserved the institution of the alcalde and resisted
demands for an easing of restrictions on land transfers. In this the
occupation authorities had to struggle with their own inclinations,
evident in their concessions over the introduction of jury trials, as
well as the demands of the inhabitants.[17] The latter increasingly
called for the introduction of elected government, with the support of
some American senators. Yet it was not only the inadequacy of indigenous institutions in the face of economic and demographic change
that challenged military government. The mining camps established
to exploit the discovery of gold were effectively beyond the control of
the military government, which simply lacked the resources to assert
its authority over them. The position of the military government
was further weakened by the lure over its own soldiers exercised by
the gold fields, leading to extensive desertion. One official confessed
that 'Government, both civil and military is abandoned . . . the
volunteers will be mustered out of service, and we shall be utterly
without resource for the protection of public property'.[18] These
peculiar constraints did not exist in Mexican territory along the Gulf
of Mexico or in Mexico City, though the American generals were

acutely conscious of the paucity of their forces. Where possible they preferred to rely on Mexican authorities, including Mexican courts. Where existing officials declined to continue in office new ones were appointed or elections permitted. The extent of intervention in local affairs varied, with an American officer taking over the control of the police in Tampico while in Pueblo the Military Governor authorised the creation of an indigenous police force. In both of these towns the Americans established chambers of commerce.[19] Despite such variations in the extent and efficacy of military government there is no doubt that this was what took place. Military officers occupied the senior positions within the administrations and senior generals took a close interest in the conduct of the administration.

The American Civil War inevitably revealed the greater complexities that could accompany military government. Ironically, the initial steps, embodied in General Butler's occupation of New Orleans, began with a manifest failure to appreciate this, for Butler proclaimed 'I desire only to govern the military forces of the department'.[20] He soon found, however, that he was to become involved in far more than the security of his troops and the authority of the Union. One unanticipated source of difficulty lay in his recurrent conflicts with foreign consuls whom he suspected of concealing financial assets for the benefit of Confederate forces. His conflicts with them drew lukewarm support from Washington, concerned as the Union government was to avoid antagonising foreign governments and encouraging recognition, or worse, of the Confederacy. It is, indeed, argued that this, rather than Butler's personal rapacity, explains the brevity of his rule in New Orleans.[21]

That military government involves an international dimension in the shape of relations to neutral powers had long been evident but the divergence in policy between Butler and Washington exposes the possibility of what comes close to an independent foreign policy pursued by a military government. That divergence became more explicit later on when Germany protested against trade restrictions imposed by the occupation authorities in the Philippines. At that time, when the United States had freed itself from the weakness brought about by the Civil War, the legal advice offered by Charles Magoon to the government was that the Germans probably

> labor under the misapprehension that the restrictions on trade with the Sulu Islands imposed by the military government of the Philippines constitute the permanent regulations and established policy of the United

States . . . If I understand the mater rightly these restrictions are imposed by the military government because . . . there is a military necessity therefor.[22]

Whatever the significance of such issues in Butler's recall, his initial expectation of a limited role for his military government foundered on numerous other difficulties. The recalcitrance of local authorities, still loyal to the Confederacy, poor sanitation and the fear of yellow fever, the proliferation of refugees and chronic shortage of food forced Butler, as they forced other military governors in the Civil War, into a series of ad hoc measures to fend off the next imminent crisis. Continuing expression of support for the Confederate cause, even in the form of the omission of positive reference to the President of the United States in church prayers, induced Butler to interfere in the conduct of religious services, despite the deep-rooted antipathy to state interference in religion in the United States.[23] Although initiated in border states still loyal to the Union, the seizure of those suspected of disloyalty became a systematic practice that swept up so many that a special commission had to be appointed to review cases. It was, a historian later observed, 'another curious bit of machinery, half military and half civil in character'.[24]

The same could be said of the military governors who were drawn from civilian life but given military rank and were thus incorporated within the military chain of command. That did not prevent disputes between them and generals in command of armies. That was at its clearest in the case of the strongest of these military governors, Andrew Johnson in Nashville. On the one hand, Johnson clamoured for soldiers to be placed at his disposal, citing the threat that Confederate forces might retake the city.[25] On the other hand, the generals resorted to the use of military commissions for trials where Johnson wanted to see an early restoration of civil justice. One such commander, General Rosecrans even instituted a secret military police force which Johnson considered both corrupt and counter-productive.[26] In part these conflicts arose because of differences over what were considered to be the appropriate policies but they also arose because of the different functions and interests of the military governors and the generals, compounded as they were by the shortage of personnel sufficient to satisfy both sides. That this was not due to the peculiar conditions of the American Civil War or recourse to governors drawn from non-military backgrounds can be seen from the Boer war and the conflict between General Pretyman and Lieutenant-General Kelly-Kenny. Pretyman had been appointed military governor of Bloemfontein with a wider remit for the administration of the Orange Free State as a whole. Kelly-Kenny took over military command as the main British army moved on. Crucially, nothing had been done to clarify their relationship. The disputes over jurisdiction were demonstrated by the fact that both generals maintained their own intelligence officer as well as their own provost-marshal.[27]

There was, though, one similarity between these two cases insofar as in each of them the victor made claims upon the loyalty of those who were defeated. This was especially acute in the American Civil War where President Lincoln pressed for early elections in Tennessee under the mistaken impression that the majority of the population had been misled but was fundamentally loyal. The mistake became apparent early on when a well-known rebel was elected as a judge, forcing Johnson to confirm his appointment only to have him promptly arrested for disloyalty. Thereafter, Johnson did his best to resist the pressure of the President for early elections and when they were held they were tightly controlled to ensure the desired result.[28]

The tension between the command of combat forces and the tasks of military government was soon increased by developments within armies, spearheaded by the formation of the Prussian general staff, which became the model for other armies. The broad strategy was to relieve the military commanders of as many tasks and concerns as possible, leaving them to focus on the conduct of the forthcoming battles. With this in mind special rear area commands were established to ensure communications and supplies. By the same token, during the Franco-Prussian war the tasks of military government were to be dealt with through this structure.[29] The reports of the General Inspector of Rear Areas (*Generaletappeninspekteur*) indicate the limited nature of activities in this phase of the occupation, which consisted of measures for the security of occupying troops, instructions to surrender weapons, to continue paying taxes and for supervision of the press by French prefects.[30] The latter provision was rendered problematic by the widespread flight of the prefects and many sub-prefects. Officials at communal level proved more willing to remain, possibly on the understanding that whereas the prefects represented the interests of the French state they only represented the interests of their communes.[31] In Alsace-Lorraine, many subordinate officials also resigned from their posts, not least because of the threat issued by the new French government that otherwise they would lose their pensions.[32] German intent had been to establish a limited supervisory administration relying on the administrative structures of occupied France to carry out most of the work. They found, however, that they had to assign German officials, especially to the vacant posts of prefect and sub-prefect. Their difficulties were succinctly summarised by the official German history of the war:

> The authority of these gentlemen, however, was not by any means recognised generally by the population, and in most cases, their orders were generally only obeyed when their was a military force to back them. But in consequence of the few troops available for these purposes, this was frequently impossible.[33]

In the absence of French officials, the collection of taxes proved problematic given the sheer scale of officialdom needed to levy them and the complexity of French taxation law.[34]

The Germans in turn aggravated the position of French officials by imposing collective responsibility in cases of attacks upon German occupation troops. In the eyes of some this amounted to turning these officials into not just agents but 'spies' for the occupation forces.[35]

In order to coordinate their occupation, the Germans established Government-Generals, eventually four in total, that supervised the activity of the various French departments under their remit. As with the experience of military government in the American Civil War there was no central coordinating agency. The outcome in both cases was that there was considerable divergence in occupation policy depending upon the attitude of the individual military governors.[36] In the case of the occupation of France, it was, according to some, less the rigid application of policy decided at general headquarters and more the lack of coordination and general rules that accounted for the arbitrary character of military government.[37]

In the wake of the armistice convention and the subsequent disbanding of most of the Government-Generals, the Germans were faced with a new problem as a revolutionary commune was established in Paris. This was a challenge to the French national government rather than to the occupier, though the French government could only mobilise sufficient force to suppress the commune with the release of French prisoners of war by the Germans. The official German view was that they were 'in view of their own security . . . ready to afford every possible aid to the authorities, although they did not feel themselves called upon to intervene actively in foreign disorders'.[38] That was more than a little disingenuous.[39] In fact it provides dramatic demonstration of the inability of the occupier to remain neutral when faced with internal divisions brought about in part at least by its own occupation.

Even more problematic were cases where internal divisions preceded the occupation, as the Americans discovered in their occupations of the Philippines and Cuba. In both cases, highly developed revolts against Spanish colonial authority had taken place before the Spanish-American war. In the Philippines, rebel forces had driven out most of the Spanish garrisons before the Americans entered Manilla and, on learning of the Americans' intent to retain the islands, launched an attack upon them. The rapid escalation of violence served as a warning to the Americans in their relationship with the Cuban Liberation Army that had played a significant role in assisting American land forces against Spanish troops.[40] Relations deteriorated as the American commander General Shafter initially relied upon Spanish officials for the continuation of government in Santiago.[41] Indeed the Americans felt obliged to compel the insurgents to respect the armistice between the Spanish and the Americans.[42]

The broader problem, as General Shafter put it, was that 'dual government can't exist here; we have got to have full sway of the Cubans'.[43] The difficulty for the Americans was how to achieve this without a direct confrontation with the Liberation Army. The strategy they pursued was to absorb as many as possible of the senior officers of Cuban forces into the higher levels of the administration, with positions lower down the hierarchy for lower ranks. A demobilisation programme providing funding for payment for the surrender of arms contributed further to the dissolution of the Cuban forces, though, in contrast to Iraq over a century later, the Americans recognised the danger of large numbers of unemployed former members of the Cuban army and eventually incorporated many into either public works programmes or a new Rural Guard.[44] That had an additional advantage in the eyes of General Wood: 'The Cubans are perfectly willing to accept the acts of their own civil officers, which, if performed by soldiers of the United States, would give rise to a great deal of bad feeling and friction'.[45] Although management of the threat of a dual system of authority initially took pride of place, Wood's military government found itself reforming everything from sanitation to marriage laws in what would subsequently be called 'state building'.[46]

Although Wood's efforts at state building were less successful than he himself suggested, and although there were attempts to improve conditions in the Philippines, the differing outcome in the relationship with the indigenous liberation armies, linked as it was to the intent to hold the Philippines as a colony but to promote a self-governing, if dependent, Cuba, had a major impact on the nature of military government in the two cases. That divergent interests held by the same occupier will produce different forms of military government received even more dramatic illustration during the First World War. Here, in the case of German occupation of Belgium, internal division was neither the product of the fact of military occupation as it had been in France in 1870–1 nor a pre-existing state of affairs as it had been in the Philippines and Cuba, but was rather fomented by the occupation authorities. That, however, was not immediately apparent. The occupation began with the proclamation of a unified Government-General under Baron von der Goltz in August 1914, though the 'dualism of occupation tasks' had an impact upon the territorial remit of the Government-General and on its internal organisation. Territorially, occupied Belgium was divided between the Government-General and the zones of operations, and the army rear areas which remained under the control of the military commanders. Internally, the Government-General was divided into a military administration and a civil administration.[47] That apparent simplicity was overridden in some areas, by, for example, assigning the Governor-General responsibility for church affairs beyond his territorial remit.[48] Nor did this division of responsibility avoid tensions between the military government and the military commanders. As one occupation official recalled, 'the legal and factual relationship between the Governor-General and the commanding officers of the army were controversial and not without friction'.[49]

There was some institutional hint of later problems in the establishment of a Political Bureau dedicated to the 'Belgian problem' and the implications of this problem for foreign nations.[50] Initially, however, the German military government worked through existing institutions, replacing Belgian Provincial Governors with Presidents of the Civil Administration, a practice, according to Belgian commentators, that was facilitated by the similarity between Belgian and German administrations.[51] In contrast, some German officials were more struck by the ignorance of their colleagues about Belgium, 'sometimes even among men in key positions'.[52]

The major challenge to the integrity of the Belgian state was foreshadowed by the division of the Department of Art and Science in October 1916 into Flemish and Walloon sections. Subsequently, in

March 1917, the entire country was divided into separate Flemish and Walloon administrations, with the latter being governed from Namur, prompting numerous resignations by Belgian officials.[53] The Germans had sought to prepare for this politically by acknowledging a self-appointed Council of Flanders, made up of Flemish nationalists, though their small number and marked unpopularity gave them no more than symbolic significance – much as the French found when, after the war, they sought to exploit separatist sentiment in the Rhineland. In Belgium, the conflict between the military government and the Belgians crystallised in the attempt by the Belgian courts to prosecute members of the Council of Flanders in 1918. The Germans then reacted by dismissing members of the Belgian Court of Appeal on the grounds that they had 'associated themselves in a political manifestation'.[54] The outcome was the effective cessation of the Belgian administration of justice throughout the country.

Despite the deterioration of the situation in the second half of the war, the German military government had initially sought to govern through indigenous structures. Only as it began to modify the basic structure of the country did it encounter a level of resistance that forced it to take over more and more of the functions of the Belgian state, exposing thereby the hollowness of the proxy Flanders Council, through which it hoped to prop up the new order. In the east, German occupation took on an entirely different form in what the Germans referred to as *Ober Ost*, an abbreviation of the title Supreme Commander in the East (*Oberstbefehlshaber Ost*).[55] In this area of military occupation adjoining the Baltic, with a population of some three million, indigenous structures were almost entirely suppressed and the indigenous peoples were rigorously excluded from an administration that grew to as many as 18,000.[56]

Here, an administration organised on the basis of rear area (*Etappe*) commands reported both to rear area inspectorates and to the central administration of *Ober Ost* until the autumn of 1917, after which they reported to the latter alone.[57] The fact that Section Four (politics) of the central administration, which set the tone for the military government, dealt with the civilian and military authorities in Germany further indicates the goal of making *Ober Ost* as autonomous as possible. That autonomy was not merely administrative, for General Ludendorff, the guiding hand behind the organisation of the administration, aspired to make *Ober Ost* self-sufficient economically as well. Also indicative of the ambitions behind this administration was the fusion of the politics section with the section responsible for *Verkehrspolitik* ('movement policy').[58] This entailed strict control and registration of people, land, animals and trade based upon a systematic subdivision of the territory within *Ober Ost*.[59]

Yet despite the complex mechanism of control and the brutality with which it was enforced, and despite the extensive network of economic enterprises which the central administration of *Ober Ost* ran, the much vaunted autarky proved elusive. The cities, or at least the non-German populations of the cities, faced starvation. In 1917, armed bands, initially composed of Russian soldiers left behind in the retreat but supplemented later from various sources, even including German deserters, attacked German troops and terrorised local villages. Loss of control in some areas was so extensive that the Germans avoided them and abandoned even the pretence of protecting the non-German population.[60] In many respects, German military government in the *Ober Ost* resembled German occupation policy in the east during the Second World War, of which it has been observed that it 'abolished all pre-existing authority and declared the entire native leadership unfit by racial criteria to exercise authority. The invaders flattened the existing local institutions in the territories they invaded . . .'.[61]

In Mesopotamia, a radically different policy was pursued, as is evident from the instructions changing the status of the Chief Political Officer in Mesopotamia to that of a Civil Commissioner:

> For the present only such minimum of administrative efficiency should be aimed at as is necessary for the maintenance of order and to meet the requirements of the Force; the amendment of laws and the introduction of reforms should be kept within the narrowest possible limits. His Majesty's Government do not wish large or controversial administrative questions raised or referred to them until the danger of Turkish attack is passed.[62]

Even initially, however, in addition to the administration of justice, a Revenue Department was established which played a prominent role in its function as a land agent and source of funds for the maintenance of mosques.[63] Nor was this merely a matter of re-establishing basic structures of government for, as a review of British administration of the area noted, 'payment of revenue is considered the measure of allegiance'.[64] Even before the armistice, the number of departments increased rapidly, so much so that quite early in the occupation Percy Cox, the Chief Political Officer, noted that 'the Political Branch [that is, the Political Branch of the Government of India] . . . is performing functions which it has never had occasion to perform before in the history of the country or of the Department'.[65]

If anything, the range of activities undertaken by the military administration of Palestine was even more extensive, extending to the provision of seed and livestock to farmers. This range of activities brought with it bureaucratic proliferation that amounted to a 'swollen military administration that . . . had steadily grown in elaboration, if not in efficiency' by the time the Mandate of Palestine was established.[66] The fact that there were three Chief Administrators in 1919, as demobilisation took its toll on personnel, as well as 'discord and divided counsels' about the contentious fate of Palestine, compounded the difficulties of the military government there.[67] In both Mesopotamia and Palestine, so far as the British deemed it possible, indigenous people were incorporated into the administration. Yet none of this, of course, could prevent the conflict encouraged by the hopes raised by President Wilson's image of a post-war world or the contradictory promises issued by the British government and its agents. Indeed, some measures, such as the improved efficiency of tax collection in Mesopotamia may have contributed to a major revolt in 1920.[68]

Whereas Ludendorff's *Ober Ost* intentially flattened existing institutions, both the German Government-General in Belgium and British military government in Mesopotamia and Palestine sought to utilise them, because they had no desire to destroy all local institutions and because they recognised that they had no choice. The resources they could devote to the task of governing were limited and overstretched, subject to recall for other duties and not always familiar with the societies which they were to govern. That still left considerable room for misjudgement, for example of the stability of the traditional structures which the British thought they could use in Mesopotamia.[69] Although such misjudgements were bound up with wider stereotypes about alien peoples and societies they were compounded by the lack of preparation for and ad hoc response to the problems of military occupation. Little notice seemed to have been taken of the experience of Japan at the time of the Russo-Japanese war of 1904–5 where a special corps of 'commissioners of the military administration of Manchuria' had been formed in advance, consisting of men with recent experience of China and knowledge of the Chinese language. The legal counsellor to the commander of one of the Japanese armies noted that this corps had been formed in the light of the need to liaise with the neutral Chinese authorities, over whose territory the war would be fought, but, he asked, 'why should one not proceed on the same basis, when an army of whatever country operates on enemy territory'.[70]

That some specialisation in the tasks of government might be desirable had occurred to many but the predominant pattern remained one of improvisation. That was true as the Allied armies entered the Rhineland following the Armistice of November 1918, which provided that it should be 'administered by the local authorities under the control of the . . . armies of occupation'.[71] As Ernst Fraenkel noted, even that provision contained hidden complications in that it was not clear whether 'local' meant subordinate, communal administration or the administrative institutions of the Rhineland as a whole. Given the hierarchical structure of German administration, the precise meaning of 'local' made a significant difference.[72]

Although Marshall Foch, as Supreme Commander of the Allied and Associated Powers, issued general instructions, including a model ordinance for police regulations, the commanding generals of the four occupation armies, French, British, Belgian and American, enjoyed considerable autonomy and often guarded their autonomy and status vis-à-vis each other.[73] Autonomy meant divergence of practice. Thus, in contrast to the other armies, which organised themselves in accordance with the territorial administrative units they were to oversee, the Americans retained their tactical military structure until the disadvantages of this induced them to follow suit in June 1919. Other differences included the formation of a '*Corps des Affaires Civiles*' by the French while the British devolved authority to individual army commanders.[74] The multilateral character of the occupation, with its divergent structures and approaches, was particularly cumbersome in dealing with the substantial problems of economic dislocation, which obliged the occupiers to extend their remit far beyond the police functions they had initially envisaged. Ad-hoc coordinating committees provided only a temporary solution and in April 1919 the occupiers established an Inter-Allied High Commission whose authority over the armies was subsequently enshrined in the Versailles Treaty, marking the transition to a supposedly civilian dominated occupation.

Occupation armies in the Second World War also faced these choices about levels of coordination, that is, about the level at which to govern, reconciling the tension between military structures and appropriate government structures and about whether, or at which point, to subordinate military command structures to civilian sources of legitimacy. They did so with varying degrees of preparation. Much of German-occupied Europe fell under civilian, that is Nazi party, or paramilitary, that is SS, supervision, but significant areas remained under military authority at least for most of the war. A belated plea for some uniformity in the mosaic of occupation regimes by Alfred Rosenberg met with a brusque dismissal: 'the Führer does not place the slightest weight on the uniform construction of the authorities and administrative organs of the various areas under German control'.[75] Yet the general character of the structure of occupation did make a difference, although all of them were subject to increasing interference from central Reich authorities, both those based on state structures and those based on party or hybrid structures.[76] Military structures enjoyed the advantage of a more unified chain of command and greater access to troops, though even the latter was not automatic. The authority of the military governor (*Militärbefehlshaber*) in that respect was far less than that of an armed force commander (*Whehrmachtsbefehlshaber*): hence the request of the military governor of France, Otto von Stülpnagel, to be designated as a *Wehrmachtsbefehlshaber.*[77] Unity of command did not guarantee access to important political figures in the Reich, especially access to Hitler who had a low opinion of the political skills of his generals.[78]

Throughout Nazi-occupied Europe, then, military governors had to deflect competing agencies if they were in reality to govern occupied territory. In the west, only the military governors of Belgium, in whose remit part of northern France was incorporated, and France, where the existence of an unoccupied zone under the control of collaborationist Vichy government of Marshall Pétain complicated matters, retained some autonomy. The established pattern was represented by General Alexander von Falkenhausen in Brussels and General Otto von Stülpngael in Paris. Both reported to Supreme Army Command, where General Brauchitsch provided some support, especially for Falkenhausen, against other agencies.[79] Subordination to the Supreme Command of the Armed Forces after December 1941 left them more exposed.

At least in Belgium, Falkenhausen's Chief of Military Administration, Eggert Reeder, had given some thought to the occupation before it took place. Reeder's recommendation was that the Germans should avoid creating the impression of any intent to annex the country, knowing full well the long-standing ambitions towards Flemish Belgium, should promise to respect the Hague Regulations and should promise to maintain a functioning Belgian economy.[80] The style of administration was intended to be supervisory and Reeder took pride in administering the area with only 472 senior officials.[81] That was only possible because it was a supervisory administration that could rely, especially initially, on an administrative structure headed by Belgian Secretary-Generals. Indeed, the Germans sought to construe the powers of these Belgian officials in terms of Belgian law, rather than powers ascribed to them by the occupying authorities, in order to enhance the status of the Secretary-Generals vis-à-vis their fellow Belgians and in an attempt to make the Secretary-Generals more compliant.[82]

These officials too hoped to exploit German dependence upon them in order to mitigate the harshness of occupation and to enhance their own room for manoeuvre. That proved to be increasingly difficult especially as German persecution of Jews, forced mobilisation of Belgian labour – of which there were bitter memories from the time of the First World War – and retaliation against acts of resistance, grew. In all of these areas, Falkenhausen and Reeder, though fully committed to the German cause, sought to moderate the policies pursued by central Reich agencies and above all by Heinrich Himmler, striving to fend off the appointment of a Higher SS and Police Leader for which Himmler had pressed from the outset.[83] That struggle was part of the wider issue of the long-term fate of Belgium in a Nazi New Order in Europe in which the various collaborationist movements were also pawns.[84]

In Paris, General Otto von Stülpnagel faced a more complex situation. Although he reached agreement that it should not interfere in matters of military administration, the existence of an armistice commission in Wiesbaden, headed by General Karl-Heinrich von Stülpnagel, and the existence of a German ambassador, Otto Abetz, albeit with an imprecise remit, increased the threats to any integrated form of government and the opportunity for Vichy France to attempt to exploit the proliferation of agencies.[85] Otto von Stülpnagel also resisted some of the intrusions of the SS, successfully excluding an SS unit after it organised the bombing of synagogues in Paris in 1941.[86] Yet as the security situation deteriorated after the summer of 1941 new opportunities were opened up for the SS, culminating in the appointment of Carl-Albrecht Oberg as Higher SS and Police Leader in Paris to coincide with a change of military governor. The new military governor, Karl-Heinrich von Stülpnagel, had already complained that the armistice commission was becoming 'ever more political' and requested a 'clear separation of his military authority from all political questions'.[87] As the historian Eberhard Jäckel put it, in the light of the structure of military administration, as it was conceived in 1940, that was basically nonsense: even that structure had moreover long since been hollowed out by the offices of German agencies set up in Paris, so innumerable as to escape oversight and which all had overlapping competencies.[88]

Military government in the west functioned at most as a temporary, and rather permeable, barrier against the competing agencies of the Third Reich. The unity of command which its adherents espoused was also undermined by the weakness of the support which they received from the higher echelons of the army command. Its ultimate failure was exposed as early as December 1941 with the Night and Fog decree, by which those deemed guilty of acts against the occupation were to be secretly transferred to Germany, leaving the population ignorant of their fate.[89] It culminated in the employment of the collaborationist militia in a campaign of political assassinations which was to be conducted without reference to the military authorities. That amounted, as Reeder put it, to the declaration of a 'war of all against all'.[90] That same sentiment was evident in the notes left on the bodies of those assassinated by the collaborationist *Parti Populaire Français*: 'Terror against terror'.[91]

In the east, much of the territory occupied by the German armies was handed over to civilian-dominated agencies, though even here, from July to October 1941 in the Ukraine for example, a period of military administration occurred. Only as German advances slowed did the army resist further transfers to civilian rule.[92] Its administration was divided into Army Group Rear Areas and Army Rear Areas, though the only substantive difference was that the former were attached to individual armies whereas the latter constituted larger regional zones.[93] Both were subdivided into field commands and subordinate city or town commands. As in the First World War, the flattening of local political structures was the standard pattern: 'with virtually no exception, indigenous administrations functioned only on the lowest level, at which no German network was established, although even here the indigenous officials were subject to "hiring and firing" by the Germans'.[94]

The difference, of course, was that in the Second World War this was linked to the genocide of the Jews. In this, army units and the death squads (*Einsatzgruppen*), which followed closely in the wake of the army's advance, cooperated closely. Reservations were largely limited to expressions of concern about the impact on discipline. The underlying motives were summed up by Field Marshall von Reichenau:

The main aim of the campaign against the Jewish-bolshevist system is the complete destruction of its forces . . . As a result, the troops have to take on tasks that go beyond conventional purely military ones. In the eastern sphere the soldier is not simply a fighter according to the rules of war, but the supporter of a ruthless racial (*völkisch*) ideology.[95]

The fact that this was based on a vicious delusion made no difference to behaviour. Ironically, part of the delusion was noted by Otto Rasch, leader of *Einsatzgruppe* C. Rasch had no objections to murdering Jews, or indeed other people, but he noted in a report in September 1941: 'The work of Bolshevism is supported by Jews, Russians, Georgians, Armenians, Poles, Latvians, Ukrainians; the Bolshevik apparatus is no way identical with the Jewish population'.[96] The ideological vision behind the war overrode such fleeting insights as it overrode all other considerations, with even economic resources directly relevant to the prosecution of the war acting as no more than a temporary brake.

Japanese occupation more clearly resembled rule by a military caste than did German occupations, where racial distinctions and resemblances were used to justify civilian rule by the Nazi party and the SS. Despite the high social status enjoyed by Japanese bureaucrats at home, especially those directly appointed by the Emperor, military superiority within the occupation regimes was paramount. In Malaya, that was evident in the pre-eminence given to the head of the General Affairs Department, a military officer, in comparison to the heads of other departments who were drawn from the civil service. As one Japanese official recorded, 'The chief of the General Affairs Department is tremendously powerful as if he were Prime Minister. The commander of a field army is divine, and the superintendent is unapproachable'.[97] This did not mean that the military was a monolithic bloc. In part, this was because of the tension between commanders of operational forces and military officials within the occupation administrations embodied in the slogans 'Operations First' and 'Politics First'. Those principles even divided central military staff from operations officers on the matter of whether to grant independence to Burma.[98]

The shape taken by specific instances of military government was also deeply affected by more specific features of the Japanese military. These were more important than the general principles drawn up in November 1941 at the Liaison Conference between Imperial Headquarters and the Government although these included the provision that 'important matters pertaining to local military administration shall be determined' by subsequent meetings of the Conference.[99] Japanese military commanders and governors enjoyed considerable autonomy in implementing the general principles, though all adhered to the injunction to make their commands self-sufficient as far as possible and to ruthlessly exploit the areas under their control. That still left sufficient scope for divergence to lead to criticism of one occupation authority by another.[100]

Japanese military structures and decision-making processes, besides being cumbersome, also gave considerable room for initiatives by junior officers while simultaneously shielding everyone in the process from responsibility and promoting plans that bore little relationship to actual conditions.[101] The potential consequences of this, especially when allied to deep-seated hostility to the Chinese, became evident in the 'sook ching' or 'purge through purification', that is, the massacre of large numbers of Chinese in Singapore.[102] The fact that the military police (kempeitai) played a significant role in this reflected their general autonomy within the Japanese occupation administration. Indeed, the military police were not even subject to the authority of local military commanders.[103]

The language of the sook ching reflected the attitude of Colonel Watanabe Wataru, head of the General Affairs Department, towards the Chinese: 'They must be held accountable for their past misdemeanours. It is my policy to make them reborn with a clean slate. Depending upon the extent of their penitence, we will allow them to live and will return their property'.[104] Towards those with whom the Japanese had had less problematic relationships there were frequent calls for a repressive policy in order to demonstrate the superiority of Japanese military force, even where the sheer fact of occupation had already done this. Yet alongside such strategies was the attempt to govern through indigenous peoples and, especially in the later stages, to deploy indigenous paramilitary forces and even military forces, such as the Malay Volunteer army.[105] Neighbourhood associations were promoted both as the basis for some of these forces and as a means of control over the population.[106]

While able to make some appeal to nationalist sentiment, especially as directed against former colonial powers, through the proclamation of a Greater East Asia Co-prosperity Sphere, the organisation of the Co-prosperity Sphere, like other aspects of Japanese occupation, betrayed its improvised nature and the vacillation of policy to which the Japanese occupation authorities were prone. Ignorance of local conditions and the complexity of relationships even within specific ethnic or religious communities, let alone between them, helped to undermine Japanese strategies. In Malaya, for example, the attempt to utilise Moslem Sultans ran aground not only on the inconsistent pursuit of the policy but also on the antipathy of many Malayan Moslems towards the Sultans.[107]

Aside from the arbitrary brutality that percolated down through the Japanese military to the lowest level, the most striking feature of the Japanese organisation of military government was the divisions within the occupation authorities. These set the army against the navy and both against the Ministry of Great East Asian Affairs, military commanders against military governors and administrators, military officers in general against civil servants incorporated into the occupation administrations and caused friction between factions within the army.[108] Although some of these conflicts are to be found in all military occupations, both the distinctive characteristics of the Japanese army and its place in the Japanese polity, as well as the sheer extent and diversity of the area occupied by Japan, made Japanese military government especially prone to inconsistency.

The caste-like appearance of the Japanese military vis-à-vis those subject to it was in some ways to be repeated as the Japanese themselves were subject to military government. According to the historian John Dower, their military rulers 'constituted an inviolate privileged caste' and 'almost every interaction between victor and vanquished was infused with intimations of white supremacism'.[109] That they might appear as 'neo-colonial overlords', with the attendant implications of racial supremacy, had not escaped the occupiers themselves and there had been plans for the involvement of Chinese troops, possibly 60,000, in the occupation of Japan to soften this appearance.[110] It was, however, general assumptions about race, aggravated by the racial overtones of the war in the Pacific, rather than the status of the army in American society, that promoted the impression. Indeed American attitudes to the status of the military establishment, accentuated by the conflict with what were seen as militaristic opponents in both theatres of the war, entailed some predisposition against military government even in instances of military occupation. That had not always been the case, and as late as 1913 the American military had unceremoniously set aside civilian governors in the occupation of Vera Cruz.[111]

President Truman was wrong when he proclaimed that the American custom was 'that the military should not have governmental responsibilities beyond the requirements of military operations'.[112]

Nor was this necessarily the sentiment of his generals. Amidst the planning for the occupation of Italy, the first enemy territory the Allies envisaged occupying, Eisenhower was insistent upon a clear military chain of command reporting through a Combined Civil Affairs Committee to the Combined Chiefs of Staff. The latter, in turn, specified that the 'military administration . . . shall contain no political agencies or political representatives of either government'.[113] While this ensured that government in Italy would be strictly military in the first phase, some concession had to be made to Winston Churchill's demand that some role be found for personal representatives of himself and President Roosevelt. The solution was to accord them the status of advisors to both the two heads of government and the Supreme Commander.[114] The preservation of the integrity of military government also involved a basic choice between two types of military government, by then well-known to the authors of military manuals. According to the American manual:

> In the operational type, commanders of combat units or of military administrative areas are responsible for civil affairs within their respective zones of operation or areas . . . The chain of civil affairs control conforms to the operational or administrative chain of command . . . In the territorial form, a separate civil affairs organization is created under the direct command of the theatre commander, or under a subordinate commander . . . The line of communication within the organization is direct from higher to lower civil affairs officers. Local civil affairs officers are not responsible to operational unit commanders stationed in their area.[115]

In Italy, preference was to be given to the territorial type.

The potential complexity of military government promptly expanded as Italy signed an armistice with the Allied invaders who formed an Allied Control Commission in order to supervise the terms of the armistice. This raised the question of the relationship between the Military Governor of Italy and the Control Commission. Only the strong protests of General Eisenhower as Supreme Commander prevented the Combined Chiefs of Staff from effectively subordinating military government to the Control Commission. The Control Commission would, however, supervise the administration of Italian territory handed back to the Italian government, creating the so-called 'King's Italy', while as a supposedly provisional measure military government was divided into two regions, Forward and Rear Areas.[116] Restoring authority to Italian administration in these Rear

Areas was more difficult than anticipated, with the Italian government being reluctant to accept responsibility for them.[117]

Even where Italian authority had been restored it was subject to the Control Commission the size of whose staff threatened the Italian government it was intended to assist. Indeed the Chief Civil Affairs Officer, Lord Rennel, protested that the

> authority of the Prefectoral Government in the provinces will never survive so numerous a staff-as is proposed shall guide and control them when they become the executive of a Central Italian Government. The mere number of such officers is a guarantee that they will interfere in matters which will render any Italian Civil Service machine inoperable.[118]

Although the dual structure of military government and Control Commission was ended in January 1944, it was not only the structure of government in occupied Italy that presented unanticipated problems. Optimistic assumptions about the relative self-sufficiency of Italy in foodstuffs and the resumption of exports proved unfounded, leaving military government with the task of organising imports.[119] Both immediate problems and longer term solutions involved not only military government but also agencies created to establish a new order after the war, including the United Nations Relief and Rehabilitation Agency as well as a United States Congress, still hostile to a former enemy state.[120] In practice, military government was sucked into the early phases not only of providing immediate relief from the threat of starvation and disease but also into the process of reconstruction – for which there had been inadequate preparation in the planning for post-war Europe.

That was to be even more true for the military government of occupied Germany. In the case of Germany, however, experience of military government in Italy induced a diametrically opposed structure of government. Instead of the 'territorial form' of organisation the intent was to adopt the 'operational type'.[121] The deficiencies of that choice were being recorded before the war had even ended. According to the staff at Supreme Headquarters, the 'strictly tactical theory of military government has broken down of its own weight under pressure of practical considerations'.[122] The difficulty was that economic regions such as the Rhineland did not coincide with the shifting boundaries of tactical military formations. Military government units were subject to changing jurisdictions as those military formations advanced. Yet there was resistance to a change to a territorial basis with one American general blaming calls for such a change on malign British influence.[123] The British, however, experienced exactly the same difficulty, with different levels of German administration subject to different levels of military command but no vertical integration of administrative structures.[124] Nor did it help that military government units at the lowest levels were subject to a plethora of often conflicting instructions.[125]

Official policy was that 'Military Government will be effected, as a general principle, through indirect rule. Mil[itary] Gov[ernment] Detachments have the responsibility of controlling the German administrative system, not of operating it themselves'.[126] Lack of an effective civil affairs chain of command, confusing and countervailing orders from above, and lack of certainty about the more specific contours of Allied policy on such matters as the restoration of political parties, combined to produce arbitrary and often detailed intervention by local units while they struggled to restore basic services amidst a background of suspicion manifest in the official prohibition of fraternisation. Yet even more important for the evolution of military government was the paralysis of the Allied Control Council which was supposed to administer Germany as a whole. In this, a key role in subsequent developments was played by General Lucius Clay, the American Deputy Military Governor. Although his suspension of reparations deliveries to the Soviet Union from the American zone in May 1946 was motivated more by frustration with the French than with the Soviet Union, this was but one of the key steps towards the administration of Germany on the basis of zones of occupation.[127]

In fact, as early as June 1945, the British had taken over an organisation henceforth known as the North German Coal Control to manage the severe shortages in this area on a zonal level.[128] This was to be followed by other such bodies. This also forced the British into more direct government than had been anticipated, if only because no German administrative structures existed on the level of the zones.[129] Although such measures were intended as provisional, as the emergent Cold War consolidated the zonal boundaries the military governors found that indirect rule could only be re-established by creating German agencies at that level.

As the example of General Clay indicates, the exigencies of military government can force military governors into playing a role on the wider international stage. This was true not only with respect to the increasingly troubled relationship within the wartime alliance but also in relation to their own governments. That was especially pronounced in the American case where Clay and the American army protested against the share of Marshall Plan aid designated for Germany and insisted upon payment in dollars for German exports while refusing to pay in dollars for her imports.[130] In effect, Clay and the army developed their own policy with respect to Germany and its role within the wider division of Europe and the integration of the western zones in the process of European reconstruction and integration.

Much, however, depended upon the position of the military governors within their respective political systems. Clay enjoyed more power than his Soviet counterpart, Marshall Zhukov. Zhukov had to contend with Soviet reparations officials, who commanded a staff of some 70,000 and overruled his attempts to reassure Germans about specific installations, and with the commanders of the five military districts who sought to protect their own soldiers from the efforts of the Soviet Military Administration to restrain at least the grosser excesses of its own army.[131] Indicative of the general confusion, in Thüringen, General Kolesnichenko found that so many different Russian agencies were inspecting factories that he ordered everyone was to be refused entry unless they had a pass signed by him.[132]

While Clay and the other military governors in the west had to improvise to create structures through which they could govern, and Zhukov struggled in vain to control the agencies of his own government, in Japan General MacArthur seemed to possess an unparalleled autonomy as head of a 'new super-government'.[133] Contrary to the rationale behind the 'commissioners of the military administration of Manchuria' at the time of the Russo-Japanese war, expertise on Japan was regarded as a hindrance since such experts were presumed to be too inclined to be conciliatory to conservative forces within Japan.[134] Yet it was a 'super-government' that was explicitly reliant for the implementation of its decrees upon existing Japanese government machinery. The suddenness of the Japanese surrender in the wake of the use of atomic weapons brought about, as MacArthur informed his subordinates, 'a major change in the concept of conditions under which the occupation of Japan will take place . . . now contemplated that the occupation will take place without violence and the Japanese government will continue to function'.[135] This meant that the early assumption of an analogy with Germany had been abandoned.[136]

The Supreme Commander of the Allied Powers (SCAP), MacArthur, and his staff, especially the Government Section of SCAP headquarters, intervened directly in the Japanese system of government, at first openly through decrees in the first year of the occupation but then indirectly through advice that was understood to be little different from instructions. That was partly a product of the desire to transfer responsibility to the Japanese government and shield the occupation authorities.[137] It was also a product of the most dramatic intervention of the occupation, namely the drafting of a new constitution for Japan. Frustrated by Japanese failure to produce an appropriate document, MacArthur informed his staff that 'in the next week the Government Section will sit as a Constitutional Convention'.[138] Their text was then presented, without warning, to a stunned Japanese government with very limited room for negotiation. Nor was this the limit of such intervention. The once all-powerful Home Ministry was dissolved in December 1947 at SCAP's insistence.[139]

That particular reform, however, had a significant impact upon the nature of military government, which consisted of more than SCAP headquarters and its edicts and advice. As in north-west Europe, military government teams had initially been included in the combat formations of the occupying army, leaving them ill-distributed in terms of the Japanese administrative system, especially the prefectures; a distribution not corrected until well into the occupation.[140] As early as September 1945, the army instructed field commanders not to issue direct orders to Japanese officials, save in emergencies, and SCAP even instructed Japanese officials to disobey any orders from local military government teams.[141] The latter were supposed to confine themselves to monitoring the behaviour of Japanese local government, reporting shortcomings that would then be corrected through centralised edicts. Dissolution of the Home Ministry, however, weakened, at least temporarily, the mechanism for implementing such edicts. As the member of one military government team subsequently asked: 'How, then could we have relied on a centralized device to serve us through a decentralized Japanese structure?'[142] His answer was that the military government teams, acting through advice understood as instruction, had played a more significant role than their official position allowed. That fact also gave the occupied Japanese some room for manoeuvre.[143]

Part of the reason for MacArthur's sense of urgency about the constitution and his desire to present it as a Japanese initiative was his concern to escape scrutiny by the Far Eastern Commission, established by the wartime allies to oversee the occupation, presenting it with a fait accompli before the Commission formally met.[144] Despite MacArthur's intent to ignore or evade any effective supervision by the Commission, he was quite ready to intimate that his position as Supreme Commander made him the agent of that body in order to strengthen his autonomy with respect to the American authorities.[145] Yet not even MacArthur could escape all constraint as was evident in the rejection of his proposal in 1947 for a rapid peace treaty.[146] Ultimately, however, MacArthur's dependence on the American chain of command led to his dismissal, albeit over his views about the Korean war rather than the occupation of Japan.

For all the intervention in Japan and Germany in the name of the supreme authority of the occupying powers, those societies exhibited considerable resilience, including that of people supportive of much of the reforms imposed by the occupiers. Existing structures as well as new ones, some initially intended by neither occupier nor occupied, meant that those societies endured in ways that also shaped the machinery of the government of the occupier. This occurred to an extent that was not possible where the occupant was intent upon not only flattening existing structures but purposefully inhibiting the emergence of new ones.

In the most prominent military occupation of the post-war world, the Israeli occupation of the West Bank and Gaza, a different pattern emerged in which existing structures were overwhelmed and eventually circumvented by the emergence of unstable new forces. In the case of Gaza, Egyptian occupation preceded Israeli occupation. Egypt's military governor had already encountered a *waqf* administration overwhelmed by the influx of refugees in 1948, and further weakened by its dependence upon the Egyptian administration as well as its isolation from sources of funds in lands claimed by Israel and from the authorities in pre-partition Palestine to which it had been responsible. Subsequent occupation by Israel meant that the Israeli army inherited this supervisory capacity though the relationship with the *waqf* administration inevitably became more problematic given the level of antipathy between Israelis and Palestinians. Preferring to keep the religious establishment weak, the Israeli authorities allowed the *waqf* administration to stagnate – until they realised that the new Islamic radical groups were becoming a challenge not only to the Palestine Liberation Organisation, but also to their authority.[147] Even earlier, it had become apparent that many in the refugee community accepted neither Egypt's nor Israel's authority over the refugee camps, nor did they accept the established local authorities who could not cope with their needs in any event.[148]

Although developments in the West Bank differed in some respects, there was a similarity in that, here too, the occupier undermined so much of the pre-existing institutions that they could not constitute a useful interlocutor but could not manage to create new institutions. Attempts to do so by, for example, relying on 'village leagues' in the supposedly less-militant rural areas, were unsuccessful.[149] That in turn was linked to an attempt to separate out civilian administration from strictly military functions, albeit without undermining the unity of command and subordination of the apparatus to the army. According to its architect, who became the first Head of Civilian Administration, it was intended to respond to 'the understanding that the separation of executive functions between military and civilian affairs would better suit the needs of the population and the policy aims of the government'.[150] Neither succeeded, giving way to recurrent attempts to licence some form of indigenous authority and to resort to brutal repression, as that authority turned against the occupier or a plethora of such aspiring authorities turned on each other.

As forms of government without meaningful constitutions or legitimacy in the eyes of those subject to them, military occupations are continually threatened by an exercise of supreme authority that provokes open revolt and a descent into the kind of warfare symbolised by the Napoleonic occupation of Spain or the Israeli occupation of Gaza and the West Bank. Yet even where this outcome is avoided the deployment of armed forces structurally ill-suited to, and often woefully ill-prepared for, government, generates a challenge to the unity and apparent omnipotence claimed in the aspiration to supreme authority. Yet the attempt to escape from such problems by resort to civilian, rather the strictly military rule, has proved to be no escape at all.

Notes

1. See for example the entry on 'Governance' in Dieter Nohlen and Rainer-Olaf Schultze (eds), *Lexikon der Politikwissenschaft*, vol. 1 (Nördlingen: Beck; 2005), pp. 323–4.
2. Robert O. Keohane, 'Governance in a partially globalized world', *American Political Science Review*, 95 (2001), pp. 1–13.
3. Franz Oppenheimer [1908], *The State* (New Brunswick, NJ: Transaction, 1999), p. 15.
4. For an example, see Vejas Gabriel Liulevicius, *War Land on the Eastern Front* (Cambridge: Cambridge University Press, 2000).
5. Eyal Benvenisti, *The International Law of Occupation* (Princeton, NJ: Princeton University Press, 2004), p. 78.

6. Article 42, Hague Regulations, 1907.
7. A. H. Carpenter, 'Military government of Southern Territory', *Annual Report of the American Historical Association*, (1901), pp. 477–8. See especially the statement by the Military Governor of the State of Louisiana: 'the city of New Orleans is in reality the State of Louisiana', p. 478.
8. Hans Umbreit, 'Towards continental domination', in Militärgeschichtliche Forschungsamt (ed.), *Germany and the Second World War*, vol. 5, part 2 (Oxford: Clarendon Press, 2000), pp. 126–7.
9. T. C. W. Blanning, *The French Revolution in Germany* (Oxford: Oxford University Press, 1983), p. 85.
10. Ibid. p. 87.
11. For the latter, see Stewart Woolf, *Napoleon's Integration of Europe* (London: Routledge, 1991), p. 62.
12. Georg Jellinek, *Die Lehre von den Staatenverbindungen* (Goldbach: Keip, 1996), pp. 145–6.
13. Woolf, *Napoleon's Integration of Europe*, p. 53.
14. William E. Birkhimer, *Military Government and Martial Law* (Kansas City, MO: Hudson, 1914), p. 102.
15. Eldridge Colby, 'The occupation of Michigan', *Michigan Law Review*, 22 (1924), p. 520. Elsewhere the British showed less hesitation.
16. Quoted in 'Cross et al. *v.* Harrison', *US Reports*, 57 (1853), pp. 183–4.
17. Myra K. Saunders, 'California legal history', *Law Library Journal*, 88 (1996), pp. 492–506.
18. Quoted in Garl Lawson and Guy Seidman, *The Constitution of Empire* (New Haven, CT: Yale University Press, 2004), p. 186.
19. Justin H. Smith, 'American rule in Mexico', *American Historical Review*, 23 (1918), pp. 295–8.
20. Quoted in Christopher G. Pena, *General Butler. Beast or Patriot* (Bloomington, IL: 1st Books, 2003), p. 67.
21. Frank Freidel, 'General Orders 100 and military government', *The Mississippi Valley Historical Review*, 32 (1946), p. 547. See also Pena, *General Butler*, pp. 106–23.
22. Charles E. Magoon, *Reports on the Law of Civil Government in Territory Subject to Military Occupation* (Washington, DC: War Department, 1903), pp. 331–2.
23. Pena, *General Butler*, pp. 133–4.
24. Carpenter, 'Military government of Southern Territory', p. 478.
25. Peter Maslowski, *Treason Must be Made Odious* (Millwood, NY: KTO, 1978), p. 38.
26. Ibid. p. 65.
27. L. S. Amery, *The Times History of the War in South Africa*

1899–1902, vol. 6 (London: Sampson Low, 1909), pp. 576–8; Keith Terrance Surridge, *Managing the South African War 1899–1902* (Woodbridge: Boydell Press, 1998), p. 85.

28. Maslowski, *Treason Must be Made Odious*, pp. 79, 88, 93.

29. Alfred Vagts, 'Military command and military government', *Political Science Quarterly*, 59 (1944), pp. 254–5.

30. Rudodlf Thierfelder, 'Die Verwaltung des besetzten französischen Gebiete 1870–1873', *Reich-Volksordnung-Lebensraum*, 4 (1943), pp. 372–3.

31. Edgar Loening, 'L'administration du Gouvernement-Général de l'Alsace durant la guerre de 1870–1871', *Revue de Droit International et de Législation Comparée*, 4 (1872), p. 642.

32. Ibid. p. 641.

33. F. C. H. Clarke (trans.), *The Franco-German War, 1870–71*, vol. 3, part 2 (London: HMSO, 1884), p. 137.

34. Loening, 'L'administration du Gouvernement-Général', p. 101.

35. G. Rolin-Jaequemyns, 'Essai complementaire sur la guerre Franco-Allemande', *Revue de Droit International et de Législation Comparée*, 3 (1871), p. 313. For one of the many French protests, see P. Deloynes, 'Droit pénal de la guerre – de la responsabilité des communes', *Revue de Droit International et de Législation Comparée*, 6 (1874), pp. 134–41.

36. For the significance of this in the context of the administration of justice, see later, Chapter 7.

37. Rolin-Jaequemyns, 'Essai complementaire sur la guerre Franco-Allemande', p. 313

38. Clarke (trans.), *The Franco-German War, 1870–71*, vol. 3, part 2, p. 167.

39. For a more astringent view, see Karl Marx, 'The civil war in France', in Karl Marx, *The First International and After* (Harmondsworth: Penguin, 1974), pp. 221–2.

40. That role was subsequently downplayed by Americans but was evident at the time; see Louis le Fur, 'Chroniques des faits internationaux', *Revue Générale de Droit International Public*, 5 (1898), pp. 796–7 and Louis A. Pérez, 'Cuba between Empires, 1898–1899', *The Pacific Historical Review*, 48 (1979), pp. 481–4.

41. Ibid. p. 482

42. Fur, 'Chroniques des faits internationaux', p. 798.

43. Quoted in Louis A. Pérez, Supervision of a protectorate', *The Hispanic American Historical Review*, 52 (1992), p. 253.

44. Ibid. pp. 254–7.

45. Quoted in ibid. p. 258. See also Wood's own recollections: Leonard Wood, 'The military government of Cuba', *Annals of the American Academy of Political and Social Science*, 21 (1903), p. 154.

46. Wood, 'The military government of Cuba', pp. 153–82. Wood's reform-
    ing zeal had disastrous consequences elsewhere; see Charles Byler,
    'Pacifying the Moros', *Military Review* (May–June 2005), pp. 41–5.
47. Ludwig von Köhler, *The Administration of Occupied Territories, Vol.
    1: Belgium* (Washington, DC: Carnegie, 1942), p. 11.
48. Ibid. p. 23.
49. Ibid. p. 24.
50. W. R. Bisschop, 'German war legislation in the occupied territory
    of Belgium', *Transactions of the Grotius Society*, 4 (1918), p. 122.
    According to von Köhler, 'it was a sort of branch office of the Foreign
    Office in Berlin': *The Administration of Occupied Territories*, p. 29.
51. Bisschop, 'German war legislation', pp. 123–4.
52. von Köhler, *The Administration of Occupied Territories*, p. 16.
53. Bisschop, 'German war legislation', p. 133; James Wilford Garner,
    International Law and the World War, vol. 2 (London: Longmans,
    1920), p. 79.
54. Garner, *International Law and the World War*, p. 90.
55. Liulevicius, *War Land on the Eastern Front*, p. 21.
56. Ibid. pp. 57–8.
57. Ibid. pp. 55, 198.
58. On the range of meanings conjured up by this term, see ibid. pp.
    89–90.
59. Ibid. pp. 62–3, 89–108.
60. Ibid. p. 79. The contrast between east and west led H. de Watteville
    to conclude: 'There can be no question that the military regime of the
    Germans failed to a large extent in the East in like proportion as it
    succeeded in the West'. 'The military administration of occupied ter-
    ritory in time of war', *Transactions of the Grotius Society*, 7 (1921),
    p. 140.
61. Jonathon Steinberg, 'The Third Reich reflected: German civil adminis-
    tration in the occupied Soviet Union, 1941–4', *The English Historical
    Review*, 110 (1995), p. 650.
62. *Review of the Civil Administration of Mesopotamia*, Cmd. 1061
    (London: HMSO, 1920), p. 74.
63. Ibid. pp. 5–9.
64. Ibid. p. 76.
65. Quoted in Philip Graves, *The Life of Sir Percy Cox* (London:
    Hutchinson, 1941), p. 208.
66. Norman Bentwich, *England in Palestine* (London: Kegan Paul, 1932),
    p. 44.
67. Ibid. p. 37, 43.
68. Toby Dodge, *Inventing Iraq* (New York, NY: Columbia University
    Press, 2003), p. 8.
69. On the latter, see ibid., especially pp. 83–100 and Amal Vinogradov,

'The 1920 revolt in Iraq reconsidered', *International Journal of Middle East Studies*, 3 (1972), pp. 123–39.

70. Nagao Ariga, *La guerre Russo-Japonaise* (Paris: Pedone, 1908), p. 70. His point was noted by J. M. Spaight, *War Rights on Land* (London: Macmillan, 1911), p. 365. His account of the existence of the corps, but not his recommendation, was noted in the British *Manual of Military Law* (London: HMSO, 1914), p. 289.

71. Quoted in Ernst Fraenkel [1944], 'Military occupation and the rule of law', in Ernst Fraenkel, *Gesammelte Schriften*, vol. 3 (Baden-Baden: Nomos, 1999), p. 152.

72. Ibid. pp. 166–7.

73. See the record of the American military commander: Henry T. Allen, *My Rhineland Journal* (Boston, MA: Houghton and Mifflin, 1923), pp. 17–35.

74. Fraenkel, 'Military occupation and the rule of law', p. 155.

75. Quoted in Czeslaw Madajczyk, 'Die Besatzungssyteme der Achsenmächte', *Studia Historicae Oeconomicae*, 14 (1980), p. 117.

76. Umbreit, 'Towards continental domination', pp. 129–30.

77. Ibid. p. 134. The more accurate translation of *Militärbefehlshaber* as 'military commander' appears in Umbreit. The less accurate 'military governor' is used here in the interest of conformity with other references to military governors in this text.

78. Ibid. p. 130. This reflected wider considerations about leadership (*Führung*) in the Third Reich. See Peter M. R. Stirk, *Twentieth-Century German Political Thought* (Edinburgh: Edinburgh University Press, 2006), pp. 91–6.

79. Werner Warmbrunn, *The German Occupation of Belgium 1940–1944* (New York, NY: Lang, 1993), p. 76.

80. Ibid. p. 71.

81. Ibid. p 74.

82. Ibid. pp. 104–7.

83. On the significance of these officers within the SS empire, see Hans Buchheim, 'Die Höheren SS- und Polizeiführer', *Vierteljahreshefte für Zeitgeschichte*, 11 (1963), pp. 362–91.

84. For a recent survey of this, see Jay Howard Geller, 'The role of military administration in German-occupied Belgium 1940–1944', *The Journal of Military History*, 63 (1999), pp. 99–125.

85. Eberhard Jäckel, *Frankreich in Hitlers Europa* (Stuttgart: DVA, 1966), pp. 71–4. See also, on Abetz, Philippe Burrin, *France under the Germans* (New York, NY: New Press, 1996), pp. 90–6.

86. Umbreit, 'Towards continental domination', p. 148.

87. Jäckel, *Frankreich in Hitlers Europa*, pp. 94–5, 195.

88. Ibid. pp. 195–6.

89. 'Aus den Richtlinien von Wilhelm Keitel vom 12 Dezember 1941',

in Ludwig Nestler (ed.), *Europa unter Hakenkreuz. Die faschistische Okkupationspolitik in Frankreich (1940–1944)* (Berlin: DVW, 1990), p. 191.

90. Warmbrunn, *The German Occupation of Belgium*, p. 147.

91. Burrin, *France under the Germans*, p. 446.

92. Alexander Dallin, *German Rule in Russia 1941–1945* (London: Macmillan, 1981), p. 95.

93. Ibid. p. 96.

94. Ibid. p. 93.

95. J. Noakes and G. Pridham (eds), *Nazism 1919–1945*, vol. 3 (Exeter: Exeter University, 1988), p. 1096.

96. Quoted in Wendy Lower, *Nazi Empire-Building and the Holocaust in the Ukraine* (Chapel Hill, NC: University of North Carolina Press, 2005), p. 83.

97. Quoted in Yoji Akashi, 'Bureaucracy and the Japanese military administration, with specific reference to Malaya', in William H. Newell (ed.), *Japan in Asia* (Singapore: Singapore University Press, 1981), p. 49.

98. Ibid. p. 68

99. Harry J. Benda *et al.* (eds), *Japanese Military Administration in Indonesia: Selected Documents* (New Haven, CT: Yale University, 1965), p. 3.

100. Miysuo Nakamura, 'General Imamura and the early period of Japanese occupation', *Indonesia*, 10 (1970), pp. 63, 67–9.

101. Akashi, 'Bureaucracy and the Japanese military administration', pp. 47–9.

102. Yoji Akashi, 'Japanese policy towards the Malayan Chinese 1941–1945', *Journal of Southeast Asian Studies*, 1 (1970), pp. 63, 67–9.

103. Paul H. Kratoska, *The Japanese Military Administration of Malaya* (London: Hurst, 1998), pp. 59–60.

104. Akashi, 'Japanese policy towards the Malayan Chinese', p. 65.

105. Kratoska, *The Japanese Military Administration of Malaya*, pp. 93–103.

106. See, for example, Elmer N. Lear, 'Collaboration in Leyte: the Philippines under Japanese occupation', *The Far Eastern Quarterly*, 11 (1952), pp. 196–201.

107. Yoji Akashi, 'Japanese military administration in Malaya', *Asian Studies*, 7 (1969), p. 109.

108. On the factions, see Akashi, 'Bureaucracy and the Japanese military administration', p. 66.

109. John W. Dower, *Embracing Defeat. Japan in the Aftermath of World War II* (London: Penguin, 1999), p. 211.

110. Takemae Eiji, *The Allied Occupation of Japan* (New York, NY: Continuum, 2002), pp. 73, 93–4.

111. Vagts, 'Military command and military government', p. 257.
112. Earl F. Ziemke, *The U.S. Army in the Occupation of Germany 1944–1946* (Honolulu, HI: University Press of the Pacific, 1975), p. 401.
113. C. R. S. Harris, *Allied Military Administration of Italy 1943–1945* (London: HMSO, 1957), p. 10.
114. F. S. V Donnison, *Civil Affairs and Military Government. Central Organization and Planning* (London: HMSO, 1966), pp. 56–7.
115. War Department, *Military Government and Civil Affairs*, FM 27-5 (22 December 1943), p. 24.
116. Harris, *Allied Military Administration of Italy*, pp. 95–6.
117. Charles Fairman, 'Some observations on military occupation', *Minnesota Law Review*, 32 (1948), p. 332.
118. Harris, *Allied Military Administration of Italy*, p. 113.
119. Ibid. pp. 376–7.
120. Ibid. pp. 364–5; John Lamberton Harper, *America and the Reconstruction of Italy, 1945–1948* (Cambridge: Cambridge University Press, 1986), p. 32.
121. Donnison, *Civil Affairs and Military Government North West Europe*, pp. 21–2.
122. Ziemke, *The U.S. Army in the Occupation of Germany 1944–1946*, p. 206.
123. Ibid. p. 273.
124. Donnison, *Civil Affairs and Military Government North West Europe*, pp. 234–7.
125. John Gimbel, *A German Community under American Occupation* (Stanford, CA: Stanford University Press, 1961).
126. SHAEF, *Handbook for Military Government of Germany*, December 1944, para. 247.
127. Anne Deighton, *The Impossible Peace* (Oxford: Clarendon Press, 1993), p. 84. Unlike the British, Clay did not presume at this stage that a division of Germany was inevitable or even necessarily desirable; ibid. pp. 118–20.
128. Donnison, *Civil Affairs and Military Government North West Europe*, p. 406.
129. Ibid. p. 242.
130. Michael J. Hogan, *The Marshall Plan* (Cambridge: Cambridge University Press, 1987), pp. 163–4, 132–3.
131. Norman M. Naimark, *The Russians in Germany* (Cambridge, MA: Harvard University Press, 1995), pp. 26–7.
132. Ibid. p. 23.
133. Dower, *Embracing Defeat*, p. 208.
134. Ibid. pp. 221–4.
135. Marlene J. Mayo, 'American wartime planning for occupied Japan',

in Robert Wolfe (ed.), *Americans as Proconsuls* (Carbondale, IL: Southern Illinois University Press, 1984), p. 471.

136. Ibid. p. 470.
137. Takemae, *The Allied Occupation of Japan*, pp. 114–16.
138. Dower, *Embracing Defeat*, p. 360.
139. Takemae, *The Allied Occupation of Japan*, pp. 304–5.
140. Ralph Braibanti, 'Administration of military government in Japan at the prefectural level', *American Political Science Review*, 43 (1949), pp. 251–8.
141. Ibid. p. 268.
142. Ralph Braibanti, 'The role of administration in the occupation of Japan', *Annals of the American Academy of Political and Social Science*, 267 (1950), p. 163.
143. Braibanti, 'Administration of military government in Japan at the prefectural level', p. 258. On these teams, see also Takemae, *The Allied Occupation of Japan*, pp. 117–20.
144. Takemae, *The Allied Occupation of Japan*, pp. 274–5. See also Hugh Borton, 'Preparation for the occupation of Japan', *The Journal of Asian Studies*, 25 (1966), p. 210.
145. Philip H. Taylor, 'The administration of occupied Japan', *Annals of the American Academy of Political and Social Science*, 267 (1950), p. 151.
146. For an example of the tensions this involved, see Walter Hixson, *George F. Kennan* (New York, NY: Columbia University Press, 1989), pp. 61–4.
147. Michael Dumper, 'Forty years without slumbering: waqf politics and administration in the Gaza Strip, 1948–1987', *British Journal of Middle Eastern Studies*, 20 (1993), pp. 174–90, especially p. 189.
148. Ilan Pappe, *A History of Modern Palestine* (Cambridge: Cambridge University Press, 2006), pp. 195–6.
149. Michael Palumbo, *Imperial Israel* (London: Bloomsbury, 1990), pp. 154–72.
150. Quoted in Joel Slinger, 'The establishment of a civil administration in the areas administered by Israel', *Israel Yearbook on Human Rights*, 12 (1982), p. 278. For the persistence of this strategy and its wider ramifications, see Raja Shehadeh, 'Negotiating self-government agreements', *Journal of Palestine Studies*, 21, 4 (1992), pp. 27–8.

Chapter 4

The Role of Civilian Governors in Military Occupation

The role of civilian governors in military occupations has been an ambivalent one. From the days of the representatives on mission of revolutionary France, civilian agents and agencies have periodically been seen as symbols of a political intent subversive of the temporary nature of military occupation and military authority.[1] Sometimes, military governments have even resisted the establishment of civilian institutions of governance on the grounds that this would imply a premature annexation of the territory.[2] Suspicion of civilian agencies culminated in this judgement of a court in the Netherlands after the Second World War: 'After the cessation of active military operations the then German Reich continued consistently to commit new violations of international law by, *inter alia*, . . . setting up in Holland a civil administration which was made independent of a military commander . . .'.[3]

Yet some role has frequently been conceded, more or less willingly, to civilian agents and agencies with limited integration into a military command structure. Hostility to the idea of authoritarian polities dominated by military bodies has encouraged the search for overarching civilian authority. More recently, the search for a level of legitimacy that, so it seems, cannot be provided by the fact of occupation and the nature of international law alone, has led to the deployment of civilian structures parallel to military structures under the aegis of the United Nations and other international bodies. Such trends have been strengthened by the frustration of military commanders with the intractability of political problems, even where these same commanders have been advocates of integrated systems of command.[4] Professed indifference to politics has pointed in the same direction, even where the profession might not be entirely sincere.[5] More important was the comment made by General Jackson in relation to his greeting the new head of the United Nations Mission in Kosovo, Bernard Kouchner: 'it seemed to me important to show that in a civilized society the military should be subject to the civil authority'.[6]

Subordination of military authority to civilian authority, and a greater role for civilian agencies, also suggests greater priority for occupation according to the rule of law rather than martial law and the dictates of military necessity. There is, of course, no guarantee that civilian agencies and authority will, without further qualification, lead to this outcome, as the occupation regime in the Netherlands condemned by the Dutch court illustrates. Moreover, even where the purposes of the civilian governors are not perverse, the virtuous circle of subordination to civilian authority and more extensive activity by civilian agencies and government according to the rule of law is no more an accurate picture than the model of military government as a caste-like phenomenon. Not the least of the complications which undermine such a picture is the relationship between the civilian agencies and the military forces without which the former would not constitute civilian governors within a regime of military occupation in the first place. As in the case of forms of military government, the nature of the society over which authority is exercised – especially the extent to which relatively centralised and hierarchical indigenous political structures persist and some form of unity of political will can be maintained – will shape the nature of the occupation regime, even where it is animated by a largely predatory intent. By the same token, the extreme fragmentation of indigenous power can undermine the intent and structure of civilian agencies, even where this fragmentation is not the intent of the occupier.[7]

The expertise that civilian agencies can provide, whether on the basis of being extensions of ministries or other agencies within the domestic structure of the occupier or on the basis of ad hoc agencies created for specific purposes related to occupations, is often invoked as a prime reason for their deployment. Yet, in principle, there is no necessity for allowing this expertise to be deployed in the form of an independent agency rather than in subordination to a military command structure, though pragmatic considerations and resource constraints, as well as more significant considerations of political ambition and legitimacy have led to such a preference.

Autonomous civilian agencies with a powerful domestic base or important political allies have played a most obvious role where such agencies have been divorced not just from military structures but also from the normal structures of the modern state. Here the party and security agencies of the Third Reich and the Soviet Union stand out as examples. Yet more mundane agencies within democratic states can play a significant and problematic role. In the American occupation of Cuba, the postal service operated under the control of the Postmaster General in Washington whose local agent in Havana 'created, in a way, a small government of his own'.[8] More importantly, financial irregularities, suspicion of the potential imperial ambitions of the President and an impending presidential election, combined to create a scandal which threatened both the re-election of the President and the reputation of the occupation regime under General Wood.[9]

Concern about the financial probity of occupation regimes has become more prominent, not surprisingly, as the financial burden upon the occupier has grown with the extent of the occupier's ambitions, leading to greater potential leverage for civilian agencies. That was evident even in the closing stages of General MacArthur's administration of the occupation of post-war Japan. In implementation of National Security Directive 13/2 of October 1948, which signalled a wide-ranging shift in occupation policy, Joseph Dodge was dispatched from Washington to oversee a deflationary economic policy and a balanced Japanese budget. According to a member of the occupation administration, Theodore Cohen, Dodge, whom he parodied as the 'Lord High Imperial Accountant', exercised enormous power through his economic brief. Dodge, Cohen wrote, 'was demonstrating that control of the budget from one small office was more powerful than the 150,000-man Occupation army commanded by General MacArthur'.[10] That was an exaggeration insofar as Dodge's power over the Japanese economy existed only because of the fact of military occupation. It was true, however, that the 'reverse course', as it came to be known, was not only a change of policy but also the resolution of a dispute over the location of authority in Japan in which Dodge, as personal representative of the President, triumphed over MacArthur.[11] It was inevitable too that the development of the Economic Cooperation Administration, established to implement the Marshall Plan in Europe, would come to be seen as a competitor to the military administration in Germany. Indeed the Military Governor, General Clay, worried that its development would mean that the 'military government may no longer have the authority and prestige which makes successful administration possible'.[12]

In each of these cases, the civilian agent or agency exerted such authority as it could by virtue of its technical function or the specific policy it was established to pursue. It did not exert the general power of the occupier or even stand alongside the military forces as a distinct partner in the task of occupations; still less did the civilian agent or agency enjoy any formal power of command over the armed forces. It is, however, when civilian agencies or agents attain sufficient autonomy vis-à-vis the military force that has established the occupation that the character of the occupation begins to take on a different form. As indicated above, the rationale for embarking on such a course has varied considerable. In the case of the occupation of the Rhineland, the decisive consideration was reaction to an initial proposal for the continuation of military government and martial law, including a wide-ranging authority to veto German legislation as well as 'industrial regulations, awards or agreements'.[13] For Pierrepont Noyes, the American representative on the existing Inter-Allied Rhineland High Commission, the proposal appeared to be 'an extremely brutal document' whose consequence would be that 'force and more force must be the history of such occupation long continued'.[14]

The outcome, intended to mitigate the harshness of the occupation regime, was for a civil commission, with even less extensive powers than Noyes himself had suggested, and the suspension of martial law, save when it was specifically invoked at the request of the commission.[15] French dissatisfaction with these constraints, above all with the principle of civilian control, was evident in the attempt to interpose a 'security committee' composed of four officers drawn from the occupation armies. That, as General Allen, commander of the American forces, noted 'would be largely in the nature of transferring civil authority to military authority'.[16]

According to the Rhineland Agreement establishing this civilian authority, the principle of civilian control reserved to the High Commission 'the power, whenever they think it necessary, to declare a state of siege in any part of the territory or in the whole of it'. It further specified that in this event 'the military authorities shall have the powers provided in the German Imperial Law of May 30th 1892'.[17] The principle of civilian pre-eminence seemed to be confirmed in 1920 when the High Commission overruled military instructions prohibiting the singing of the *Deutschlandlied* on the grounds that they had no authority to issue such general instructions. Yet the French general, Mordaq, objected to what he described as the '"unbearable" dualism of governmental powers' and proved reluctant to remain within the remit ascribed to him by the High Commission or even, on some occasions, to obey the direct and specific instructions of the Commission.[18]

The dependency of the Commission's authority upon international agreements further complicated the situation. The Rhineland Agreement specified that the High Commission should consist of the representatives of four nations, France, Belgium, Britain and the United States. The latter, however, failed to ratify the Treaty of Versailles, implementation of part of which was the purpose of the Rhineland Agreement. Formally, the United States was not a member of the Commission, though adept initiatives by the American general, Allen, mitigated that particular difficulty. More problematic was the role of the Commission in wider Allied policy towards Germany and the enforcement of the payment of reparations and fulfilment of other conditions by Germany imposed by the Treaty of Versailles. In this context the Commission became not only a body that implemented the Rhineland Agreement but also an agent of the London Conference of Allied Governments, in which capacity it established committees regulating customs, alcohol and import and export licenses. As Ernst Fraenkel pointed out, this meant that 'two systems of occupation control, of wholly different legal character, were administered by the same body'.[19] Franco-Belgian occupation of the Ruhr, territory which lay outside the remit of the Rhineland Agreement, a policy approved by neither the British nor the American governments, met with the withdrawal of the American forces from the Rhineland while the British declined to participate in the occupation of the Ruhr. That left a military government in the Ruhr which met with a policy of passive resistance by the Germans.[20] As this resistance was extended to the Rhineland, the High Commission, acting with the abstention of the British, replicated decrees issued by the French commander of Franco-Belgian forces in the Ruhr.[21] Not only did this amount to a fragmentation of the occupation regime in terms of its legal remit, territorial extent and composition, but it also distorted the principle of civilian control that the Rhineland Agreement had established.

Within the Rhineland itself, the High Commission was confronted not only with a robust German bureaucracy with links to administrative and political agencies in unoccupied Germany and the recalcitrance of specific officials but also with a discrepancy between Allied, especially American, understanding of the nature of government and German understanding. According to Fraenkel, the powers of the High Commission had been formulated on the basis of the presumption of a division of powers, with the High Commission acting primarily as a legislative organ whose ordinances were to be implemented by a German bureaucracy. Provision for the removal of officials who failed to implement ordinances was to be the prime means of enforcement. Here, however, the High Commission had conceded more ground than it realised:

> By restricting the disciplinary power of the High Commission to cases of non-conformance with the ordinances, it relinquished control over all those activities of the German administrative agencies that were not based on statutes but on an almost unrestricted general jurisdiction.[22]

Having conceded this power, the High Commission, especially through its French chairman, Tirard, tried to claw back the power it had conceded, by, for example, granting itself a general power of veto over all official appointments. The fact that this veto was exercised in order to promote separatist tendencies in the Rhineland inevitably made the Germans more resentful.

At the same time, Germany attempted to bolster the integrity of its administration vis-à-vis the High Commission by appointing a *Reichskommissar* for the occupied territories whom they attempted to interpose between the High Commission and the various German administrative agencies. In this Germany had limited success for the occupation authorities refused to channel their instructions to German agencies through the *Reichskommissar*, though they accepted that he could coordinate initiatives from German agencies to the High Commission.[23] In practice, the *Reichskommissar* saw his task largely as one of obstruction, as did the senior officials of the German National Property Administration.[24] Given German attempts to centralise their interaction with the High Commission it is not surprising that Germany took particular exception to the appointment of local representatives of the High Commission with vague, but in fact extensive, powers. This meant, moreover, that German officials were subject to two potentially competing authorities, their superiors within the German bureaucracy and the local representatives of the High Commission. The fact that these representatives were sometimes civilians failed to reduce the tension, as one representative noted:

> The fact that the German preferred that power to be exercised by soldiers rather than by civilians showed how the local delegates must have been detested. So much so, that Gaye and I were ordered always to wear uniform on duty so as never to be mistaken for civilians.[25]

Ironically, the attempt to mitigate the rigours of military occupation by establishing a civilian-dominated regime increased the resentment which inevitably accompanied it. In Fraenkel's judgement:

> If an occupation statute is too 'liberal', if it underestimates the strength
> of the bureaucratic forces in the occupied country, and overlooks the
> necessity for an efficient control of these agencies, there is a danger that
> those entrusted with its application will be led to adapt even its most vital
> provisions to the demands of expediency.[26]

To this must be added the extent of French ambition and the wider
function of the occupation of the Rhineland in guaranteeing French
security. The occupation was itself a substitute for separation of the
Rhineland from Germany, but was not a substitute for the Anglo-
American guarantee that the French had been promised.[27] Both in
matters of the organisation of the government of the occupation and
its wider policy objectives, the French became implicit revisionists in
relation to the treaties and agreements they claimed to be enforcing.[28]
It was also a diminishing asset. The limitation of its duration by the
Treaty of Versailles meant that the power of the occupying forces
declined as the scheduled end of the occupation grew closer.[29]

The introduction of civilian administrations into occupied
Netherlands and Norway during the Second World War was not
constrained by international agreements and was driven by an
even more radical, and futile, political ambition. In both cases, the
administrations – headed by a *Reichskommissar*, Terboven in Norway
and Seyss-Inquart in the Netherlands – were intent upon a replication
of the 'legal revolution' that they believed had led to the Nazi seizure
of power in Germany and which was supposed to prepare these
Germanic peoples, as they saw them, for incorporation into a Greater
Germanic Reich.[30] Both were aware that the indigenous national
socialist movements, led by Vidkun Quisling and Anton Mussert
respectively, were small and bitterly opposed by many of their fellow
nationals. Both were also aware that they had to maintain a difficult
balance. Seyss-Inquart, for instance, was torn between the competing
pressure of 'the far reaching suppression of all possible forms of
public activity' in the interests of the security of the occupier and the
desire to 'awaken and control the political will . . . to concede such
freedoms as will make the final result into a decision which the Dutch
have made for themselves'.[31]

While Seyss-Inquart concealed the intended perpetuation of
German hegemony and denial of any meaningful independence to the
Netherlands, he was sincere in his intent to win over the majority of
the population to a policy of collaboration and to allow some measure
of political freedom in the process. This amounted to sufficient scope
for the formation, by a small non-party group, of the Netherlands

Union, which had attracted 800,000 members by February 1941. The Union, committed to a programme of renewal in the political and social structures of the Netherlands, was also intended as a rejection of the claim of the indigenous National Socialist Movement to represent Dutch society to the occupation forces.[32] Despite the sudden growth of the movement, there was uncertainty on the part both of the members of the movement and the occupation authorities. Despite concessions made by the Netherlands Union, including the omission of any reference to maintaining the royal house, the underlying disagreement about the future of the Netherlands culminated in the dissolution of the Union by Seyss-Inquart in December 1941. Hence, when at his trial Seyss-Inquart confessed that amongst the 'errors of judgement' he had made was the presumption 'that in an occupied country, an independent political will can develop', he erred again, for it was the independence of the Netherlands Union, despite its compromises, that condemned it in the eyes of the occupier.[33]

Seyss-Inquart had also sought to attain his goal through reshaping the institutional and, even more so, the associational structure of Dutch society. Formal governmental structures, aside from the representational bodies, remained relatively unaffected. As in the military government of occupied Belgium, German General Commissars operated through the Secretary-Generals of the Dutch ministries, endowing the latter with enhanced powers.[34] There was some innovation in the centralisation of the police force and a division of the Department of Education, Arts and Science, part of which became a Department of Propaganda and Arts, in imitation of Joseph Goebbels' ministry in Berlin.[35] That was linked with the creation of a Chamber of Culture, a Netherlands Land Estate, a Foundation Winter Help Netherlands with a monopoly of charitable work, and a Construction Service, later replaced by a Labour Service; these all replicated similar institutions created in the Third Reich as part of the *Gleichschaltung* that formed part of the Nazi seizure of power. With varying degrees of compulsory membership and coercive power, they too formed part of Seyss-Inquart's attempt to control public life.[36] A similar strategy was followed in Norway, though there the fact that the indigenous national socialist leader, Quisling, had attained a greater role, despite the opposition of *Reichskommissar* Terboven, proved to be an obstacle to the policies of the occupier; Quisling feared inciting so much dissent that Terboven might use this as an excuse for reasserting his authority over Quisling.[37] In retrospect, at his post-war trial, Seyss-Inquart confessed that this strategy had also failed, though he claimed that the structure of Dutch associational life had forced the strategy upon him:

> With the prohibition of political parties, most of the organisations of the free professions became impossible, since right down to the chessplayers' club everything in the Netherlands was organised on a political basis. In the interests of the occupational forces I had to create new supervisory bodies. Maybe it was due to lack of imagination that these organisations were, in part at least, very similar to their prototypes in the Reich.[38]

In the case of civilian administration in the German occupied east, the official position stressed the importance of ensuring that 'the peoples of the eastern area are confronted with a single legislator and that all decrees are issued by one unified political will'.[39] That was combined with a policy of refusing to recognise that the populations of the occupied territories had any rights, as opposed to duties, dismantling as much of the existing indigenous political structures as possible and instituting a form of political rule by party agents. In the eyes of these agents it appeared that 'the party's ideal of an administrative tabula rasa was about to be realized'.[40] Consistent with this ambition, Hans Frank, Governor-General of Poland, established twelve, and later fourteen, departments rather than the much smaller number typical of other German occupation regimes.[41] To some degree there were limits to the extent to which the German occupiers could dispense with all the administrative structures and personnel, if only because of the shortage of German personnel and the sheer scale of the territories and populations under occupation. In the Government-General of Poland large numbers of Poles were required as lower level administrators and even as mayors. Similarly, up to 16,000 were employed in a Polish police force though, unlike western Europe, these policemen were excluded from higher ranks and their stations strictly subordinated to German police officials.[42] Yet, despite this ideological emphasis upon unity and the deliberate flattening of indigenous structures, the reality of civilian rule in the east was chaotic. Seyss-Inquart, who had been briefly Deputy Governor of the General-Government, contrasted conditions there with the relatively centralised control he claimed to have exercised in the Netherlands, denying that anything similar could be found in the east.[43] Later commentators have been so struck by the chaotic reality as to find it 'puzzling that this rather small contingent of German colonizers was so divided. They lived, after all, in the midst of a hostile population and, after 1942–1943, lost their self-assurance and grew to feel endangered'.[44] The chaos was rooted, in fact, in a rabid competition for power, restrained neither by traditional understanding of military occupation nor by notions such as Seyss-Inquart's hopes for a 'legal revolution' in the Netherlands, and driven forward by the racial agenda that culminated in the Holocaust.

Here it was a hybrid civilian-military agency, Himmler's SS, which emerged as the dominant force.[45] It was not, however, the only source of competition. The *Arbeitsbereich* (area of work activity) of the Nazi party was an extension of the party into occupied areas where the regime had a specific political programme. This, although nominally subordinate to Governor-General Frank, developed some autonomy, even if its size, some 16,000 in 1940, was not matched by the quality of its personnel.[46] Some disjunction between Frank's administrative structure and the *Arbeitsbereich* followed automatically from Nazi commitment to the distinct roles of the Nazi party on the one hand and state structures on the other. Both shared an antipathy to Himmler's SS, as in part did the army with which Frank initially had problems as well.[47] Backed by the range of commissions and offices bestowed on Himmler by Hitler in the east, the SS and police system threatened to acquire the 'character of an autonomous territorial regime' in the face of which the 'sovereign position granted to Frank as General-Governor by Hitler proved to be . . . a paper supremacy'.[48]

Although the Nazi civilian administration in the Netherlands and Norway, like their military counterpart in Belgium, degenerated into a terroristic regime as collapse approached, civilian rule, motivated as it was by Nazi racial ideology, provided some scope for manoeuvre to indigenous political structures and forces, in a way that was excluded at the outset from the racially motivated civilian administrations in the occupied east. It was the latter, however, which proved to be not only far more destructive and barbarous but also more chaotic, much more so than the military administration of the *Ober Ost* in the First World War, which had also been based upon the flattening of indigenous social structures. All these, however, also contrast sharply with the occupation of the Rhineland, and not only because of the obvious differences between the political ambitions of the occupiers. The fact that the occupied Rhineland had strong political and bureaucratic structures rooted in the structures of unoccupied Germany also shaped the nature of the occupation regime.

A still stronger contrast occurs where it is the intent of the occupier to positively foster such strong indigenous political structures.

Here, too, civilian governors have been seen to have a distinct attraction, symbolising the transition from strictly military government. Nevertheless, it does not automatically follow that such civilian governors are weak. In the case of post-war Germany, the authority of the occupier was perpetuated as military government was formally ended, with the military governors of the three western zones being replaced by high commissioners. Under the Occupation Statute, the high commissioners retained unilateral legislative power in their respective zones, enjoyed joint legislative authority as the Council of the Allied High Commission, and possessed a power of review of German legislation until this provision was amended in September 1950.[49] Although the review power was exercised with some restraint, the legislative activity of the Commission was quite intensive.[50] Moreover, the Allied commissioners, especially the American High Commissioner, exerted extensive influence by virtue of their general authority, backed by the threat to assert their powers under the Occupation Statute, in such key issues as the devaluation of the currency and the structure of the German coal and steel industries.[51] The power exercised by the High Commission was rooted not just in the provisions of the Occupation Statute and the continued presence of large American forces, but also in the ability of their respective governments to sanction, or break, international agreements, especially those that could bring about an end to the Occupation Statute. That was finally achieved in 1955, with German rearmament and integration into the western alliance system. In this case, however, much of the work had already been carried out under a military government, before the appointment of the high commissioners and the promulgation of the Occupation Statute.

Although the intention of military occupation to develop, in part at least, indigenous political structures is not new, as the American occupation of Cuba at the end of the nineteenth century demonstrates, the flurry of occupations that followed the end of the Cold War illustrate the difficulties that this ambition brings with it, especially where existing structures have disintegrated. They also illustrate the peculiar constraints which civilian governors face when they are divorced from a military chain of command. In this respect, however, the United Nations Transitional Administration for Eastern Slavonia, Baranja and Western Sirmium (UNTAES) from 1996 to 1998 was distinctive, for here civilian and military authority was combined. That meant that the Transitional Administrator was able to demonstratively deploy military force in order to enhance the occupier's authority, especially when confronted with paramilitary challenge, most notably over control of the Djeletovici oil fields.[52] Even so, it was notable that, despite the lack of violence, this action caused some disquiet in the United Nations in New York.[53] The task there was eased by the fact that despite the inter-ethnic violence that had led to the deployment of UNTAES in the first place, local government structures were sufficiently intact to allow UNTAES to exercise a supervisory administration, taking direct control only over the police force.[54] Indeed, Derek Boothby, the Deputy Administrator, later noted that its 'tasks may be described as supervision and oversight, but they are not governing, which implies the direction and control over the actions and affairs of a community'.[55] This is, of course, not peculiar to civilian governors. Both military and civilian governors have typically preferred to rely on supervisory administration where possible, unless ideologically committed to the destruction of indigenous political structures. Supervisory administration was also eased by the limited purpose of the occupation, namely the reintegration of the area into an independent Croatia while avoiding a renewal of violence and providing some protection for ethnic Serbs in the area.[56]

The presumption that supervisory administration would suffice was sufficiently strong for it to be taken as the basis for the occupation regime even where, for different reasons, it turned out to be unsound. In the case of Bosnia, even supervisory administration seemed to be subordinate to a facilitative role, for the Dayton Peace Agreement of 1995 provided that the High Representative was 'to facilitate the Parties' own efforts and to mobilise and . . . co-ordinate the activities of the organizations and agencies involved in the civilian aspects of the peace settlement'.[57] The 'Dayton model' mistakenly presumed that the parties desired to cooperate. The assumption made in Iraq about a rapid transition to Iraqi government of a functioning state was even less plausible, but again issued in preparation for very limited supervisory administration. The outcomes were, however, significantly different insofar as in Bosnia existing structures, namely the governments and institutions of the Federation of Bosnia-Herzegovina and, even more so, the Republika Srpska, proved strong enough to resist the efforts of the supervisory administration whereas in Iraq the problem became one of a fragmentation of the state.[58] Elements of the supervisory model were still present in the failed Rambouillet agreement for Kosovo of February 1999. The reality after the NATO bombing campaign was the flight of Yugoslav officials leaving a vacuum partially filled by the attempted seizure of authority by Albanian paramilitary forces in all those communes with an ethnic Albanian majority.[59] Only in East Timor was the level of destruction and dislocation so drastic that the irrelevance of the supervisory model was unmistakable. That was evident in the effective recognition of the need to establish a de facto government.[60] In all of these cases, however, government far beyond the supervisory model became the practice for a greater or lesser duration.

As in instances of rule by military governors, civilian governors are present by virtue of the military forces that support their presence. In all of these cases, however, the relationship between the military forces and the civilian governors proved to be a cause of the weakness of the occupation regime. In Bosnia, not only was the role of the High Representative restricted but there was also opposition from the United States to a powerful International Police Task Force for fear that the military Implementation Force (IFOR) would be called in to support the authority of the police if it were challenged.[61] Separation of military command from structures of civilian authority meant that little could be done when IFOR took a restrictive view of its role. According to one report, it

> refused to deploy on the streets . . . or to impose a curfew . . . refused to arrest indicted war criminals . . . was reluctant to enter any situations where it might be forced to confront a mob of civilians, believing it had no capacity to respond effectively.[62]

Failure to prevent the intimidation of Serbs in Sarajevo, leading to the effective expulsion of between 60,000 and 100,000, 'sent a powerful signal that the country's pluri-ethnicity was a thing of the past'.[63] Yet as frustration with the reluctance of the indigenous parties to cooperate grew, it was military force in the shape of IFOR's successor, the more assertive Stabilization Force (SFOR), which gave substance to the considerable enhancement of the High Representative's powers by the Peace Implementation Council in 1997 at its Bonn summit.[64] By the same token the marked reduction of international armed forces weakened the prospect of continued exercise of these 'Bonn powers', especially under a High Representative with a pronounced public reluctance to use them.[65]

Civilian-military coordination had proven to be weak in East Timor as well, notably between the UN humanitarian operations centre of the UN Transitional Administration in East Timor (UNTAET) and the civil-military operations centre of the International Force in East Timor (INTERFET).[66] Despite INTERFET's vigour in establishing security and the borders of East Timor it took a limited view of its role beyond these areas. Although it went further than some critics liked in establishing a detention centre it declined to extend its remit to civil policing or the judicial process. Nor had adequate preparation been made for coordination between the police element of the UNTAET and INTERFET.[67] Similar problems arose in Kosovo, reinforced by the disavowal of any concern about 'mission creep' by the Kosovo Force (KFOR) commander.[68] Concern about preventing the return of the departed Yugoslav army, slow deployment of the international police force and indeed of the other components of the UN Interim Administration Mission in Kosovo (UNMIK), overstretched KFOR.[69] That was aggravated by the fact that 'within the hastily drawn up structure of UN administration in Kosovo, UNMIK, not KFOR, was to be responsible for the everyday maintenance of public order'.[70] Again there was a reluctance to extend KFOR's remit to judicial functions.[71] A special problem was presented by the existence of the Kosovo Liberation Army, parts of which were incorporated into a new Kosovo Protection Corps, whose precise role was open to different interpretations. Equally significant, the Kosovo Protection Corps became a major source of disagreement within the international administration.[72] Riots in March 2004 exposed a chronic lack of coordination and mutual mistrust. In retrospect at least it seemed that the 'division of responsibility [between UNMIK and KFOR] is ambiguous, and the response to the March 2004 riots was consequently disastrous'.[73]

While the separate organisation of UNTAET and UNMIK, on the one hand, and the respective military forces on the other, might be seen as a source of some of these problems, it is notable that recognisably similar problems occurred in Iraq where both the military force and the civilian agency, the Coalition Provisional Authority (CPA) were the agents of the same power and the head of the CPA, Paul Bremer, reported to the Department of Defence. Given the lack of certainty about the process by which the CPA had been authorised, even some time after the event, it is less surprising that there was some uncertainty about the relationship between the military forces and the CPA.[74] Although a broad division of responsibility between security, the task of the armed forces, and political reconstruction, the task of the CPA, readily suggests itself such a separation proved impossible. This made the relationship between them crucial yet there was disagreement between the military and civilian agencies about which, if either, was senior to the other.[75] In fact, they existed as separate structures with their own chains of command and channels of communication.[76] This organisational autonomy could not, however, be translated into autonomy of policy, for each could impinge on the other, either by taking initiatives or by being resistant to them. The CPA, for example, initiated a policy on border security without consulting the military command and made no change after it had, belatedly, consulted it.[77] Yet the CPA was dependent upon the military command structure, most obviously in crucial decisions about how to respond to the emergence of an insurgency and especially the challenge posed by the radical cleric Muqtada al-Sadr. Indeed Bremer recalled being unable even to compel military lawyers to supply evidence that might have warranted Muqtada's arrest.[78] More broadly, the CPA was dependent on the military by virtue of its lack of control over military escorts, without which its personnel could not move, and by virtue of the sheer discrepancy in the size of the two organisations.[79]

In all of these operations the fact that a governing structure had to be constituted in the first place, compounded by tendencies towards centralisation, weakened the ability of these authorities to extend their remit throughout the occupied territory and undermined their own plans to decentralise authority. Initially, at least, 'UNITAET invested primarily in building its own capacity to function as a de facto state'.[80] In East Timor, the intended decentralisation to district administrators exercising control over all non-military agents faltered: 'the subordination of civilian elements to the DA [District Administrator] was unravelled with independent chains of command reasserting themselves from the capital'.[81] In Kosovo, UNMIK still lacked a presence in some communes a full three months after the end of the war.[82] In Iraq, the problem was less one of excessive centralisation and more the shortage of personnel, paucity of resources, and a lack of central coordination, leaving governate coordinators to improvise, despite their lack of substantive power.[83]

Even at the centre, the power wielded by civilian governors, though it could appear to be near absolute, was not as unrestrained as might appear. This is not to deny that it was substantial. The military force that stood behind them, albeit without being under their direct control, their power of appointment to the various provisional and consultative bodies that they established or their power of dismissal, have readily attracted attention. That impression is consolidated by the observation of the UN Special Envoy, Lakhdar Brahimi, shortly before the formation of an interim Iraqi government and the formal end of the CPA in June 2004: 'I'm sure he doesn't mind my saying it – Mr. Bremer is the dictator of Iraq'.[84] The authority explicitly claimed by the CPA bore out Brahimi's assertion for Bremer, in the first CPA regulation, had proclaimed that

> *Pursuant* to my authority as Adminstrator of the Coalition Provisional Authority . . . I hereby proclaim the following . . . The CPA is vested with all executive, legislative and judicial authority necessary to achieve its objectives . . . Regulations shall be those instruments that define the institutions and authorities of the CPA. Orders are binding instructions issued by the CPA . . . Regulations and Orders . . . shall take precedence over all other laws and publications.[85]

Not only was this a rejection of any division of power and the assertion of a plenitude of power but, by definition of CPA regulations, it was an assertion of the competence of the CPA to determine its own competence. The latter has often been taken as the mark of sovereignty.[86] Elsewhere, it was the arbitrary nature of power that stood out. Thus, the widespread dismissal of elected and appointed officials in Bosnia led to protests against the exercise of power without accountability to those over whom it is exercised:

> The Bonn powers had become instruments of bureaucratic convenience, their sweeping use justified in public on vague and general grounds, and little restrained by basic principles of individual responsibility and due process. All of this was happening, moreover, in the name of 'strengthening the rule of law'.[87]

In part, however, it is precisely the presumption that the rule of law, including 'individual responsibility and due process', ought to prevail that enhances the arbitrary and unrestrained nature of power. That was already evident in Ernst Fraenkel's reflections on the occupation of the Rhineland:

> From a purely psychological point of view, the co-existence of two systems of government – a rule of arbitrariness and a rule of law, is probably harder to endure than an outright rule of martial law . . . if legal procedures are presumably respected, extra-legal measures appear arbitrary and the activities of courts hypocritical.[88]

Ironically, however, despite the undeniable fact that this power is arbitrary in this sense, uncertainty about its exercise, and awareness of the fact that it is not legitimate power in the eyes of those subject to it, can also enhance the tendency to rely upon it. Thus, according to the Head of the Office of District Administration in East Timor, UN officials 'stated openly that since UNTAET was not a representative government, it could not tolerate other bodies in the country being more representative'.[89]

The perceived illegitimacy of government by an occupation regime, whether openly admitted military occupation or government in the name of international administration, was enhanced by what has been called a dual mandate in the case of the Security Council Resolution authorising UNTAET: namely, the injunction to establish a de facto government and to promote self-government.[90] The same pressure induced early national elections in Bosnia in September 1996, allowing the main nationalist parties to consolidate their hold on their respective ethnic clientele.[91] Even when less haste was exercised, as in Kosovo, where province-wide elections were delayed until November 2001, the result was the consolidation of the divisions that had led to the occupation and 'created institutions that further undermined UNMIK's limited power to coax change'.[92]

Yet if promoting early national elections risked creating a counterweight to the occupation regime, one that could claim to embody the principles that the occupier proclaimed as its own goal, so too avoidance of elections, for fear of such an outcome, was not without its own dangers. The temptation has been not only to delay national elections but to delay local or municipal elections as well while resorting to the appointment of advisory bodies. In East Timor, where UNTAET reluctantly conceded local elections under pressure from the Asian Development Bank as part of its programme for local development, UNTAET insisted that the elected councils 'shall not exercise legislative, executive or judicial power of government'.[93] Whereas many occupiers had seen local administrative structures, including sometimes elected bodies, as agencies through which to rule or at least as agencies which would relieve the occupier of the task of governing, UNTAET seemed to see them as a potential threat to its own legitimacy. At the same time, however, UNTAET created a National Consultative Council, consisting of appointed members, whose proximity to the indigenous population was said to potentially confer greater legitimacy on the administration; however, substantive power was denied to it on the grounds that UNTAET should, in the words of Transitional Administrator Vieria de Mello, 'be cautious about delegating power in the interest of avoiding furthering any particular party'.[94] In fact, that proved impossible with Vieria de Mello clearly favouring the leader of the National Council of Timorese Resistance that had opposed Indonesian rule.[95] Neutrality faced with a divided population is, as Ernst Fraenkel had noted, not necessarily an option. More important here, however, is the dynamic that drove UNTAET to search for the legitimacy of its own authority in the approval of the occupied while denying indigenous structures any power, and preferably, any electoral legitimacy for fear that such representative structures would challenge its own legitimacy.

A similar dilemma operated in Iraq, but with more dramatic and destructive consequences. The intent there had been for power to be handed over to an Iraqi Interim Authority, in fact, a group of exiles selected by the United States, followed by an elected Iraqi government. Amidst the chaotic post-invasion developments, as central institutions disintegrated, this original plan was abandoned in favour of recognition that the occupiers would have to exercise their authority directly. One of the casualties of this rapid reversal was the local administrative authorities, which were to have been elected well in advance of any national body and whose purpose was to 'complement the role of the Transitional Authority'.[96] Now suspicious of any elected body, the new CPA moved to a process characterised more by selection. Where local military commanders had, on their own initiative, set about organising elections they were instructed to desist.[97] Later in the year, the CPA decided upon a 'refreshment' of local and provincial councils, as well as the establishment of new councils where none had been formed. Again, however, this was a controlled process dominated by selection, supposedly on the basis of a model developed in the Muthanna governate. The reality was a haphazard process that 'yielded councils that were viewed as neither legitimate not representative'.[98] Earlier, the CPA, intending a prolonged period of occupation, had instituted an Interim Governing Council; the Security Council Resolution that acknowledged it described it as 'broadly representative'.[99] Bremer publicly proclaimed that it was 'a balanced representative group of political leaders' that 'will represent the diversity of Iraq'.[100] In fact it was perceived as being neither representative, because it was appointed, nor balanced, skewed as it was to the exiles, was given little real power and its members were privately derided by Bremer: 'There's not one of them who is a true democrat, who represents much more than his own group's narrow interests, who has any support except from his own people'.[101] There was only one sense in which the Council had any significance and that was as a brake upon the CAP's freedom of action in the light of the representative character the CPA had ascribed to it. Much the same was true of the local representatives who often had an added interest in resisting the assertion of control by any fledgling Iraqi state.[102] Despite the lack of substantive power granted to these bodies they acted as restraints upon the power of the occupier because, while the CPA could over-rule them on particular issues, the CPA also needed at least some semblance of cooperation from them given the representative status ascribed to them.

This was not the only constraint upon the power of the civilian governors. Even in the case of Iraq, the occupation authorities needed some level of sanction from the UN, at least after the invasion. The CPA also needed the UN to broker an agreement with the influential Ayatollah Ali al-Sistani, who pressed throughout for prompt direct elections. As one observer noted, however, 'Bremer was wary both of the risk of diluting or ceding some of his authority and of the danger that a UN mission might radically revise the method for choosing a transitional national assembly'.[103] In Bosnia and Kosovo, the position was more complex given the number of international agencies involved, the changing remit of these agencies and the relationship between them. In Bosnia, especially initially, the Office of the High Representative established in implementation of the Dayton Peace Agreement amounted to little more than first among equals alongside several other international agencies and missions, including the Organisation for Security and Cooperation in Europe (OSCE), the UN Mission in Bosnia and Herzegovina, and the UN High Commissioner for Refugees (UNHCR). Attempts to establish the High Representative's authority over these bodies met with resistance as each sought to maintain its accountability within its own hierarchy, and hence autonomy, vis-à-vis the High Representative.[104] Not all of these bodies had precise remits, with the OSCE changing 'from one new role to another as necessary'.[105]

The disadvantages of the organisation of this multi-agency form of government were clear enough to induce some attempt to avoid them in establishing the international regime for Kosovo. In the latter case, Security Council Resolution 1244 sanctioned the creation of a 'Special Representative to control the implementation of the international civil presence' and specified that other international organisations would provide 'assistance' to the Secretary General.[106] The Secretary General went further in trying to assert the authority of his organisation, though not without attempts by the heads of others, notably the OSCE, to expand the remit of their own organisation.[107] He identified separate leading organisations for different tasks,[108] yet the hierarchy of authority was not clear to even experienced officials:

'It still wasn't clear who UNMIK was accountable to . . . The UN Security Council – yes – but also the UN Department of Peacekeeping Operations? The UN Department of Political Affairs? The Contact Group? The [European] Commission?'[109] Lack of clarity about accountability was compounded by lack of authority over the component elements of the 'civil presence', with the Special Representative unable to control the physical location of the staff of some of them, let alone dismiss them.[110]

As in other instances of military occupation, the major limitation to the apparently untrammelled governmental power of the civilian governors has been the population subject to their authority, especially given the ambitious goals ascribed to these governors and the constraints imposed upon them. In several recent cases, civilian governors have also had to deal with the fact that the commitment of these populations to the integrity of the territory under occupation has been questionable, to a greater or lesser degree. Whereas in the case of the occupation of the Rhineland it was one of the occupiers who sought to promote separatism, in the case of Bosnia, Kosovo and Iraq separatist tendencies have existed in the populations themselves. The occupier has been in the position of holding a population together against the will of at least part of the population of the occupied territory. In all three cases, the occupation regime has been constrained by the desire to promote an indigenous central state authority and yet also to promote some degree of decentralisation of authority, either as a goal in its own right or as a means of reassuring those who felt threatened by strong central institutions.[111]

Commitment to a political vision based upon the occupiers' own domestic political regime, or upon the goals enshrined in the international organisations involved, has variously worked to restrict the range of options open to the occupier and has continually threatened to undermine the legitimacy of the occupation, whilst not in the least detracting from the fact that these too are instances of alien rule. The fact that a part of each population has felt only limited, if any, obligation to the occupier has been compounded by reservations about the degree of obligation towards the existing polity. As has increasingly been the case, where control of the military force – upon which the occupier's presence ultimately rests – has been separated from control of government functions, creating in practice a form of dual government, the occupation regime has shown a tendency to fragment. Such fragmentation can, as has been indicated above, pave the way for predatory agencies within the occupation regime, as it did in the Nazi occupation of eastern Europe. Even where the occupation regime is far removed from such predatory intent, the weakness of the occupation regime, especially if it has exhibited doubts about its own authority, does not necessarily benefit the population subject to it. Nor can the alien nature of occupation be avoided by the 'rhetoric of ownership', which tries to obscure this fact, albeit in the interests of transforming the occupied society into the kind of polity that both the occupier and some, but rarely all, of the inhabitants of occupied territory desire.[112]

Notes

1. Carl Schmitt, *The Nomos of the Earth* (New York, NY: Telos, 2003), pp. 207–8.
2. As in the case of California.
3. '*In re* Rauter', *Annual Digest*, 16 (1949), p. 540.
4. See, for example, the protest of General Eisenhower: 'The sooner I can get rid of these questions that are outside the military in scope, the happier I will be!', quoted in Eyal Benvenisti, *The International Law of Occupation* (Princeton, NJ: Princeton University Press, 2004), p. 82
5. See Rory Stewart, *Occupational Hazards, My Time Governing in Iraq* (London: Picador, 2006), p. 214.
6. Mike Jackson, *Soldier* (London: Bantam, 2007), p. 290.
7. Iraq provides a prime example. See Eric Henning and Glen Rangwala, *Iraq in Fragments* (London: Hurst, 2006).
8. Ralph H. Gabriel, 'American experience with military government', *American Political Science Review*, 37 (1943), p. 432.
9. Ibid. pp. 432–3.
10. Theodore Cohen, *Remaking Japan. The American Occupation as New Deal* (New York, NY: The Free Press, 1987), p. 432.
11. Ibid. p. 428. For an assessment of the 'reverse course', see also Takemae Eiji, *The Allied Occupation of Japan* (New York, NY: Continuum, 2003), pp. 468–85.
12. Quoted in Thomas Alan Schwartz, *America's Germany. John J. McCloy and the Federal Republic of Germany* (Cambridge, MA: Harvard University Press, 1991), p. 33.
13. Ernst Fraenkel, 'Military occupation and the rule of law', in Ernst Fraenkel, *Gesammelte Schriften*, vol. 3 (Baden-Baden: Nomos, 1999), pp. 202–3.
14. Quoted in ibid. p. 203.
15. Ibid. p. 204.
16. Henry T. Allen, *My Rhineland Journal* (Boston, MA: Houghton and Mifflin, 1923), p. 48.

17. Article 13 of the Rhineland Agreement, in Fraenkel, 'Military occupation and the rule of law', p. 322.
18. Ibid. pp. 214–15.
19. Ibid. p. 222.
20. According to a French document 'Passive resistance consisted in rejecting collaboration in any shape or form with the French and Belgians, in refusing all their demands, in not complying with any of their orders, in leaving them to their own resources while, if necessary, yielding them possession of the field where they presented themselves'; quoted in B. T. Reynolds, 'A review of the occupation of the Rhineland', *Journal of the Royal Institute of International Affairs*, 7 (1928), p. 204.
21. Ibid. p. 204.
22. Fraenkel, 'Military occupation and the rule of law', p. 237.
23. Ibid. p. 231.
24. On the latter, see James E. Edmonds, *The Occupation of the Rhineland 1918–1920* (London: HMSO, 1987), pp. 194–5.
25. Quoted in Fraenkel, 'Military occupation and the rule of law', pp. 218–19.
26. Ibid. p. 219.
27. French policy towards separatist tendencies was based on the mistaken belief, contrary to their own intelligence, that it was pro-French in motivation, whereas it was anti-Bavarian and anti-Prussian. See Margaret Pawley, *The Watch on the Rhine* (London: Tauris, 2007), pp. 57–8.
28. See Walter A. McDougall, *France's Rhineland Diplomacy, 1918–1924* (Princeton, NJ: Princeton University Press, 1978).
29. See the perceptive assessment and prediction of Reynolds, 'A review of the occupation of the Rhineland', p. 211.
30. Hans-Dietrich Loock, 'Zur "Grossgermanischen Politik" des Dritten Reiches', *Vierteljahreshefte für Zeitgeschichte*, 8 (1960), pp. 42, 46–7.
31. Quoted in Gerhard Hirschfeld, *Nazi Rule and Dutch Collaboration* (Oxford: Berg, 1988), p. 56. See also Seyss-Inquart's proclamation of 14 May 1940, in Raphael Lemkin, *Axis Rule in Occupied Europe* (Washington, DC: Carnegie Endowment for International Peace, 1944), p. 448.
32. Hirschfeld, *Nazi Rule and Dutch Collaboration*, pp. 73–4. On the idea of renewal, see J. C. H. Blom and W. ten Have, 'Making the New Netherlands: ideas about renewal in Dutch politics and society during the Second World War', in M. L. Smith and Peter M. R. Stirk (eds), *Making the New Europe* (London: Pinter, 1990), pp. 87–97.
33. International Military Tribunal, *Trial of the Major War Criminals*, vol. 15 (Nuremberg: International Military Tribunal, 1948), p. 645.

34. Werner Warmbrunn, *The Dutch under German Occupation 1940–1945* (Stanford, CA: Stanford University Press, 1963), pp. 36–7.
35. Ibid. p. 38.
36. Ibid. pp. 45–7.
37. Paul M. Hayes, *Quisling* (Newton Abbot: David & Charles, 1971), p. 271.
38. International Military Tribunal, *Trial of the Major War Criminals*, vol. 15, p. 645.
39. Walter Labs, 'Die Verwaltung des besetzten Ostgebiete', *Reich-Volksordnung-Lebensraum*, 5 (1943), p. 139.
40. This is the assessment of Dietrich Orlow, *The History of the Nazi Party*, vol. 2 (Newton Abbot: David & Charles, 1973), p. 295.
41. Jan Tomasz Gross, *Polish Society under German Occupation* (Princeton, NJ: Princeton University Press, 1979), p. 51.
42. Klaus-Peter Friedrich, 'Collaboration in a "land without a Quisling"', *Slavic Review*, 64 (2005), pp. 716, 722. By comparison, the Dutch police under occupation reached a maximum in excess of 18,000. Hirschfeld, *Nazi Rule and Dutch Collaboration*, p. 165.
43. International Military Tribunal, *Trial of the Major War Criminals*, vol. 15, p. 647.
44. Gross, *Polish Society under German Occupation*, p. 70.
45. For this characterisation, see Bernd Wegner, *Hitlers Politische Soldaten* (Paderborn: Schöningh, 1982).
46. Orlow, *The History of the Nazi Party*, vol. 2, pp. 295–6.
47. Martin Broszat, *Nationalsozialistische Polenpolitik 1939–1945* (Stuttgart: DVA, 1961), pp. 75–6.
48. Ibid. pp. 57, 80.
49. For a brief summary of the complex provisions, see H. E. Bathurst, 'Legislation in the Federal Republic of Germany', *International and Comparative Law Quarterly*, 1 (1952), pp. 40–58.
50. See, for example, the summary 'Allied High Commission for Germany', *International Organization*, 4 (1950), pp. 535–8.
51. On devaluation, see Schwartz, *America's Germany*, pp. 61–5; on steel and coal, see J. Gillingham, *Coal, Steel and the Rebirth of Europe* (Cambridge: Cambridge University Press, 1991), pp. 268–80.
52. Richard Caplan, *International Governance of War-Torn Territories* (Oxford: Oxford University Press, 2005), pp. 39–40; Derek Boothby, 'The political challenge of administering Eastern Slavonia', *Global Governance*, 10 (2004), pp. 39–40, 45–6.
53. Ibid. p. 46.
54. Caplan, *International Governance of War-Torn Territories*, p. 88.
55. Boothby, 'The political challenge of administering Eastern Slavonia', p. 41.
56. For somewhat divergent assessments of UNTAES, see ibid. pp.

48–50; Sally Morphet, 'Current international civil administration', *International Peacekeeping*, 9 (2002), pp. 145–7; and Simon Chesterman, *You, the People* (Oxford: Oxford University Press, 2004), pp. 71–2.

57. Quoted in International Crisis Group, 'Kosovo: let's learn from Bosnia', ICG Balkans Report 66 (17 May 1999), p. 2.

58. See Richard Caplan, 'International authority and state building: the case of Bosnia and Herzegovina', *Global Governance*, 53 (2004), pp. 55–6; and Henning and Rangwala, *Iraq in Fragments*, pp. 48–55.

59. International Crisis Group, 'Kosovo: let's learn from Bosnia', p. 5; International Crisis Group, 'Waiting for UNMIK: local administration in Kosovo', ICG Balkans Report 79 (18 October 1999), pp. 2–5.

60. See Joel C. Beauvais, 'Benevolent despotism', *New York University Journal of International Law and Politics*, 33 (2001), pp. 1108–11.

61. Caplan, 'International authority and state building', p. 55; Caplan, *International Governance of War-Torn Territories*, pp. 47–8.

62. European Stability Initiative, 'Reshaping International Priorities in Bosnia and Herzegovina', part 2 (30 March 2000), p. 38.

63. Elizabeth Cousins and David Harland, 'Post-Dayton Bosnia and Herzegovina', in William J. Durch (ed.), *Twenty-First-Century Peace Operations* (Washington, DC: United States Institute of Peace, 2006), p. 91.

64. Ibid. pp. 39–40; Gerald Knaus and Felix Martin, 'Travails of the European Raj', *Journal of Democracy*, 14 (2003), p. 64.

65. See the damning judgement of the International Crisis Group, 'Ensuring Bosnia's future', Europe Report 180 (15 February 2007).

66. Michael G. Smith and Moreen Dee, 'East Timor', in Durch (ed.), *Twenty-First-Century Peace Operations*, p. 416.

67. Ibid. pp. 420, 428–9.

68. For the disavowal, see John G. Cockell, 'Civil-military responses to security challenges in peace operations', *Global Governance*, 8 (2002), p. 487.

69. Iain King and Whit Mason, *Peace at any Price* (Ithaca, NY: Cornell University Press, 2006), pp. 54–7.

70. Espen Barth Eide and Tor Tanke Holm, 'Postscript: towards executive authority policing?', *International Peacekeeping*, 6 (1999), p. 213.

71. Caplan, *International Governance of War-Torn Territories*, p. 62.

72. King and Mason, *Peace at any Price*, pp. 147–50; International Crisis Group, 'Collapse in Kosovo', Europe Report 155 (22 April 2004), pp. 8–9.

73. International Crisis Group, 'An Army for Kosovo?', Europe Report 174 (28 July 2006), p. 2.

74. Elaine Halchin, 'The Coalition Provisional Authority (CPA)', CRS Report RL32370 (6 June 2005).

75. Christopher M. Schnaubelt, 'After the fight: interagency operations', *Parameters*, 20 (2005–6), pp. 49–50.

76. Andrew Rathmell, 'Planning post-conflict reconstruction in Iraq', *International Afffairs*, 81 (2005), pp. 1030–1.

77. Schnaubelt, 'After the fight', pp. 54–6.

78. L. Paul Bremer, *My Year in Iraq* (New York, NY: Threshold, 2006), pp. 129–30. See also his comment: 'That afternoon I discovered that the Marines were also lobbying at the Pentagon against the arrest', p. 131. See also Larry Diamond, *Squandered Victory* (New York, NY: Henry Holt, 2005), p. 228.

79. Henning and Rangwala, *Iraq in Fragments*, pp. 99–101. See their conclusion: 'the Coalition military became the *de facto* senior agency to the civil administration', p. 102.

80. Beauvais, 'Benevolent despotism', p. 1114.

81. Jarat Chopra, 'Building state failure in East Timor', *Development and Change*, 33 (2002), p. 989.

82. King and Mason, *Peace at any Price*, p. 55.

83. Stewart, *Occupational Hazards*, pp. 29–30, 119.

84. Quoted in Diamond, *Squandered Victory*, p. 259.

85. CPA/REG/16 May 2003/01.

86. For the variety of meanings of this 'competence-competence', see Carl Schmitt, *Constitutional Theory* (Durham: Duke University Press, 2008), pp. 402–3.

87. Quoted in Knaus and Felix, 'Travails of the European Raj', p. 65. For an earlier critique in a similar vein, see David Chandler, *Bosnia. Faking Democracy after Dayton* (London: Pluto, 2000), especially pp. 201–4.

88. Fraenkel, 'Military occupation and the rule of law', p. 244.

89. Chopra, 'Building state failure in East Timor', p. 992.

90. Beauvais, 'Benevolent despotism', pp. 1107–8. See also the reference to the 'UN's dual role as both a mission and an embryonic government', Caplan, *International Governance of War-Torn Territories*, p. 102.

91. 'Thereby providing a legal framework for the results of ethnic cleansing'. Cousins and Harland, 'Post-Dayton Bosnia and Herzegovina', p. 95.

92. King and Mason, *Peace at any Price*, p. 247.

93. Quoted in Caplan, *International Governance of War-Torn Territories*, p. 124.

94. Quoted in Beauvais, 'Benevolent despotism', p. 1120.

95. Ibid. pp. 1123–4.

96. According to the Final Report on the Transition to Democracy in Iraq, as quoted in International Crisis Group, 'Iraq: can local governance save central government', Middle East Report 33 (27 October 2004), p. 1.

97. David L. Phillips, *Losing Iraq* (Boulder, CO: Westview, 2005), pp. 170–1.
98. International Crisis Group, 'Iraq: can local governance save central government', pp. 11–12. See also Henning and Rangwala, *Iraq in Fragments*, pp. 110–11.
99. S/RES/1500 (2003).
100. International Crisis Group, 'The next Iraqi war?', Middle East Report 52 (27 February 2006), p. 10.
101. Quoted in Phillips, *Losing Iraq*, p. 174.
102. Henning and Rangwala, *Iraq in Fragments*, pp. 125–7.
103. Diamond, *Squandered Victory*, pp. 83–4. He also noted that Bremer supported the UN mission when it did arrive, p. 136.
104. International Crisis Group, 'Bosnia: reshaping the international machinery', Balkans Report 121 (29 November 2001), pp. 10–11.
105. Cousins and Harland, 'Post-Dayton Bosnia and Herzegovina', p. 113.
106. S/RES/1244 (1999).
107. International Crisis Group, 'The new Kosovo protectorate', Balkans Report 69 (20 June 1999), pp. 4–5.
108. Report of the Secretary General, S/1999/779 (12 July 1999).
109. Quoted in King and Mason, *Peace at any Price*, p. 126.
110. Ibid. pp. 249–52.
111. On this dilemma, see Charles Tripp, 'The United States and state-building in Iraq', *Review of International Studies*, 30 (2004), pp. 545–58.
112. On the 'rhetoric of ownership', see Chesterman, *You, the People*, pp. 5–6.

Chapter 5

Occupation and Obligation

As suggested in the discussion of the definition of military occupation there is a prima facie case that inhabitants of occupied territory are under an obligation to obey the occupying authorities. There is indeed explicit, if qualified, reference to this idea in the current British *Manual of the Law of Armed Conflict*:

> While the orders of the authorities of an occupying power may be lawful, and while the occupant is entitled to require obedience to lawful orders, it does not necessarily follow that failure to comply with such orders is illegal under the law of armed conflict. However, the inhabitants are liable for punishment by the occupying power should they disobey legislation, proclamations, regulations, or orders properly made by that power.[1]

Yet, despite the recurrent appearance of this expectation of obedience in the law and practice of military occupation, explicit attention to the problems associated with it has been far more fitful than that devoted to the problem of political obligation in general.[2] So much is this the case that it was possible to identify an article by Richard Baxter published in 1950 as 'pathbreaking'; to which it might be added that the path has remained largely untrodden.[3] That is hardly surprising for Baxter's article was a condemnation of the doctrine. Neglect of the correlative concept of the authority of the occupier has not been as marked, though here too wider considerations, in this case the tendency to confound authority with power, have contributed to the neglect.[4] The reason for this is not difficult to detect. As a relatively rare study of the authority of international administrations has put it, such authority 'seems to be at odds with contemporary conceptions of legitimate government. While the legitimacy of government is rooted in notions of self-determination and increasingly democracy, international administrations, at least temporarily, deny both to people over whom they govern'.[5] Such sentiments can be strengthened where they are linked with notions of resistance to military force, especially if linked to either claims to self-determination or the establishment of democratic governance. The presumption that such resistance is justified in general, within domestic regimes, seems only to make resistance to occupiers more self-evident, for if there is a right 'to oppose tyranny and domestic oppression, then surely such a right exists in relation to *alien* forms of oppression'.[6]

While contemporary understanding of legitimate government in terms of self-determination and democracy undoubtedly militates against the notion of a duty of obedience to occupiers, such an understanding is not necessary in order to make a duty of this kind problematic. By definition, the occupier is not the legitimate government. The occupier is present by virtue of the force at the occupier's disposal, regardless of whatever authorisation the occupier may claim. Disavowal of obedience, as the resistance to Napoleon's occupation of Spain demonstrates, requires neither a commitment to democracy nor a commitment to self-determination, at least not in any modern understanding of either term. The occupier resembles the usurper and as Locke observed of usurpers: 'Whoever gets into the exercise of any part of the Power, by other ways, than what the Laws of the Community have prescribed, hath no Right to be obeyed, though the Form of the Commonwealth be still preserved'.[7] Usurpers who go further, embark upon tyranny, thereby justifying further resistance.

Even where tyranny is not practiced, and few if any occupiers have escaped all taint of tyranny, the occupier like the usurper seems to stand condemned simply by virtue of what he is rather than what he does. The resort to force that accounts for the occupier's presence seems, indeed, to entail that he lacks properly understood authority. For as Hannah Arendt argued: 'Since authority always demands obedience, it is commonly mistaken for some form of power or violence. Yet authority precludes the use of external means of coercion; where force is used, authority itself has failed'.[8] In the same spirit, Cicero specified that, in a republic,

> unless there is in the State an even balance of rights, duties and functions, so that the magistrates have enough power, the counsels of the eminent citizens enough authority, and the people enough liberty, this kind of government cannot be safe from revolution.[9]

The occupier's nature is wholly incompatible with any such separation of power and authority. The maintenance of the occupier's status ultimately depends upon the ability to deploy force even if the display of such power need not be omnipresent. As the British *Manual of Military Law* of 1914 put it,

> If the invader is driven out of a district by the enemy or voluntarily evacuates it, or if the district frees itself from the exercise of his authority by a *levée en masse*, so that the legitimate government is able to resume its authority, occupation at once ceases.[10]

Yet it remains true that for both the occupier and those subject to occupation the authority of the occupier is the only alternative to recourse to violence if the occupier is determined to assert their authority. By the same token, an unqualified right of resistance, a rejection in principle of the idea that an occupier may have authority, and the assertion that all have a right to resist and none any duty to obey may be equally destructive. As H. Sutherland Edwards observed of such sentiments at the time of the Franco-Prussian war:

> If the apparently noble, but really barbarous, principle be recognized, that every man has, without condition, a right to defend his native land, his village, and the house in which he was born, then it follows that an invading army must, for its own safety, imprison or destroy all inhabitants thus claiming an absolute right to resist it.[11]

There are, of course, intermediate positions. Occupiers, especially modern ones in the form of international administrations, facing little direct challenge to evict them, may lapse into passivity rather then enforce their edicts. That, according to some observers, was the outcome in Kosovo: 'As the mission aged, UNMIK made more and more rules but then took no action when they were broken'.[12] It may be the case that occupiers lack the resource or the willingness to use it to face challenges to their authority.[13] More strikingly, occupiers, or at least sections of their forces, may fail to grasp the extent and nature of the authority that international law arguably assigns to them.[14] Yet acceptance of the possibility that populations of occupied territory have obligations to occupiers does not necessarily mean that those obligations are unlimited, any more than the existence of political obligation in general entails unlimited obligation. That point was accepted by Halleck who unequivocally advocated obligations to occupiers:

> The general duty of obedience to the laws results from the protection they afford to the lives and property of the citizens and subjects; but when a civil government fails to afford that protection, and obstinately persists in a course injurious to the people, and when the probable evils accompanying the change are not greater than the blessings to be obtained by it, revolution becomes a duty as well as a right. So also, with respect to the military government of occupation.[15]

Significant though these factors are it is the idea that occupied populations are under any obligation to occupiers at all that is the most problematic. According to Hall any such supposition rests on the belief that 'the fact of occupation temporarily invests the invading state with the rights of sovereignty, and dispossesses its enemy, so as to set up a duty of obedience to the former and of disregard to the commands of the latter'.[16] He held, however, that this is an

> inconsistent and artificial theory . . . [and that] though it is certain that invaders have habitually exercised the privileges of sovereignty, it is equally certain that invaded populations have generally repudiated the obligation of obedience whenever they have found themselves possessed of the strength to do so with effect.[17]

Hall argued that not only had invaded populations demonstrated their rejection of a duty of obedience but the courts of the great powers had repudiated the association of mere invasion with the assumption of sovereignty since the days of the Napoleonic wars, thereby repudiating the doctrine on which the duty of obedience was founded.[18] Hall was in fact merely reflecting the opinion which had formed in the nineteenth century that invasion did not by itself entail the acquisition of sovereignty. He was unusual, however, in deducing from this that there could be no obligation to occupying forces.

Military manuals and commentators more typically asserted or assumed an obligation to obey, though there was significant variation in the vigour with which this was expressed and the extent and precision of the supposed obligation. The Lieber Code of 1863 held that 'the people and their civil officers owe strict obedience to them [the occupiers] as long as they hold sway over the district or country, at the peril of their lives'.[19] This emphasis upon obedience in the face of the power of the occupier and the prospect of severe punishment is also found in the French military manual of 1893 and in the works of several French authors.[20] Halleck, writing shortly before the Lieber Code, expressed the obligation in terms of a reciprocity between the occupied and occupier:

> If the conquered are under an implied obligation to make no further resistance to the conqueror, it is only in consideration of the favors and privileges they are to derive from a relaxation of the extreme rights of war, by being allowed peacefully to pursue their ordinary occupations, without any further restraint than may be necessary for the safety of the conqueror.[21]

While still emphasising reciprocity, more emphasis was placed on the positive duties of occupiers in the British manual of 1914, though this still derived from it an extensive range of obligations:

> to behave in an absolutely peaceful manner . . . to take part in no way in the hostilities, to refrain from every injury to the troops of the occupant, and from any act prejudicial to their operations and to render obedience to the officials of the occupant.[22]

The contemporaneous American *Rule of Land Warfare* also referred to the 'reciprocal obligations of inhabitants' and placed a similar emphasis on the obedience necessary for the occupier to fulfil its duties.[23] The German manual assimilated the position of the occupier to that of the legitimate power: 'The inhabitants of the occupied territory owe the same obedience to the organs of Government and administration of the conqueror as they owed before the occupation to their own'.[24]

These variations, emphasising fear created by the overwhelming power of the occupier, the relaxation of the 'extreme rights of war', the reciprocity of obligations or the exercise of public power by the occupier, clearly have different implications for the understanding of the nature of military occupation and also have varying degrees of plausibility. They are united, however, in being emphatic assertions of the existence of an obligation on the part of the occupied populations. Yet none of them amounted to the assertion of unlimited obedience. It was, moreover, less the reservations about the general assumption of an obligation and more the specific demands or expectations that led to growing disquiet about the wider principle of such an obligation. Prominent here are the imposition of oaths of one kind or another and the doctrine of war treason. To these may be added the problem posed by a *levée en masse* against an occupier and the extent to which occupiers can call upon the occupied population to work for the occupier.[25] Although reservations about the threat to the rights of individuals and recourse to excessive and cruel retaliation played a part in consideration of these problems, the central and recurring issue was the extent to which they posed a threat to the allegiance or patriotism of the occupied population which lay at the heart of the disputes.

That the imposition of oaths might prove problematic as well as tempting to occupiers is easy to see. Again it is the fundamental weakness of the position of the occupier that is central. Despite the assertion of a duty to obey, Hall was right that occupied populations had all too frequently repudiated any such obligation. The fact that occupation forces were typically thinly spread in relation to the occupied territory magnified the problem. Just as fundamentally weak states with extensive claims to obedience had been tempted to resort to oaths to bridge the gap, so too were occupiers.[26] It was precisely this to which Spaight took exception:

> Any attempt to make the moral sanction of an oath supply the material deficiencies of an occupant's material power – to substitute, as it were, the restrictive force of the inhabitant's conscience for that of an effective garrison – is as much to be deprecated as the abandoned German system of occupying districts 'theoretically'.[27]

Yet the imposition of oaths had been frequent. The Lieber Code provided that 'commanding generals may cause the magistrates and civil officers to take the oath of temporary allegiance or an oath of fidelity to their own victorious government or rulers', though it added that both magistrates and the population in general owed obedience regardless of whether an oath was imposed.[28] Oaths were imposed during the American Civil War, including a draconian one imposed by General Halleck during his military government of Richmond – though that was at the end of the war.[29] Similarly, they were deployed in the conquest of New Mexico, in at least one case having the effect deplored by Spaight.[30]

Much, however, turned on what the oath specified. The general presumption amongst those who sanctioned the imposition of oaths on the population of occupied territories was that they should not be 'inconsistent with their general and ultimate allegiance to their own state'.[31] The attempt to evade this stricture during the Boer war, by demanding that populations in occupied territories take an oath of neutrality rather than an oath of loyalty, was itself evidence of disquiet about demanding oaths at all; it was precisely this practice during the Boer war that called forth Spaight's condemnation of oaths as a substitute for the inadequate power of the occupier. Oaths to be imposed on officials proved to be equally difficult to sustain. While not providing explicitly for an oath, the Brussels Conference of 1874 retained a fairly strong version of the obligations of officials in Article 4: 'They shall not be dismissed or subjected to disciplinary punishment unless they fail in fulfilling the obligations undertaken by them, and they shall not be prosecuted unless they betray their trust'.[32] Even that proved to be too much by the end of the century. Shortly before the First World War, Pasquale Fiore proclaimed that it was 'disloyal and arbitrary to impose an oath of fidelity on magistrates or civil functionaries of the occupied country'.[33] At the Hague in 1899, despite general agreement that it was to the benefit of the occupied population as well as the occupier that administrative officials remain in office, the smaller powers were so opposed to anything that might create the presumption that they were obliged to do so that the article was dropped entirely.[34] That left only the explicit prohibition of any assertion of allegiance in Article 45, which was retained unaltered in 1907: 'It is forbidden to compel the population of occupied territory to swear allegiance to the hostile power'.[35]

As in many other aspects of military occupation, however, it is not only the occupier who can create doubt about matters of allegiance. That was evident in the Franco-Prussian war of 1870–1 after the French revolt against the imperial system that had failed them in the war. French courts, especially at Nancy, proclaimed that they could no longer pronounce justice in the name of the Empire and asserted their right to pronounce justice 'in the name of the people and the French government'.[36] The Germans objected that this would amount to their recognition of the French Republic, which their governments had not done. According to Westlake, referring explicitly to Article 45 of the Hague Conventions, the Germans were entitled and obliged to do this, for the principle enshrined in that article 'prohibits every thing which would assert or imply a change made by the invader in the legitimate sovereignty'.[37] The formula suggested by the Germans, 'in the name of the High German Powers occupying Alsace and Lorraine', was predictably rejected by the French and was regarded by even contemporary German authors as excessive.[38] Even the formula which many commentators found unobjectionable, 'in the name of the law', met with resistance on the grounds that both supreme executive authority and supreme legislative authority had been inherited by the new French Republic and that only the formula proclaimed by the Republic was acceptable.[39]

Although some found the sensitivity of the French judges to be exaggerated, the dispute symbolises how the issue of allegiance raised by the imposition of oaths readily surfaces in other ways. That is even more striking in the responses to the prospect of the *levée en masse* and the doctrine of war treason. Again, the Lieber Code is clear about the latter category:

> If the citizen or subject of a country or place invaded or conquered gives information to his own government, from which he is separated by the

hostile army, or to the army of his own government, he is a war-traitor, and death is the penalty of his offense.[40]

So too were the military manuals of the major powers. The British *Manual of Military Law* of 1914 was not deterred by the fact that the 'Hague Rules do not refer to cases in which inhabitants of invaded or occupied territory . . . furnish, or attempt to furnish, information to the enemy' for it added that 'such persons should be charged with war treason . . . for although treason as such is not mentioned in the Hague Rules, belligerents are by customary international law empowered to punish treason by death'.[41] Some disquiet was evident in the attempts to mitigate such approaches by referring to the diverging motives which could lead to individuals providing such information: those who acted for patriotic reason were given preferential treatment compared with those who acted for financial gain. Others, however, dismissed such qualifications as irrelevant to the fact that the informant violated his or her status as a non-combatant by providing the information, or even by attempting to do so.[42] It was left to Spaight, however, to meet the obvious charge that treason supposes some allegiance, indeed a very high degree of allegiance, and that since the very definition of military occupation precludes allegiance to the occupying power, there can be no charge of treason. The point had been made forcibly by Westlake, who added the objection, similar to Spaight's own objection to oaths of neutrality, that

> to introduce the notion of moral fault into an invader's view of what is detrimental to him serves only to inflame his passions, and to make it less likely that he will observe the true limit of necessity in his repression of what is detrimental to him.[43]

Spaight, however, replied to the main argument by claiming that

> we have got long distance from the stage when treason implied infidelity to a personal sovereign . . . Today treason means a conspiracy against the *established authority* in a State. Now the established authority in an occupied territory is the *de facto* ruler, the occupant . . . he is the 'war ruler' and as it is 'treason' to conspire against the ordinary ruler, it is 'war treason' to conspire against the 'war ruler'.[44]

Spaight was right about the general trend in terms of the nature of allegiance but equally clearly misses the point in another sense. As the example of the French courts in the Franco-Prussian war shows it was quite possible to disavow the personal sovereign, the Emperor Napoleon III, while refusing to equate the status of the military government of the occupier with that of the legitimate government.

The intractability of the doctrine of war treason – the fact that it stood in the military manuals of the day and was endorsed by so many commentators yet that it seemed to fly in the face of the allegiance to one's own country, an allegiance that none disputed – emerged most forcefully in an exchange during the First World War, against the backcloth of the German occupation of Belgium, and specifically the execution of a British nurse, Edith Cavell, presumably on the charge of war treason. Here, J. H. Morgan attacked Lassa Oppenheim, a leading international lawyer of the day, for supposedly introducing a peculiarly German doctrine into the English-speaking world.[45] An agitated Morgan turned his attack into a general denunciation of the notion that the populations of occupied territories owe any obedience to the occupier: 'What is "obedience" here but that spurious allegiance which lies at the bottom of this detestable and illicit conception known as war treason?'[46] Oppenheim had little difficulty in refuting Morgan's dubious historiography and in demonstrating the widespread support for the doctrine of war treason.[47] Yet Oppenheim was as insistent as anyone else in mitigating the implications of the doctrine. There is, he insisted, a difference between treason understood in the normal sense and the doctrine of war treason, adding: 'Nor has, as far as I can remember, any writer who adopted the term ever maintained that war treason committed by an inhabitant of occupied territory makes him guilty of a *moral* crime'.[48] This was the prelude to a wider attack on the general notion of any duty to obey the occupier. The whole notion, he argued, is based on an erroneous extrapolation of duties of inhabitants from rights possessed by the occupier. Relying upon the notion that international law exists purely between states, he insisted that the only duty correlative to the right of the occupier to administer occupied territory was the 'duty of the legitimate government to recognize, after the occupation has ceased, all the legitimate acts of administration carried out by the occupant'.[49]

Ironically, Baxter's article, which did much to silence the debate while condemning Oppenheim, also illuminates the problem. He wrote,

> If a person committing acts of resistance is guilty of a violation of international law, it seems strange that the individual's own government may inspire or demand such acts without being subjected to similar penalties. Yet it has never been suggested that a state is guilty of an international delinquency if it calls for acts of resistance or avails itself of the fruit of the forbidden tree.[50]

Although the expectation of resistance does in fact most readily arise in the case of the demands of an exiled government, it arises even where the nature and status of the legitimate government is in doubt, as was the case during the Napoleonic occupation of Spain. Citing an example from that time Hall, who as Morgan noted was 'not wanting in latitude to the rights of an occupying army',[51] protested with respect to participants in a *levée en masse*:

> The customs of war no doubt permit that such persons shall under certain circumstances be shot, and there are reasons for permitting the practice; but to allow persons shall be intimidated for reasons of convenience from doing certain acts, and to mark them as criminals if they do them, are wholly distinct things. A doctrine is intolerable which would inflict a stain of criminality on the defenders of Saragossa.[52]

The largely civilian defenders of that city against Napoleonic armies symbolised for Hall a fine expression of patriotic duty and sentiment. Much the same attitude had been evident at the Brussels Conference of 1874. There Baron Lambermont expressed his concern about proposed provisions relating to a *levée en masse*:

> Events take place during war which will continue to take place, and which must be accepted. But the question before them [the participants in the conference] is that of converting them into laws, into positive and international laws. If citizens are to be sacrificed for having attempted to defend their country at the peril of their lives, they need not find inscribed on the post at the foot of which they are about to be shot the Article of a Treaty signed by their own government which had in advance condemned them to death.[53]

Baxter, Hall, Lambermont and Oppenheim all shared the same dilemma. They expected that occupiers faced with armed resistance in an established occupation would repress the rising and refuse to accord those who rose against them the status of lawful belligerents, yet saw such people as morally admirable and even duty bound to act as they did. The impossibility of resolving that dilemma led them, in varying degrees, to be suspicious of, and mostly explicitly hostile to, the wider assumption about a duty to obey the occupier.

Subsequent developments add little to the nature of this dilemma save in the sense there was a greater inclination to provide protection for at least some types of resistance movement in the Geneva Convention of 1949. Thus Article 4 of the Third Convention explicitly included members of 'organized resistance movements, belonging to a Party to the conflict and operating in or outside their own territory, even if this territory is occupied'.[54] This response to the fate of some members of such movements during the Second World War was criticised as amounting to the proclamation of an *'ius insurrectionis'*, though the leading commentator on the conventions, Jean Pictet, insisted that the intent was to maintain the core principles of the Hague Conventions.[55]

For most members of occupied populations the question of whether to obey the occupier was likely to arise not in the case of the call to join a *levée en masse* or a resistance movement but in more apparently mundane matters, especially in the provision of goods and services to the occupier. Some services clearly could not be construed as mundane, such as serving in the armed forces of the occupier or acting as guides to the occupier's forces. While condemnation of the latter easily became the consensus, the former proved more problematic.[56] This was because defining what was excluded by such language as the Hague Regulations' restriction of the requisitioning of goods or services to those 'of such a nature as not to involve the inhabitants in the obligation of taking part in military operations against their own country' was not necessarily straightforward.[57]

The constraints that could be faced by members of populations under occupation in this respect were, however, severe. On the one hand, according to the Belgian Rolin-Jaequemyns, a 'systematic and collective refusal' to provide services demanded by the occupier could be taken as a 'positive act of hostility' towards the latter.[58] On the other hand, the absent legitimate power, or other members of the population, could regard the services as evidence of support for the enemy and hence as treasonable. The tension between these two constraints was evident in the Lieber Code which provided that 'no person having been forced by the enemy to serve as a guide is punishable for having done so', but also that 'a citizen serving voluntarily as a guide against his own country commits treason'.[59] That logic induced those who had volunteered to guide American forces in the Philippines to ask to be tied by ropes to create the impression that they were acting under compulsion.[60] Even where the service was not provided voluntarily, demonstrating that this was the case was not always easy. Indeed one of the reasons suggested for issuing receipts for requisitioned goods and services was to enable the recipients to prove that they had acted under compulsion.[61]

In these cases, the problem arises from the difficulty in determining the voluntary nature of the act. On other occasions occupiers have sought to conceal the compulsion they have exercised, or to proffer some justification of departure from what they know to be prohibited practices: in the First World War, Germany attempted to justify its deportation of Belgian workers on the grounds of extensive unemployment in Belgium.[62] That practice, especially on the scale and under the conditions of the deportations during the Second World War, led to explicit condemnation of such practices in the Geneva Conventions.[63]

While it has been argued that the labour of these deportees can be construed as something that 'objectively' constitutes treason, that claim was made only to condemn the deportation as immoral.[64] More problematic are cases where there is a fundamental divergence between the occupier and the absent legitimate power about what is a legitimate demand, or where there are divisions among the population of occupied territories about the legitimacy of such demands. Such conflicts arose during the Franco-Prussian war of 1870–1 over the German administration of public forests. Although much of the dispute concerned German management of the resources of the forests, French citizens working in the forests were caught in the dispute when the French government in unoccupied France threatened them with sever penalties if they did not withdraw their labour. The German authorities and German publicists protested vigorously about this but it was the comment of an English writer, Hall, defending the legitimacy of the French government's acts, who brought out the nature of the dilemma: 'It was only guilty of forcing them to choose between the alternatives of immediate punishment by the Germans, and of possible future punishment, with the brand of unpatriotism added, from the courts of their own nation'. Hall added that 'such acts are generally unwise and even cruel, but they are none the less clearly within the rights of a government'.[65] It might be added that the position to which Hall consigned the hapless inhabitants of occupied territory is also intolerable.

If anything, divisions within the population pose even crueller dilemmas for, being typically unable to resort to established courts, those who see the acts of their fellow citizens as treasonable can turn only to covert violence to inflict the punishment they believe to be due. It was precisely because of such prospects that some international codes and military manuals specified that the occupying authorities were obliged to protect officials who consented to remain in office.[66] It is, of course, not only public officials who face suspicion of treasonable collaboration for acts that the occupier regards as legitimate, as the recent case of interpreters acting for the occupying forces in Iraq demonstrates.

Even where there is a possibility of a resort to the courts, as in the case of Belgian attempts to prosecute separatists for treason in the First World War, the occupiers have intervened to suppress such proceedings. According to Ernst Fraenkel, they can do no less, for

> high-treason proceedings represent, in legal form, political measures taken by a government against those whom it considers enemies of the state . . . An occupying power, enforcing a regime of martial law, cannot allow its friends to be treated as enemies by the authorities of the occupied territory.[67]

In general, any such cases, along with a series of other lesser judgements about the extent to which obligations are owed to occupiers, come before domestic courts only after the end of the occupation. When this has happened, similar dilemmas to those faced in the debate leading up to the Hague Conventions of 1907 have recurred. That became apparent especially in the judgments of Dutch courts after the Second World War, which paid more specific attention to the issue of obligation.[68] Thus, the Special Criminal Court argued in 1946 that 'legal measures of the occupant did not, in general, create legal obligations for the inhabitants and were not in conscience binding upon them'.[69] The court then made an exception for instances where the measure's 'only purpose' was in the interests of the occupied country, in which event the citizens 'were, perhaps . . . bound to obey the ordinances' though they still had to bear in mind 'the higher duty, resting on every Dutchman, to remain faithful to his lawful Government, to defend his country and to abstain from assisting the enemy'.[70] Another court added that 'inhabitants could not be said to owe specific obligations to the enemy'.[71] Yet another court held that the 'temporary lack of sanctions' available to the legitimate government gave no exemption from the 'emergency decrees of the Crown which were not regularly promulgated in Holland'.[72]

The equivocation of Dutch courts was understandable both in terms of the tradition of that country in seeking to curtail the authority of occupying powers and in terms of their revulsion against the occupation regime during the Second World War and against those of their fellow citizens who had collaborated with its repressive policies. They were, however, no more successful in making sense of the idea of an obligation to obey occupiers in general. Nor is it in any way evidently clear how such an obligation might be justified. Yet, if there is no such plausible justification this can only contribute to either the clash of assertions of authority revealed in the intolerable dilemma to which Hall consigned members of populations under occupation, or to a hesitancy to exercise the authority which falls to occupying powers by virtue of the fact of military occupation.

Commentators and courts have in fact invoked a range of arguments and analogies drawn from the established repertoire of justifications for political obligation more generally, albeit with limited success. Nor is this surprising, for if one takes as a starting point the most prevalent type of justification of political obligation, namely consent theory, the prospects do not appear immediately promising. Yet consent in some form or another has frequently been invoked in justifying both the authority exercised by occupiers and the obligations of populations subject to occupation. Insofar as it is express consent that is at issue, it is worth noting first that it was this possibility that made the Belgian Auguste Beernaert worried about legitimating 'a *régime* of defeat' in the Hague negotiations in 1899.[73] Similar reservations lay behind Baron Lambermont's concern about his government's possible consent to legitimating punishment of a *levée en masse* by its own citizens against an occupying power. It is more typical, however, to look for state consent in specific cases, especially in recent years in occupations authorised by the United Nations or subsequently sanctioned by it. There are, of course, earlier cases of occupation that seem to be based on some element of consent, namely those based on treaties. Leaving aside the fact that these are only a subset of the phenomenon of military occupations it is notable that many (for example, the occupation of the Rhineland) were based on greater or lesser measures of duress and were beset by bitter wrangling over the powers of the occupier. Even in what might be the most promising of the older cases, the west European countries liberated by the Allied powers at the end of the Second World War, the consent was not even that of a recognised exiled government in the case of France.[74] Nor did the consent of the exiled governments, or the French National Committee, alter the nature of the relationship between the occupation authorities and those subject to them. This point was well put by the historian F. S. V. Donnison:

> The French were to be allowed little or no more say, at first, in the use of their own resources than they had been by the Germans. It was not so difficult to bear such treatment as a part of the natural lot of a vanquished people: it was hard when it followed 'liberation' by its friends. It is probable that the French never tasted the full bitterness of defeat until they had been 'liberated'.[75]

Although consent is more frequently invoked in occupations authorised by the United Nations, or subsequently sanctioned by it, the plausibility of this justification is even more doubtful than in France in 1944. In these cases it is far from clear that it is those subject to this authority who can be said to have consented. In Kosovo, for example, the consent was expressed in the agreement between NATO and Yugoslavia for the withdrawal of the Yugolsav army.[76] State consent here is a dubious justification 'if one considers that it was the lack of government authority that has made it necessary in the eyes of the international community to establish international administrations in the first place'.[77]

Leaving aside the more general considerations that beset consent theory, including the impossibility of showing how all subject to the authority are supposed to have consented, it might also be added that consent theory in the form of express consent would prove too much in the case of military occupation, supposing that it could be made more plausible. Military occupation has been defined in terms of the contrast between the legitimate power and the occupying powers into whose hands the authority of the former has passed. If both could be justified in the same way the difference would fall away.

In implicit recognition of the implausibility of express consent, explicit justification of obligations on the part of the occupied has relied more typically on some form of tacit consent. The general assumption, as Doris Graber summarised it, was that by 'remaining with their property in occupied territory people impliedly accede to the terms imposed by the occupant'.[78] That logic was affirmed in the 1819 judgement of the US Supreme Court in 'The United States v. Rice', though there the presumption was not just of the incurring of obligation but of an albeit temporary transfer of allegiance. According to the Court,

> The sovereignty of the United States was, of course, suspended and the laws of the United States could no longer be rightfully enforced there, or be obligatory upon the inhabitants who remained and submitted to the conquerors. By the surrender the inhabitants passed under a temporary allegiance to the British government, and were bound by such laws, and such only, as it chose to recognise and impose.[79]

Similarly, Birkhimer dismissed the fact 'that the inhabitants do not by visible signs join with their military ruler in arranging the details of his government' on the grounds that 'their covenant is implied; but it is none the less binding because it consists in silent acquiescence in the new order of things'.[80] As with the Supreme Court, Birkhimer held that the fact that the population remained in the territory was decisive. There were even attempts to invoke the classic illustration of tacit consent: 'The relationship is analogous to that which exists between aliens domiciled in a state and the government of the latter'.[81]

The difficulty with such arguments, as Baxter pointed out, was that there was little prospect that those subject to military occupation would accept that they had consented, either expressly or tacitly.[82] Consent theory in cases of military occupation too readily looks like 'at best a fiction designed to explain away an unpalatable situation'.[83] Moreover, the obvious alternative to 'silent acquiescence' is not departure from the occupied territory but the resumption of resistance that doctrines of obligation had sought to condemn. Flight may be an option on the approach of an invader, though scarcely for the entire population, any more than it was in the day when David Hume criticised this argument, but once the occupation is established, occupiers have tended to exert as much control over border movements as their resources allow.[84] In the case of the occupation of Japan, for example, this meant protracted prohibition of foreign travel.

Nor does it help that departure from occupied territory has been seen as a penalty for those desiring to remain but presumed to be prone to disobey, suggesting that occupiers have been unwilling to rely on tacit consent. Thus the American *Rules of Land Warfare* of 1914 specified that 'any official considered dangerous to the occupant may be removed, made a prisoner of war, or expelled from the occupied territory'.[85] The combination of a prohibition on leaving occupied territory with the penalty of an extended period of expulsion for those that did, imposed by the German occupation authorities in Alsace and Lorraine, brings out the implausibility in the context of military occupation of a consent theory that rests on a right and ability to emigrate.[86] Moreover, wholesale expulsion or ethnic cleansing has changed the debate to the extent that occupiers are not only prohibited from engaging in expulsion but are seen as having an obligation to resist those within occupied territory who resort to it for their own purposes. Even here, however, in reaction to the population transfers of the Second World War, the Fourth Geneva Convention specified that 'individual or mass forcible transfers, as well as deportations of protected persons from occupied territory to the territory of the Occupying Power or to that of any other country, occupied or not , are prohibited, regardless of motive'.[87] The intent of the emphasis upon 'forcible transfers' was to leave open the possibility of 'persons belonging to ethnic or political minorities who might have suffered discrimination or persecution' wishing to leave.[88] The presumption more recently is that occupiers have a duty to positively resist all such transfers, encouraging minorities to remain and guaranteeing their security. Indeed this played a major role in both justifications and assessments of the occupations of Bosnia-Herzegovina and Kosovo.[89]

That development suggests that there may be greater plausibility in the justification of obedience in terms of the protection offered by the occupier, though advocacy of the 'responsibility to protect' that emerged amidst the 'new interventionism' tended to neglect any correlative discussion of a duty to obey on the part of those protected.[90] The link between protection and obedience is, of course, a longstanding one, both in terms of general theories of political obligation and in the shorter history of military occupation. As Carl Schmitt put it:

> Given that the occupying army maintains public security and protects the population in the occupied territory, the latter is obliged to obey the occupying authority. In this case, the direct relation between protection and obedience is obvious. It is based on a clear spatial relation between an effectively present occupying authority and the population of the occupied territory.[91]

The same sentiment was expressed in Halleck's argument about the limits of obligation. It also appears in many of the accounts that suggest some form of consent or contract. Explicit assertion of the extension of protection, and of safeguards for specific establishments, has also appeared in military proclamations, such as that of General Scott in Mexico in 1847.[92]

The difficulty here is that this protection readily invokes the response that potentially meets all benefits which are imposed, that is that they are unwanted and that no gratitude, let alone duty of obedience, can be extracted from them.[93] The fact that the protection offered by the occupier is typically imposed against the manifest will of the occupied only aggravates the general problem. In many cases, Baxter's objection to justification by virtue of protection seems readily applicable: 'not only have the inhabitant and his government never consented to it but the populace has not benefited by the substitution of the occupant's uncertain protection for that of its own government'.[94]

Yet there are cases where the inhabitant's own government has been the source of a threat rather than protection, where the flight of officials and the depredations of retreating armies have been so extensive or where internecine conflict has been so endemic that the protection of the occupier is the only effective protection available. Yet this does not really strengthen the argument based on consent. It serves rather to reveal that though the justification was often couched in the language of presumed or hypothetical consent, the consent is actually fictitious and irrelevant to the argument. This can be seen in the statement of Secretary of State James Buchanan on 7 October 1848 concerning the situation in California:

> The termination of the war left an existing government, a government de facto . . . and this will continue, with the presumed consent of the people . . . The consent of the people is irresistibly inferred from the fact that no civilized community could possibly desire to abrogate an existing government when the alternative presented would be to place themselves in a state of anarchy, beyond the protection of all laws, and reduce them to the unhappy necessity of submitting to the dominion of the strongest.[95]

If the consent can be 'irresistibly inferred' whether inhabitants do or do not consent, then consent in any meaningful sense of the term is immaterial.

There are also other objections to Buchanan's argument. Amongst the most prominent is the fact that submission to the 'dominion of the strongest' is an apt description of the source of the authority of the military government established by the United States. What Buchanan assumed, of course, was that American military government could provide a more effective and benign government than was likely to emerge from an unregulated struggle for power within the territory.[96] That is essentially the same argument that is used to justify the authority of international administration in recent instances authorised by the United Nations, though, of course with far higher ambitions than prevailed in Buchanan's day.[97]

The necessity of government, and hence the existence of its authority and some duty of obedience too it, is what lies behind the argument from protection, though the language of protection has other connotations which reveal both the strength of the argument from protection and the reason why it is potentially so problematic. Some of those connotations emerge in the definition in the Fourth Geneva Convention of protected persons:

> Persons protected by the Convention are those who, at a given moment and in any manner whatsoever, find themselves, in case of conflict or occupation, in the hands of a Party to the conflict or Occupying Power of which they are not nationals.[98]

By definition, it is the occupying power alone that is in a position to ensure that the protections promised by the Convention are redeemed and yet these protections are meant to guard against the threat that usually comes predominantly from the same occupying power.

Yet it may be that this paradox also contains the source of the political obligation of the inhabitants of occupied territory. Such a possibility is suggested by Oppenheim, despite his flat denial of any obligation towards occupiers. Though insisting on this, Oppenheim added:

> Nor do I deny that *individual* inhabitants are morally bound not to resort to hostilities in arms and the like, while the occupation lasts; but this is not the outcome of a moral duty towards the occupant but towards their fellow-citizens, for he who resorts to such hostilities endangers the safety of the other inhabitants, because he gives the occupant an excuse for resorting to reprisals and all other kinds of repressive measures.[99]

Oppenheim was right to see the importance of duties to fellow citizens and right to see that these have a bearing on relations with the occupiers. He erred, however, in seeing these relationships purely in terms of the potential harm that an occupant might do in response to rash acts by individuals, though that is not to deny that this potentiality is an important consideration. He erred because he failed to see that the inhabitants' obligation is rooted not just in these utilitarian considerations but in their continued membership of a political community, albeit under the de facto government of a military occupier. The moral duty of which Oppenheim wrote is in fact a political obligation, that is, it is a 'moral obligation [which] has to do with a person's membership of a particular community'.[100] The notion that obligations arise from membership of particular communities is most evidently plausible where it is possible, as it normally is, to tie together obligations towards 'my' community with obligations towards 'my' government.[101] The government of the occupier cannot, by definition, enjoy that designation. It is for this reason that suggestions that the occupier and the inhabitants of occupied territory form a temporary legal community are misleading.[102]

The significance of the persistence of community even under conditions of military occupation can be seen by contrasting the conditions of the inhabitants with the fate of stateless people, as described by Hannah Arendt. In their condition, she wrote:

> The conception of human rights, based upon the assumed existence of a human being as such, broke down at the very moment when those who

professed to believe in it were for the first time confronted with people who had indeed lost all other qualities and specific relationships – except that they were still human. The world found nothing sacred in the abstrat nakedness of being human.[103]

This is not, or should not be, the condition of the inhabitants of occupied territory. That it is not could be said to be the intent of the Geneva Conventions as expounded by Pictet, namely that it was to ensure that 'every person in enemy hands must have some status under international law'.[104] Indeed, they acquire a new specific status as 'protected persons' in the language of the Geneva Conventions. This designation was not novel. It is recognisably the same in principle as that of the persons 'placed under the special safeguard of the faith and honour of the American Army', in the words of General Scott in 1847.[105] Inhabitants of occupied territory do not lose all the other 'qualities and specific' relationships that they previously enjoyed. That had long been recognised in nineteenth century courts, although it was expressed in terms of private law, especially property law, and in terms of assumptions about changes in allegiance expressly ruled out by later conceptions of military occupation. Thus, in 'Leitendorfer et.al. *v.* Webb', the US Supreme Court held in the case of the conquest of New Mexico,

> By this substitution of a new supremacy, although the former political relations of the inhabitants were dissolved, their private relations, their rights vested under the Government of their former allegiance, or those arising from contract or usage, remained in full force and unchanged . . .

Similarly, the Court cited a British judgement according to which

> the inhabitants of a conquered territory change their allegiance, and their relation to their former sovereign is dissolved; but their relations to each other, and their rights of property not taken from them by the orders of the conqueror, remain undisturbed.[106]

A later Court judgement specified that these relations included

> the preservation of order, the maintenance of police regulations, the prosecution of crimes, the protection of property, the enforcement of contracts, the celebration of marriages, the settlement of estates, the transfer and descent of property, and similar or kindred subjects.[107]

The same sentiment lies behind the Hague Regulations' prescription that the occupier shall 'restore and maintain public order and civil life'.[108]

The practice of occupiers and the prescription of codes and manuals has, as shown above, often gone further than this, allowing the persistence of municipal government, if only for the convenience of the occupier. Especially, but not only, more recently, occupiers have promoted the development of political institutions and other associations, albeit for highly diverse purposes. Insofar as the community persists – and it is the duty of the occupier, having assumed authority over it, to ensure that it does – it is arguable that the inhabitants have a duty not to frustrate the authority of the occupier. They have a derivative duty to obey arising from their membership of the community, while the occupier has a direct duty to protect arising from the occupier's assumption of authority.

The persistence of community is of course threatened by the occupier. The maintenance of the authority of the occupier requires some restrictions. These restrictions need not amount to what Arendt described as the 'fundamental deprivation of human rights' experienced by the stateless, namely 'the deprivation of a place in the world which makes opinions significant and actions effective', though some restriction in these respects is inevitable.[109] Yet some occupiers have embarked upon an occupation regime intended to substantially destroy all the distinctive 'qualities and specific relationships' enjoyed by the inhabitants and any possibility of effective opinion and action. They have become the tyrants indicted by Halleck. Just as occupiers may deliberately reject the duty of protection so too inhabitants of occupied territory may abandon their obligations to each other, not only in the sense which Oppenheim feared, bringing down the wrath of the occupier upon their fellow citizens, but in the sense of rejecting the persistence of the integrity of the community, seeking its fragmentation instead.[110]

Just as military government seems archaic so too the idea that the inhabitants of occupied territory have a duty to obey occupiers will continue to seem archaic. Yet that does not mean that military occupation can be understood without it; moreover, can any form of government be understood without some notion of political obligation, which is an obligation, in part at least, to a government? It is inherently more problematic because it is an obligation to an alien government and because all too frequently occupiers have resorted to practices which would vitiate the claim of any government, whether alien or not, to authority properly understood.

Notes

1. UK Ministry of Defence, *The Manual of the Law of Armed Conflict* (Oxford: Oxford University Press, 2004), p. 281.
2. For the wider problem, see John Horton, *Political Obligation* (Houndmills: Basingstoke, 1992), pp. 1–4.
3. Richard A. Falk and Burns H. Weston, 'The relevance of international law to Palestinian rights in the West Bank and Gaza: in legal defense of the Intifada', *Harvard International Law Journal*, 32 (1991), p. 154. Baxter's article is entitled 'The duty of obedience to the belligerent occupant', *British Yearbook of International Law*, 27 (1950), pp. 235–66.
4. On the confusion, see Carl J. Friedrich, 'Authority, reason and decision', in Carl J. Friedrich (ed.), *Nomos 1. Authority* (Cambridge, MA: Harvard University Press, 1958), pp. 24–48. See also Hannah Arendt, *Between Past and Future* (Harmondsworth: Penguin, 1977), 'What is authority?', pp. 91–141.
5. Dominik Zaum, 'The authority of international administrations in international society', *Review of International Studies*, 32 (2006), pp. 455–6.
6. Falk and Weston, 'The relevance of international law to Palestinian rights', p. 154.
7. John Locke, *Two Treatises of Government* (New York, NY: Mentor, 1965), pp. 445–6. Occupiers also resemble usurpers in that even where it is conceded that the usurper might have authority, it is evident that this authority, like that of the occupier, extends only to those within the territory controlled and not to those who managed to depart prior to the seizure of the territory. See August Wilhelm Heffter, *Das Europäische Völkerrecht der Gegenwart*, ed. Heinz Geffecken (Berlin: Müller, 1888), p. 404.
8. Arendt, 'What is authority?' pp. 92–3.
9. Marcus Tulius Cicero, *De Re Publica, De Legibus* (London: Heinemann, 1928), p. 169.
10. War Office, *Manual of Military Law* (London, HMSO, 1914), p. 87.
11. H. Sutherland Edwards, *The Germans in France* (London: Stanford, 1874), p. 153.
12. Ian King and Whit Mason, *Peace at Any Price* (Ithaca, NY: Cornell University Press, 2006), p. 254.
13. As seems to have been the case in the confrontation with Muqtada al-Sadr in Iraq. See L. Paul Bremer, *My Year in Iraq* (New York, NY: Threshold, 2006), pp. 130–1.
14. Lyle W. Cayce, 'Liberation or occupation?', USAWC Strategy Research Project (Carlisle Barracks, PA: US Army War College, 2004), p. 2.
15. H. W. Halleck, *International Law* (San Francisco, CA: Bancroft, 1861), p. 795.

16. William Edward Hall, *A Treatise on International Law* (Oxford: Oxford University Press, 1924), p. 557.
17. Ibid. p. 558.
18. Ibid. pp. 555–6.
19. Article 26, Lieber Code.
20. Doris Apel Graber, *The Development of the Law of Belligerent Occupation 1863–1914* (New York, NY: AMS, 1949), p. 75.
21. Halleck, *International Law*, 793–4.
22. War Office, *Manual of Military Law*, p. 292.
23. War Department, *Rules of Land Warfare* (Washington, DC: War Department, 1917), pp. 112–13.
24. J. H. Morgan [1915], *War Book of the German General Staff* (Mechanicsburg, PA: Stackpole, 2005), p. 111.
25. Graber, *The Development of the Law of Belligerent Occupation*, p. 70.
26. David Martin Jones, *Conscience and Allegiance in Seventeenth Century England. The Political Significance of Oaths and Engagements* (Rochester, MI: University of Rochester Press, 1999), pp. 259–60.
27. J. M. Spaight, *War Rights on Land* (London: Macmillan, 1911), p. 373.
28. Article 26, Lieber Code.
29. The oath is reproduced in William Winthrop, *Military Law and Precedents* (Washington, DC: War Department, 1920), pp. 813–14.
30. The alcalde of Las Vegas publicly cited his oath as the basis for refusing to join the uprising against the occupier. David Yancy Thomas [1904], *A History of the Government in Newly Acquired Territory of the United States* (Honolulu, HI: University Press of the Pacific, 2002), p. 120.
31. Richard Dana in his notes to Henry Wheaton [1866], *Elements of International Law* (Oxford: Clarendon Press, 1936), p. 367.
32. Article 4, Brussels Code.
33. Pasquale Fiore, *Le Droit International Codifié* (Paris: Pedone, 1911), p. 687.
34. Graber, *The Development of the Law of Belligerent Occupation*, p. 149.
35. Article 45, Hague Regulations, 1907.
36. The incident and associated correspondence is surveyed in Charles [Carlos] Calvo, *Le Droit International* (Paris: Guillaumin, 1888), pp. 223–34.
37. John Westlake, *International Law. Part II. War* (Cambridge: Cambridge University Press, 1907), p. 92.
38. Spaight, *War Rights on Land*, pp. 358–9.
39. Calvo, *Le Droit International*, pp. 226–7.
40. Article 92, Lieber Code.

41. War Office, *Manual of Military Law*, p. 259.

42. See Henry Bonfils, *Manuel de Droit International Public* (Paris: Rousseau, 1894), pp. 639–40; A. Mérignhac, *Traité de Droit Public International*, vol. 3 (Paris: Librairie Générale de Droit et de Jurisprudence, 1912), pp. 290–1.

43. Westlake, *International Law*, p. 90.

44. Spaight, *War Rights on Land*, pp. 334–5.

45. J. H. Morgan, 'War treason', *Problems of the War*, 2 (1916), pp. 161–5.

46. Ibid. p. 164.

47. L. Oppenheim, 'On war treason', *Law Quarterly Review*, 33 (1917), pp. 266–86.

48. Ibid. p. 284.

49. L. Oppenheim, 'The legal relation between an occupying power and the inhabitants', *Law Quarterly Review*, 33 (1917), p. 367.

50. Baxter, 'The duty of obedience to the belligerent occupant', p. 260.

51. Morgan, 'War treason', p. 165.

52. Hall, *A Treatise on International Law*, p. 91.

53. *Correspondence Respecting the Brussels Conference on the Rules of Military Warfare* (London: House of Commons, 1875), p. 264.

54. Quoted in Jean S. Pictet, *Commentary: Third Geneva Convention* (Geneva: ICRC, 1960), p. 44.

55. Ibid. p. 58.

56. See Graber's assessment of the lingering uncertainty at the time of the 1907 Hague Congress, *The Development of the Law of Belligerent Occupation*, p. 107.

57. Article 52, Hague Regulations, 1907.

58. G. Rolin-Jaequemyns, 'Essai complementaire sur la guerre Franco-Allemande dans ses rapports avec le droit international', *Revue de Droit International et de Législation Comparée*, 3 (1871), p. 334.

59. Articles 94 and 96, Lieber Code.

60. Spaight, *War Rights on Land*, p. 371.

61. Graber, *The Development of the Law of Belligerent Occupation*, p. 99.

62. John H. E. Fried, 'Transfer of civilian manpower from occupied territory', *American Journal of International Law*, 40 (1946), pp. 308–12.

63. Jean S. Pictet, *Commentary: Fourth Geneva Convention* (Geneva: ICRC, 1958), pp. 277–80.

64. Fried, 'Transfer of civilian manpower from occupied territory', p. 329.

65. Hall, *A Treatise on International Law*, p. 571.

66. Graber, *The Development of the Law of Belligerent Occupation*, pp. 129–30, 155.

67. Ernst Fraenkel [1944], 'Military occupation and the rule of law', in Ernst Fraenkel, *Gesammelte Schriften*, vol. 3 (Baden-Baden: Nomos, 1999), p. 179.

68. As pointed out by J. H. W. Verzil, *International Law in Historical Perspective*, part IX-A (Alphen aan den Rijn: Sijthoff & Noordhoff, 1978), pp. 213–14.

69. '*In re* van Huis', *Annual Digest*, 13 (1946), p. 350.

70. Ibid. pp. 350–1.

71. '*In re* Contractor Worp', *Annual Digest*, 13 (1946), p. 353.

72. 'Nederlands Beheersinstituut *v.* Robaver', *Annual Digest*, 14 (1947), p. 240.

73. See Chapter 2 of this text.

74. For a contemporary view of the status of the exiled governments, see F. E. Oppenheimer, 'Governments and authorities in exile', *American Journal of International Law*, 36 (1942), pp. 568–95.

75. F. S. V. Donnison, *Civil Affairs and Military Government. North-West Europe 1944–1946* (London: HMSO, 1961), p. 101.

76. Zaum, 'The authority of international administrations in international society', p. 460.

77. Ibid. p. 460.

78. Graber, *The Development of the Law of Belligerent Occupation*, p. 76.

79. 'The United States *v.* Rice', *US Reports*, 17 (1819), p. 254.

80. Birkhimer, *Military Government and Martial Law*, p. 23.

81. Edgar Loening, 'L'administration du Gouvernement-Générale de l'Alsace', *Revue de Droit International et de Législation Comparée*, 4 (1872), p. 633. For the classic exposition, see Locke, *Two Treatises of Government*, pp. 392–4.

82. Baxter, 'The duty of obedience to the belligerent occupant', p. 259.

83. Ibid. p. 259.

84. For Hume's comments, see Henry D. Aiken, *Hume's Moral and Political Philosophy* (New York, NY: Hafner, 1948), pp. 363–4.

85. War Department, *Rules of Land Warfare*, p. 117.

86. Edgar Loening, 'L'administration du Gouvernement-Générale de l'Alsace', *Revue de Droit International et de Législation Comparée*, 5 (1873), pp. 84–5.

87. Article 49 quoted in Pictet, *Commentary: Fourth Geneva Convention*, p. 277.

88. Ibid. p. 279. The only people conceded a 'right to leave' are 'protected persons who are not nationals of the Power whose territory is occupied', Article 48, ibid. p. 276.

89. See, for example, the condemnation reflected in the title of King and Mason, *Peace at Any Price*, p. 97: '"Security" was achieved only at the price of effectively allowing nationalists to achieve their aims without

violence. In practice this meant that UNMIK came to accept the *fait accompli* of ethnic cleansing'.

90. See International Commission on Intervention and State Responsibility, *The Responsibility to Protect* (Ottawa: International Development Research Centre, 2001).

91. Carl Schmitt, *The Nomos of the Earth* (New York, NY: Telos Press, 2003), p. 318.

92. See the text of Scott's proclamation in Birkhimer, *Military Government*, pp. 581–3.

93. Horton, *Political Obligation*, pp. 101–2.

94. Baxter, 'The duty of obedience to the belligerent occupant', p. 259.

95. Myra K. Saunder, 'California legal history', *Law Library Journal*, 88 (1996), p. 509. Buchanan's statement was widely quoted, see, for example, and 'Cross et. al. *v.* Harrison, *US Reports*, 57 (1853) pp. 184–5.

96. For vigorous refutation of this claim, see Gary Lawson and Guy Seidman, *The Constitution of Empire* (New Haven, CT: Yale University Press, 2004), pp. 184–5.

97. Zaum, 'The authority of international administrations in international society', pp. 465–8.

98. Article 4, quoted in Pictet, *Fourth Geneva Convention*, p. 45.

99. Oppenheim, 'The legal relation between an occupying power and the inhabitants', p. 369.

100. Horton, *Political Obligation*, p. 15.

101. Ibid. pp. 151–67.

102. See Chapter 2.

103. Hannah Arendt, *Origins of Totalitarianism* (London: George Allen and Unwin, 1967), p. 299.

104. Pictet, *Fourth Geneva Convention*, p. 51.

105. Birkhimer, *Military Government and Martial Law*, p. 583.

106. 'Leitendorfer et. al. *v.* Webb', *US Reports*, 61 (1857), p. 177.

107. 'Baldy *v.* Hunter', quoted in Shanker, 'The law of belligerent occupation in the American courts', p. 1079.

108. Article 43, Hague Regulations, 1907.

109. Arendt, *Origins of Totalitarianism*, p. 296. See also the interesting question raised by John Quigley, 'The relation between human rights law and the law of belligerent occupation: does an occupied population have a right to freedom of assembly and expression?' *Boston College International and Comparative Law Review*, 12 (1989), pp. 1–28.

110. For a good summary of the complexity the latter option may exhibit, see Eric Henning and Glen Rangwala, *Iraq in Fragments* (London: Hurst, 2006), pp. 270–2.

Chapter 6

Sovereignty and Occupation

The concept of sovereignty has played a key role the emergence of the idea of military occupation as a distinctive phenomenon, in the various definitions of it and in the contentious notion that inhabitants could be under an obligation to obey occupiers. Unlike the latter notion, the concept of sovereignty has remained central to reflection on military occupation even where the fact of military occupation has been denied. The persistent relevance of the concept of sovereignty has been ensured by its presumed centrality to the international order and by the fact that the function of the concept of military occupation, paradoxically, was to account for the persistence of sovereignty despite the physical presence of the occupier. Here, the existence of the ousted sovereign or the ousted sovereign's government served as evidence of the threatened continuity of the state. It was paradoxical because the fact of occupation entailed the assertion of the authority of the occupier, prevented the exercise of sovereign power, and could form the prelude to the cession of the territory, in whole or part. The threat posed by occupation was enhanced by the tendency to identify sovereignty as essential to a state and simultaneously to identify whatever governmental functions states typically exercised as manifestations of the concept of sovereignty.[1] Yet, by the same token, the occupier, even if not understood as a temporary sovereign, also served as a placeholder for the threatened sovereignty, preserving the existence of government; without this the state would dissolve into anarchy, which it was presumed the international community could not tolerate.[2] A recognisably similar logic is now used to justify international administration of 'failed' states.[3]

When the concept of military occupation began to crystallise, it was evident that the continued existence of the sovereign ruler was not the only guarantee of continuity. The persistent refusal of the population to submit, save under direct threat of the use of force, could fulfil the same function. That argument was invoked in a case which commanded attention for over a century, namely the fate of the Republic of Genoa. Genoa, having been conquered by France in 1797 and incorporated into the French empire in 1805, was subsequently occupied by British forces. Its population was encouraged to re-establish a republic by the British commander, only for Genoa to be annexed by Sardinia in accordance with the peace treaty. Protest against this turned in large part on British refusal to recognise French sovereignty throughout the period of French control and Britain's previous status as an ally of the Republic, but the leading critic of the annexation, James Mackintosh, also invoked the refusal of the Genoese to genuinely submit as evidence of the persistence of an oppressed nation.[4] A century later, the principle of the persistence of a nation under occupation, now explicitly stripped of any connection to its previous constitutional form or requirements of the absence of state recognition, was invoked in favour of the Polish nation, which had been partitioned by its neighbours before the French had conquered the Republic of Genoa. The Polish academic Siegmund Cybichowski even took exception to the wording of the treaty of 28 June 1919, by which 'the Allied and Associated Powers have by the success of their arms restored to the Polish nation the independence of which it had been unjustly deprived'.[5] He did so on the grounds that 'sovereignty, as the highest power, cannot be at the disposal of foreign states'.[6] That was consistent with a modern understanding of sovereignty as rooted in a people, and with the principle of the law of occupation that the occupier is not the legitimate power, and hence can no more restore the sovereignty it never possessed than it can assign it to a third party. It was consistent with the principle that the mere duration of occupation cannot transform it into another condition. It also conveniently ignored all other considerations of the kind that had figured in the protest of Mackintosh at the treatment of Genoa.

This abstract sovereignty, construed as an indeterminate highest power tied to the persistence of the nation, seems immune to anything short of some catastrophe bordering on genocide.[7] That, of course, was also its weakness. Sovereignty is not a timeless concept inherent in a body of people, however such a body might be defined. It, along with the state system it defines, is 'based on . . . the production of a normative conception that links authority, territory, population (society, nation), and recognition in a unique way and in a particular place'.[8] Those linkages can, however, be loosened to the point where little is left save a tentative recognition. Such a possibility is not a recent phenomenon. It was described well by Georg Jellinek towards the end of the nineteenth century: 'It is not only a theoretical consequence of the concept of sovereignty that it can exist as a *nudum jus* but also something demonstrable in the practical world'.[9] Shortly before Jellinek made this observation, two cases had provided ample evidence: the occupation and administration of Cyprus by Britain and of Bosnia-Herzegovina by Austria-Hungary, in 1878. In both cases, the occupying powers acknowledged the continuing sovereignty of the Ottoman Empire and initially administered them through their Foreign Offices, though their longer-term intent was already indicated by transfer of the administration to the Colonial Office and Ministry of Finance, respectively. Both were subsequently annexed.[10]

An inflated concept of sovereignty, presuming strong hierarchical states, is still seen as prevalent and problematic by some commentators.[11] An alternative view was expressed in the widely quoted words of UN Secretary General Kofi Annan: 'State sovereignty, in its most basic sense, is being redefined . . . States are now widely understood to be instruments at the service of their people'.[12] The conclusion drawn from such statements is that sovereignty is conditional upon the state's responsibility to protect its own peoples and where it violates this responsibility other states have a responsibility to intervene. Today, so it is argued, there is a 'marked disregard for sovereignty *traditionally construed* as a barrier to humanitarian intervention'.[13] According to others, sovereign states may be said to involuntarily waive their sovereignty where they fail to protect their own peoples.[14] Although the precise formulation, theoretical context and above all constraints about who is to decide that such a condition has arisen vary considerably, it is the range of such advocacy that is striking.[15] It has also become increasingly common to write, for example, about 'quasi-states' whose existence is 'primarily juridical' and which lack the ability to protect their populations or ensure adequate socio-economic conditions.[16] Stephen D. Krasner has unpacked the concept of sovereignty into no less than four components:

> domestic sovereignty, referring to the organisation of public authority within a state and to the level of effective control exercised by those holding authority; interdependence sovereignty, referring to the ability of public authorities to control transborder movements; international legal sovereignty, referring to the mutual recognition of states or other entities; and Westphalian sovereignty, referring to the exclusion of external actors from domestic authority configurations.[17]

Others have turned back to Grotius and models of divisible sovereignty and even suggested that such notions are applicable to the military occupation of Iraq.[18] Similarly, a notion of a 'disaggregated sovereignty' has been put forward as a better conceptualisation of the role of the UN Mission in Kosovo.[19] Of Krasnser's four components, only international legal sovereignty would clearly survive military occupation, although, as will be shown below, not even this has remained unproblematic. Since the occupier is by definition an external actor intent upon asserting its authority within the occupied state, and since occupiers attempt, with varying degrees of success, to control borders, the implication appears to be that occupiers could acquire in substantial part the thing that distinguishes conquest from occupation: sovereignty. It would seem that, at least under certain conditions, the sovereignty of the occupied state is diminished while the occupier becomes, in some respects at least, the sovereign.

Any such implication should be resisted, of course. It illustrates in modern form, however, a recurrent problem, namely the difficulty often encountered in making intelligible and meaningful the idea of a sovereignty that eludes the potential grip of the occupier and preserves the continuity of the state under occupation. Conceptually it might appear simple to do so. If Jellinek's claim that theoretically and practically sovereignty can shrink to a *nudum jus* is accepted, and if the occupier declines to assert sovereignty or other states refuse to acknowledge any assertion of sovereignty (especially where the inhabitants of occupied territory also refuse to acknowledge it, as Mackinstosh believed the Genoans had demonstrated), the persistence of sovereignty might seem straightforward. Analytically, indeed, it is straightforward. There has also been some recognition of this in the discussion of the meaning of sovereignty under conditions of military occupation. Typically, however, such recognition has been qualified, frequently leading to confusion and inconsistency. Such confusion and inconsistency is not primarily the product of carelessness but has arisen because military occupation divides legitimate authority from territory and population and thereby poses a threat to the integrity of the community that is defined precisely by their normative linkage. The nature of the threat is well illustrated by John Horton's speculation on the refusal of French citizens to accord the Vichy regime anything more than the status of a de facto government while retaining loyalty to a French state represented by General de Gaulle:

> In this situation political obligation seems entirely consistent with the denial of the authority of the *de facto* government; but how long an

intelligible sense of *political* obligation could survive this sundering from the effective government of the community is a moot point.[20]

That was the question faced by Cybichowski's ancestors during what he regarded as Poland's prolonged occupation.[21] Failure to recognise and accept that sovereignty under conditions of military occupation shrinks to a *nudum jus*, serving as no more than a marker for the fact that the occupier is not sovereign, has produced an unending catalogue of equivocation and confusion, tempting occupiers to exalt their status to the point where it is difficult to discern the difference between occupiers and legitimate powers, whilst occupied populations, exiled governments and even third parties have struggled to gloss over the precarious status of occupied territory.

As the example of de Gaulle demonstrates, the existence of a sovereign exiled government or, in de Gaulle's case, the existence of a claimant to the status of an exiled government that physically eludes the grip of the occupier has provided the traditional reference point for the persistence of sovereignty. Yet such sovereigns and governments have often shown themselves to be all too well aware of the precariousness of sovereignty as a *nudum jus*. Nor indeed, have they always managed to escape the grip of the occupier. Rather than being ousted sovereigns or governments, in any physical sense, they have more closely resembled captive sovereigns or governments; sometimes there has been no plausible candidate for either an ousted or a captive sovereign or government. That is a fact which occupiers sometimes sought to turn to their advantage, blurring the line between occupation and conquest.

Even where occupiers have disavowed any intent to annex territory, the extent of their assumption of authority has been so extensive as to render the difference between their authority and that of a legitimate power difficult to maintain, either in their own eyes or those of others. At the other extreme, occupiers eager, for various reasons, to divest themselves of the status and responsibilities of occupiers have hastened to restore the sovereignty of a legitimate power. Yet that too can prove to be unpersuasive as the discrepancy between the status of the sovereign power and the persistent reality of the power of the occupier merely exposes the fragility of the former and undermines the legitimacy that is supposedly its prerogative.

Such considerations are evident in the language used to describe the sovereignty that is supposed to persist during the period of occupation even where an identifiable ousted sovereign was presumed to exist. At one extreme, the loss of power seemed so striking that even those concerned to assert the difference between occupation and conquest wrote of the extinction of sovereignty: 'military government takes the place of a suspended or destroyed *sovereignty* . . . the laws created by the sovereignty and dependent upon that sovereignty pass away with it'.[22] Others were attracted by the logic that two sovereigns could not exist in the same place at the same time, with the presumption that as one was pushed out the other, invading sovereign, must take its place.[23] Towards the end of the nineteenth century, Frantz Despagnet allowed for the existence of two sovereigns, albeit of a different kind. According to Despagnet, the 'sovereignty of the country invaded persists *in right*' though 'on certain points' it is 'replaced *in fact* by that of the invading country'.[24] A similar position was adopted by Fauchille who referred to 'the sovereignty in fact of the occupant being entirely provisional and the legal sovereignty of the invaded state not being destroyed'.[25] A little later, Arthur Lorriot provided a more eccentric version of two types of sovereignty. According to Doris Graber, 'Lorriot states that the occupant cannot possibly be the true sovereign of the occupied region since sovereignty can arise only from the consent of the governed. Lorriot believes that the occupant brings his own sovereignty with him'.[26] The solution to such equivocation is to deny that the occupier is sovereign in any sense but to acknowledge that the occupier possesses authority.

That, however, still leaves the problem of how to understand the sovereignty of the ousted sovereignty. According to Raymond Robin it 'is impossible . . . for that sovereignty to be publicly manifested, but it *does not disappear* on that account. Though *paralyzed in fact*, at least within the limits of the necessities of war, *in law it continues to exist*'.[27] It is notable that Robin had some difficulty maintaining the sharp contrast between factual paralysis and continued legal title for in considering the British occupation of Egypt, whose nominal sovereign remained the Ottoman Empire, he wrote that Britain had been able 'to establish little by little her authority over Egypt, and finally to substitute in fact her own sovereignty for that of the occupied state'.[28] Hall noted an even more equivocal formulation, claiming that the 'continuance of sovereignty over its occupied parts is affirmed, though in the subordinate shape of a kind of "latent title" by Klüber'.[29] Here, even the status of the title which Robin asserted is downgraded. Bonfils had emphasised earlier the public dimension of sovereignty that also played a role in Robin's formulation. According to Bonfils the legal sovereign was faced by the fact of occupation with 'the impossibility of *publicly* exercising his authority'.[30] Bonfils, however, no more explained how authority could be exercised other than publicly than Robin explained how sovereignty could be made manifest other than publicly.

Others have invoked the idea of the suspension or displacement of sovereignty, without such nuances. However, the language of suspension had also been associated with the ascription of sovereignty to the invader, most notably in the American Supreme Court decision of 1819:

> By the conquest and military occupation of Castine, the enemy acquired that firm possession which enabled him to exercise the fullest rights of sovereignty over that place. The sovereignty of the United States over the territory was, of course, suspended.[31]

Suspension of sovereignty could however be invoked without assigning the occupier, even temporarily, the status of a sovereign. The language of suspension seemed to correspond to the reality of the power of the occupier whilst also suggesting that, ineffective though this legitimate sovereignty was, it would resume in due course, in accordance with the temporary nature of military occupation. Indeed the language of suspension has continued to be deployed. Thus, Richard Caplan has noted that 'UN Security Council Resolution 1244 (1999), while reaffirming "the commitment of all Member States to the sovereignty and territorial integrity of the Federal Republic of Yugoslavia"' was, by virtue of the range of powers ascribed to the UN administration, 'an act tantamount to the virtual suspension of Yugoslavia's sovereignty over Kosovo'.[32]

Ousted sovereigns, however, have not always accepted the suspension of their sovereignty or have sought to heavily qualify any such notion. This was already indicated by the Belgian suggestion that reference to the suspension of the authority of the legitimate power be struck from the text of the Hague conference in 1899. That sentiment was reaffirmed in a Belgian court judgement of 1919 when 'the Court held that in law national sovereignty subsisted in the occupied territory during the occupation, even when the occupying Power exercised *de facto* authority'.[33] The most that a later court conceded was that legislation by the ousted sovereign intended to harm the occupant was 'not capable of application in districts where a military occupation has been established'.[34]

Similar sentiments were invoked by Germany in response to the occupation of the Rhineland. On the basis that Germany remained the sovereign of the occupied territories and that legislative power is inherent in sovereignty, it insisted that German legislation came into effect immediately in the Rhineland. The fact that, in accordance with the first Ordinance of the High Commission, German legislation had to be submitted to the High Commission (which had the power to veto the application of such laws in the Rhineland), was interpreted as a 'condition subsequent' to the validity of the legislation. The High Commission, on the other hand, insisted equally firmly that this vetting procedure was a 'condition precedent' to the application of the laws.[35]

German courts subsequently argued that the authority of the High Commission in Germany was based upon the fact that the Rhineland Agreement had been 'transformed' into German law. They deduced from this that German courts had a right to review High Commission ordinances with a view to assessing their compatibility with the Agreement.[36] In reality, Germany was no more able than Belgium had been to block the authority of the occupier. Indeed the assertion of sovereignty served more as a protest against, and simultaneously as a proclamation of, its impotence.

Despite these precedents, there was limited reflection on the position of ousted sovereigns; yet, during the Second World War, they were notable by virtue of both their number and the extent of their activity, especially in London. Eight exiled governments were recognised in London: Belgium, Czechoslovakia, Greece, Luxembourg, the Netherlands, Norway, Poland, and Yugoslavia. In addition to these, the British government recognised the National Committee as the 'executive organ' of the Free French Movement, though this amounted to less than the acknowledgement of its sovereignty.[37] One peculiar consequence of these recognitions was the apparent existence of several sovereign bodies within the British capital. As one observer noted at the time, the 'co-existence of two or more sovereign governments on the same territory has created a number of unprecedented legal problems'.[38] Yet these governments were dependent upon the goodwill and recognition of Britain and the United States for their status, as the more precarious position of General de Gaulle's Free French Movement and his prolonged and often bitter struggle for recognition demonstrated.[39] In the case of France, the situation was complicated by the existence of the Vichy government of Marshall Pétain, which also claimed sovereignty and had some constitutional basis for doing so. However, critics disputed its capacity to enter into treaties, notably treaties relating to the transportation of French workers to Germany, on the grounds that 'the Pétain Government did not acquire that measure of stability and independence as to be capable of concluding international treaties' and that it 'owed whatever authority it possessed to the physical power of Germany'.[40] Nor was the fact that the Vichy regime had been recognised by other states accepted as proof of its sovereignty.[41] It is far from clear, however, that the exiled governments in London were any less dependent upon the physical power and recognition accorded them by their hosts than was Pétain's government upon the power and recognition of Germany.

Despite this dependence, the exiled governments displayed a high level of activity, especially within the diplomatic field. They concluded agreements and treaties with Britain, the United States and later Russia, as well as amongst themselves. In the case of Poland and Czechoslovakia, this even included an agreement to form a Confederation albeit of a limited intergovernmental nature, though that foundered on residual reservations on both sides and, more significantly, on Russian antipathy.[42] Other states also acknowledged the authority of these governments, not only over such armed forces as remained outside occupied territory but also individual citizens, at least in certain respects. As an American court put it in the case of the exiled government of the Netherlands, as 'the sovereign it could endeavour to preserve the interest of its nationals in properties situated beyond enemy control, especially where those residing within the occupied territory might find themselves powerless to protect those interests'.[43] This was consistent with the restriction of the authority of the occupier to the territory and inhabitants under its effective control and the denial of sovereignty to the occupier.

It was, however, the significance of the recognition of these sovereign governments to attitudes to occupied territory that was more important. Here, too, Britain or the relevant authority within the British Empire that constituted the exiled government showed no more restraint than the dispossessed governments of continental Europe. The scale of legislation for enemy-occupied territory was indeed striking. In the case of Burma, this included eight ordinances and six acts relating to the army of Burma and legislation concerning the University of Rangoon and the Railways Board.[44] Faced with this surge of activity, but finding no British judicial precedent or even extended commentary on the legislative power of ousted sovereigns, British commentators joined exiles from continental Europe in defending the ousted sovereign. According to a leading British authority, Arnold D. McNair, 'an English Court will continue to treat an allied and dispossessed Government as the *de iure* and *de facto* Government of all its normal territory in spite of the occupation of a part or the whole of it'.[45] The Czech exile, Egon Schwelb, commenting on British practice, welcomed the principle that 'this law-making capacity is unrestricted' as a rejection of wars of aggression.[46] Understandable though these reactions are, it is difficult to see how they can be reconciled with the condition of belligerent occupation. Moreover, as Eyal Benvenisti has observed, these laws 'of governments in exile were aimed at disrupting occupation policies regardless of possible hardships caused to the population'.[47]

It is not surprising that, as the Allies became occupiers, they took a dimmer view of the legislative power of absent sovereigns, even where the sovereign was not an enemy of the Allies. Indeed a post-war American court held that so far as it had been

> able to discover, throughout World War II the United States has adhered to its position that, as a matter of law, the decrees of an absent sovereign, even a friendly one, were a nullity in the areas occupied by the United States except to the extent that the United States chose to implement them.[48]

A stark illustration of that occurred in the case of death sentences passed by a court of the Allied military government in occupied Italy, after the end of the war, despite the fact that the Italian government had abolished the death penalty. Although the military government commuted the sentences it did not do so in recognition of any legislative power of the Italian government as the absent sovereign of the territories in which the crimes took place, but solely as a discretionary act of clemency.[49]

A somewhat eccentric twist was given to the relationship between the concept of sovereignty and the status of the putative absent sovereign in the case of Israeli occupation of Palestinian territory, amounting to at least an approximation to a claim that Israel was itself the sovereign. This 'missing reversioner' argument remains important because it was adopted by the Israeli government. It was put forward by Yehuda Blum in the context of divergent responses from magistrates in territory seized from Jordan to the appointment of Israeli advocates in local courts. For Blum, however, the key issue was the common presumption of the magistrates that Jordan was the ousted sovereign. Against this Blum argued that Jordan had come into possession of this territory in violation of Article 2(4) of the Charter of the United Nations in 1948.[50] Jordan, he concluded, could not be the sovereign. Jordan's subsequent 'annexation' of the territory had, he noted, not even escaped criticism from other Arab states. The most that could be said for Jordan's status before Israeli occupation of the territory after 1967 was that Jordan had been a belligerent occupier. The key in his argument, however, was that

> the rules of international law governing belligerent occupation are based on a twofold assumption, namely (a) that it was the legitimate sovereign which was ousted from the territory under occupation; and (b) that the ousting side qualifies as a belligerent occupant with respect to the territory.[51]

Since Jordan, he had argued, had never been the legitimate sovereign, title to these territories could not revert to Jordan in the event of an Israeli withdrawal. He went on to suggest that of the possible claimants to title Israel had a better claim but the key in his argument was the presumption that the concept of military occupation was primarily about the reversionary rights of the legitimate sovereign. The fact that Blum made this claim in the context of the Geneva Convention relating to civilians made it easier for his critics to attack him.[52] The critics also focused on the broader distortion evident in Blum's reduction of the normative understanding of military occupation to one of the reversionary rights of ousted legitimate sovereigns. It is true that such rights often played a prominent part in the understanding of military occupation, but as the occupations of the American Civil War demonstrates it is also possible to conceive of military occupation carried out by a power that considered itself to be the legitimate sovereign.[53]

This was not the only difficulty encountered in the attempt to make the concept of sovereignty central. Even Blum's sympathisers often resorted to equivocation faced with the logic of his argument, which would have assigned sovereignty to Israel, invoking, for example, 'the quasi-sovereign status of Israel within the West Bank area'.[54] The state of Israel preferred to conclude, in the words of Benjamin Netanyahu, that the area constituted 'disputed territories that Israel won in a defensive war in 1967'.[55] That was explicitly rejected by the International Court of Justice in 2004 in its opinion on the construction of a defensive barrier inside territory that it deemed occupied territory.[56] Indeed, by then some justification of that defensive barrier was sought on the grounds of the fact that the West Bank was very much distinct from Israel, though of a problematic status. The problem, it was claimed, arises because the occupied territories are recognized as a separate and distinct entity that simultaneously lacks, to an undefined extent, sovereignty. Hence the source of the flow of activities which are derived from these territories . . . cannot be traced to a state.[57]

The difficulties encountered in applying the language of sovereignty, and even statehood, in the case of Palestinian territories occupied by Israel are sometimes described as unique.[58] Yet such problems are evident elsewhere, not least where occupiers have asserted sovereignty, or something close to it, only to have to qualify that claim. This can be seen from Halleck's assertion in 1861 that conquered territory, at least in respect of the United States:

> is under the sovereignty and authority of the union; but it is not a part of the United States; nor does it cease to be a foreign country, or its inhabitants cease to be aliens in the sense in which these words are used in our laws . . . But while such territory forms no part of the union, and while its inhabitants have none of the rights, immunities and privileges of citizens of the United States . . . nevertheless, other nations are bound to regard the conquered territory, while in our possession, as territory of the United States, and to regard its inhabitants as under our protection and government.[59]

Such distinctions had already been employed in the case of the occupation of the Mexican port of Tampico, which was held by American courts to have remained a foreign port for revenue purposes despite asserting that the United States exercised 'sovereignty and dominion'.[60] By virtue of such sovereignty, however, other nations were obliged to treat it as American territory 'as exclusively as the territory included in our established boundaries'.[61] That judgement was expressly reiterated in the case of the occupation of Puerto Rico in 1898, where the Assistant Attorney General proclaimed before a court that American military government had 'absolutely displaced Spanish sovereignty and required no further treaty to confirm its supremacy'.[62] By the same token, territory occupied by enemies of the United States was held to be enemy territory. Consequently, Birkhimer concluded that the prohibition on trading with enemies 'extends not only to every place within his dominions . . . but also to all places in his possession or military occupation, even though such occupation has not ripened into a conquest or changed the national character of the inhabitants'.[63]

Treaty-based occupation produced the most dramatic assertion of powers qualified only by the bare assertion that sovereignty itself was not being claimed. In the case of the Panama Canal this was accompanied by the secession of the new Republic of Panama from Columbia, a secession secured by the United States. The same treaty by which the United States guaranteed the independence of the new Republic provided that a ten-mile-wide zone around the canal be assigned in perpetuity to the United States with 'all the rights, power and authority . . . which the United States would possess and exercise if it were the sovereign . . . to the entire exclusion of the exercise by the Republic of Panama of any such rights, power and authority'.[64] All that arguably remained to the Republic was the negative right prohibiting the United States from disposing of the zone to a third party. Panamanian sovereignty over the zone had shrunk to the *nudum jus* envisaged by Jellinek.

It was, however, the fate of Cuba that induced the greatest contortions. While Spain had relinquished any title to sovereignty by the peace treaty with the United States there had been no explicit transfer of sovereignty. Indeed the Joint Resolution of Congress of 1898 had expressly disavowed 'any disposition or intention to exercise sovereignty, jurisdiction or control over said island except for the pacification thereof'.[65] Consequently, Cubans did not become citizens of the United States and Cuba was regarded by the courts as a foreign country, though, as before, other states were obliged to treat it as if it were American territory. In fact, Cuba's situation in many ways resembled that of Palestine. Spain had been the legitimate sovereign of Cuba but given its explicit renunciation of any such title there was then no reversioner in the case of an end of American occupation. The position of the Cubans seemed so precarious that even the court's insistence that Cuba was a foreign country seemed dubious for, it was suggested, 'if we attribute to Cubans a sort of citizenship they are neither citizens or subjects of a "foreign state" for there is no "state" of Cuba'.[66] The only escape from such embarrassment was found, at least to the satisfaction of the Supreme Court, in the notion that 'as between the United States and Cuba, that island is held in trust for the inhabitants of Cuba, to whom it rightfully belongs'.[67] The same status of trustee was later claimed for Israel in its relation to occupied Palestinian territory.[68]

Such attempts to deal with the apparent evaporation of sovereignty were not the only possible responses to the impact of military occupation. In some circumstances at least, simple denial that a problem existed at all seemed preferable. That was the strategy adopted in the second American occupation of Cuba in 1906. On that occasion the explicit provision in the Cuban constitution for intervention was used to deny that the presence of American troops amounted to any infringement of Cuban sovereignty. The fiction of the integrity of Cuban sovereignty was maintained by the fact that Cuba conducted apparently normal diplomatic relations even with the United States.[69] While the United States connived in this fiction in the second occupation of Cuba it expressly ruled it out in the occupations of Germany and Japan at the end of the Second World War. The Japanese government, however, resisted the instruction to close its overseas missions in neutral states and neutral missions in Japan on the basis that there was no such requirement in the Potsdam declaration that formed the basis for Japan's surrender. The attempt to construe the surrender as contractual, and hence to salvage Japanese sovereignty, was not without sympathisers in the United States.[70] Even more recent commentators have suggested that, since the closure of the missions was eventually brought about indirectly through instructions to the Japanese government rather than directly by the occupation authorities, the manner of their closure confirms the continuation of Japanese sovereignty.[71] Yet the Japanese government clearly intended to claim more than such nominal status. Its attempt to set limits to the authority of the American occupier met instead with a firm rebuttal in the instructions to General MacArthur on the extent of his power: 'Our relations with Japan do not rest on a contractual basis, but on unconditional surrender . . . Since your authority is supreme, you will not entertain any question on the part of the Japanese as to its scope'.[72]

The fact that there was no German government to resist an analogous dissolution of diplomatic missions was taken as evidence that Germany's claim to the status of a sovereign state was even weaker. Even before the war had ended, Hans Kelsen had outlined the two conditions that might prevail, namely belligerent occupation (*occupatio bellica*) or subjugation (*debellatio*). Although he claimed to argue from a strictly legal perspective, Kelsen was clearly motivated by a desire to avoid a repetition of the Treaty of Versailles, which, in his eyes, left not only a resentful Germany but also a regime discredited and open to nationalist attack by its association with the treaty and its conditions.[73] His recommendation and prediction was the establishment of a condominium of the Allied powers and the subsequent establishment of a new German state which would have no legal continuity with the old one. From a post-war perspective this was exactly what had transpired, or so Kelsen claimed. In a variation on what would become the missing reversioner argument, he argued that the utter destruction of the German government made the existence of the condition of belligerent occupation impossible.[74]

Kelsen effectively took the three traditional components of the concept of the state, namely a governing power, a territory and a people, in order to argue that none of these could be ascribed to a sovereign German state. In respect of the first he quoted the Allied declaration of 5 June 1945: 'there is no central government or authority in Germany capable of accepting the responsibility for the maintenance of order, the administration of the country, and compliance with the requirements of the victorious powers'.[75] On the basis that there can be no state in international law without a government he concluded that 'Germany has ceased to exist as a state in the sense of international law'.[76] He noted, however, the obvious obstacle to his account, that is the express renunciation of an intent to annex Germany, for annexation had been assumed to be the consequence of subjugation. To this he objected that since the territory was not subject to German sovereignty, which it could not be in the absence of a German state, and since it could not be 'no state's land', it must be subject to the sovereignty of the victors. The renunciation of annexation merely signified a political intent not to hold the territory permanently.[77] There was, he noted, some precedent for such a condition in the American occupation of Cuba in 1898. It was a comparison which occurred to others, including advisers to the American military government.[78] Consistently, Kelsen dismissed the Supreme Court's assertion that Cuba belonged to the inhabitants on the grounds that in international law 'a territory "belongs" to a state, not a people, that is to say, only a state, not a people, can be the territorial sovereign'.[79] He was more equivocal in his description of the status of the inhabitants. They had become 'subjects' of the occupier but not its 'citizens', though he conceded that they could be granted certain rights, for example relating to local government, in which case they could be viewed as citizens. In elaborating the distinction between subjects and citizens, Kelsen included, though he did not stress, a crucial limit to the extent that they could be construed as citizens. According to Kelsen, a 'citizen of a state (in contradistinction to mere "subjects") is he who has political rights in, the duty of military service for, and the diplomatic protection abroad by the state concerned'.[80] While the occupier can grant political rights and offer protection abroad it cannot impose a duty of military service. Kelsen's ascription of sovereignty to the occupying powers falters at one of the earliest points on which a consensus was reached about the distinction between sovereigns and mere occupiers: the duty of military service.

Not surprisingly Kelsen's argument met with bitter resentment amongst most German commentators who devised various arguments to assert the continuity of a German state, though the desperation with which they did so was evident in the assertion of one of Kelsen's critics that 'Germany persist as a state because we want it to persist as a state'.[81] There was more substance to the attempt to distinguish between 'territorial supremacy' and territorial sovereignty, not least because it recalled the language of the Panama Treaty of 1903. As Josef Kunz recalled, this ascribed to the holder of territorial supremacy 'all the rights "as if he were sovereign", but not *of* the sovereign; the right of sovereignty, although perhaps only a *nudum jus*, can be in another state'.[82] Kunz promptly conceded that even this was more difficult to maintain in the case of Germany than it had been for the Republic of Panama: not only had the victorious powers asserted the right to determine Germany's boundaries they had also ceded parts of Germany 'at least for administration, to the Soviet Union and Poland, and that constitutes an exercise of the *jus disponendi* by the territorial sovereign'.[83]

Others tried to evade the unwelcome implications of the apparent assumption of sovereignty by the Allied powers by claiming the 'supreme authority', which they had assumed was somehow less than full sovereignty, indicated only by some such formula as 'all rights and *title*'.[84] Jennings, who also invoked that argument, tried to make sense of the situation by starting from the unrestricted authority of the Allies:

> if as a result of the Allied victory and German unconditional surrender Germany was so completely at the disposal of the Allies as to justify them in law in annexing the German state, it would seem to follow that they are by the same token entitled to assume the rights of supreme authority unaccompanied by annexation.[85]

Jennings invoked the sovereign right to dispose of territory, a right incompatible with the status of an occupier, in order to justify the Allies' express refusal to make use of the right.

The difficulty inherent in dealing with the situation was embodied in the assertion of the sometime Legal Adviser to the American Military Government in Germany, Charles Fahy, that it was quite clear that the Allies exercised 'full sovereign power', only for him to immediately add that 'it may well be that in theory sovereignty in an ultimate sense resides in the people of Germany but was suspended in exercise by them'.[86] In reality, that ultimate sovereignty amounted to no more than a placeholder for the continued existence of a German state or states, for some form of community, not necessarily determined by Germans, for the continued existence of people organised as a community who did not owe allegiance to the victors. In all other respects that ultimate sovereignty was no more than a *nudum jus*.

The position of Japan, which it had been assumed would resemble that of Germany, seemed to offer far less difficulty. Article 8 of the Potsdam Declaration of 26 July 1945 specified that 'Japanese sovereignty shall be limited to the islands of Honshu, Hokkaido, Kyushu, Shikoku and such minor islands as we determine'.[87] The Japanese reply sought to bolster this concession by making acceptance of the surrender terms of the Potsdam Declaration conditional upon the notion that the terms did not 'comprise any demand which prejudices the prerogatives of His Majesty as a Sovereign Ruler'.[88] The reply by the American Secretary of State, James Byrnes, made clear that no restraint would be accepted upon the authority of the Supreme Commander of the Allied powers, but avoided explicitly repudiating the Japanese reference to a sovereign Emperor, while the Japanese deliberately mistranslated Byrnes note to modify its impact.[89] While a modified imperial system survived, not by virtue of any concession about a sovereign Emperor but because of General MacArthur's assumptions about the role of the Emperor in ensuring a stable political system, it did seem clear that the principle of continued Japanese sovereignty had been accepted.[90] American courts had little difficulty in accepting that this was the case: 'The occupation has been, essentially, provisional and temporary; Japan has continued as a sovereign with its rights and powers of sovereignty limited only by the directives of the Supreme Commander'.[91] Yet even strident advocates of the continuation of Japanese sovereignty acknowledge that there was little scope for the Japanese government to exercise that sovereignty.[92]

This relative clarity related only to homeland islands specified in the Potsdam. Other territory, most notably Okinawa, presented an entirely different picture. That became clear when an American court had to define its status and the nature of sovereignty over it. The court appeared to cut off one escape route by declaring that 'at the outset it must be assumed that sovereignty is never held in suspense'.[93] It considered the possibility that the American occupation of the island, being temporary, left sovereignty in the hands of Japan, but ruled this out on the grounds that the United States had expressed no such intent – but had rather expressed the intent to exclude it from Japanese sovereignty. It then considered the possibility that American intent was to create an independent state of Okinawa, in which case 'it could be said that, in a sense, sovereignty passed to the people of Okinawa, the government being administered for the people by the occupant as a sort of trustee'.[94] Again, that solution was frustrated by the absence of the requisite intention. Convinced, nevertheless, that Okinawa was still a 'foreign country', the court concluded that the United States exercised 'what may be termed a *de facto* sovereignty' over it. That this did not really resolve the issue was evident when the court added that the status of the island 'offers a persuasive illustration of the observation that "the very concept of 'sovereignty' is in a state of more or less solution these days"'.[95] Diplomatic attempts to steer between the American desire to retain control, without formal annexation and the extension of American citizenship to the inhabitants, and the Japanese desire for an acknowledgement of their claim to sovereignty, led to the concession that Japan retained 'residual sovereignty' while America would continue to administer the island. It amounted in fact to the adoption of a version of the model found for the Panama Canal.[96]

It is arguable that the fact that the model proved unsustainable in the long run is evidence of what has been called a second revolution in sovereignty, generalising the system of sovereign states originally developed in the context of European international relations into a global system.[97] The subsequent challenge to the unreserved triumph of the principle of the sovereign state, in the shape of ideas of the conditional sovereignty of governments and the possibility of an involuntarily waiver of their sovereignty, has however led to a sovereignty vacuum; such notions have not extended to the point of substituting the sovereignty of the invader for that of the government or state, which would amount to the dissolution of the distinctive status of military occupation. Hence, it is argued, 'suspension of sovereignty does not imply that the UN has assumed sovereignty over East Timor. Suspension of sovereignty signifies rather that sovereignty is not an applicable concept any more'.[98] To rest there, with the sovereignty of the previous state or government being suspended or (as might be more accurately said of the case in East Timor) destroyed, but not assumed by the occupier and hence no longer applicable, would seem to amount to a relapse to a supposedly abandoned doctrine. It would seem to ignore the 'principle that sovereignty lies in a people, not in a political elite' and hence that 'the fall of a government has no effect whatsoever on the sovereign title over the occupied territory, which remains vested in the local population'.[99] It was precisely this language that Alan Gerson used in the case of occupied Palestinian territory in elaboration of his notion of the occupier as a 'trustee-occupant': 'no res nullius in the West Bank came into effect . . . sovereignty resided in the inhabitant Arabs' or was 'vested in the Palestinian Arabs'.[100] Yet this sovereignty was also said to be in a 'state of suspension' or, in the much-quoted judgement of McNair on the status of Southwest Africa, to be 'in abeyance; if and when the inhabitants of the territory obtain recognition as an independent state . . . sovereignty will revive and vest in the new state'.[101]

All of the various elements of these attempts to salvage the concept of sovereignty in the absence of a clearly recognisable ousted sovereign continue to be tenuous. The approximation of the occupier to a sovereign has been evident not only in the powers which many have assumed but sometimes even in the manner in which they have been treated by other international actors. According to Jarat Chopra, that was the case when the International Development Association of the World Bank insisted on treating the UN administration in East Timor as a sovereign government for the purposes of establishing a reconstruction fund.[102] However, it is the notion of sovereignty vested in a people, but in suspense or abeyance, that remains the most elusive. In part, the problem has been dispute over what constitutes the people or the 'local population'. In the case of the Palestinian people, this is complicated by the long-standing demand of a right of return for refugees evicted from their lands at the creation of an Israeli state and the fact that, even if this demand remains frustrated, substantial numbers of Palestinians will remain within the borders of Israel.[103] In both Bosnia-Herzegovina and Kosovo, the 'people' or 'local population' have been defined on the basis of a mixture of old sub-state administrative divisions and external imposition. In Kosovo, an initial commitment to respect the 'sovereignty and territorial integrity of the Federal Republic of Yugoslavia' was put aside by those responsible for the administration of the territory when they acquiesced in the proclamation of an independent Kosovo by the Albanian majority, whose declaration of independence had to proclaim that it 'is a special case arising from Yugoslavia's non-consensual break-up and is not a precedent for any other situation'.[104]

Whether what was proclaimed as an independent state in both these cases qualified as such, let alone as a sovereign state, was contentious. One commentator complained,

In Bosnia, the fiction of Bosnian sovereignty is rhetorically observed, but the state that is supposed to be the agent of that sovereignty has no army and allows the two constituent parts of the state the sole right to maintain armed forces.[105]

The even more precarious status of the Palestinian authority (PA) was exposed when it tried to invoke the defence of sovereign immunity before an American court. The latter, arguing from the 1933 Montevideo Convention on the Rights and Duties of States, found that it was 'transparently clear that the PA has not yet exercised sufficient governmental control over Palestine' to qualify as a state.[106]

The occupation of Iraq combined the explicit denial of assumption of sovereignty by the occupier, and the attempt to locate sovereignty in the Iraqi people and in Iraqi institutions, with rhetoric that presumed that sovereignty somehow lay in the hands of the occupier – in the sense condemned decades earlier when Siegmund Cybichowski protested about the formulation according to which Polish sovereignty was restored. Security Council Resolution 1483 of 22 May 2003 reaffirmed the 'sovereignty and territorial integrity of Iraq' while recognising the United States and Britain as occupying powers and the 'Authority', that is the Coalition Provisional Authority as their unified command.[107] Security Council Resolution 1511 of 16 October 2003 added a new dimension by specifying that the Iraqi Governing Council 'embodies the sovereignty of the State of Iraq . . . until an internationally recognized, representative government is established and assumes the responsibility of the Authority'.[108] Resolution 1546 of 8 June 2004 acknowledged the dissolution of this Governing Council and welcomed the imminent formation of a 'sovereign Interim Government' that would 'assume full responsibility . . . while refraining from taking any actions affecting Iraq's destiny beyond the limited interim period until an elected Transitional Government of Iraq assumes office'.[109] It appears that the presumption, in the absence of any Iraqi government at all, that sovereignty lay with the Iraqi people had given way to the embodiment of this sovereignty in a government that was neither representative nor worthy of international recognition. That in turn had given way to a 'sovereign Interim Government', which was put under a set of constraints that, as Adam Roberts noted, put it in 'a position analogous to that of an occupying power'.[110] Worse still, on the day sovereignty was supposedly transferred, George Bush declared that 'we have been making a transfer of sovereignty all along'.[111] Since the occupier is by definition not the sovereign, it is not at all clear how any such transfer is to be understood.

Such language served several purposes. In the first place, it served the purpose of identifying a military occupation. It subsequently reflected the desire to find some institutional embodiment or manifestation of Iraqi sovereignty, despite the persistence of military occupation. It then sought to bolster that institutional manifestation of sovereignty by according it a status and set of, albeit highly limited, powers. Sovereignty in abeyance or in suspension had turned out to be regarded as an intolerable condition. Yet the precariousness of the sovereignty of a territory under military occupation has been evident for as long as the concept and phenomenon of military occupation have acquired any clarity. That precariousness is rooted in the simple fact that without effective government, the existence of a state and any claim to sovereignty is itself precarious, that in military occupation the only effective government must be that of the occupier and the occupier is not the sovereign. Sovereignty in this condition serves at most as a *nudum jus* or as a marker for the fact that the occupier is not the legitimate power. That, of course, is unlikely to deter many from trying to construe it as something more.

Notes

1. For criticism of such conflation, see Georg Jellinek, *Allgemeine Staatslehre* (Berlin: Julius Springer, 1929), pp. 484–5.
2. See Thomas Baty, 'Can an anarchy be a state?, *American Journal of International Law*, 28 (1934), pp. 444–55.
3. The term 'failed states' is often used without any great precision. For an attempt to remedy this, see Jean-Germain Gros, 'Towards a taxonomy of failed states', *Third World Quarterly*, 17 (1996), pp. 455–71.
4. Charles [Carlos] Calvo, *Le Droit International*, vol. 5 (Paris: Guilaumin, 1888), 401–2.
5. US Department of State, *The Treaty of Versailles and After* (New York, NY: Greenwood, 1968), p. 792.
6. Siegmund Cybichowski, 'Die völkerrechtliche Okkupationsrecht', *Zeitschrift für Völkerrecht*, 18 (1934), p. 322.
7. Long before the emergence of anything resembling modern concepts of nationhood, this possibility was accepted by Hugo Grotius as a limit to the right of postliminium: 'But if the body of the people that constitute the State, be dissolved, it is more reasonable to say, that they are not esteemed to be the same people; nor the Things formerly

belonging to that State to be restored to them by the Law of Nations'. *The Rights of War and Peace*, vol. 3 (Indianapolis, IN: Liberty Fund, 2005), pp. 1393–4.

8. Thomas J. Biersteker and Cynthia Weber, 'The social construction of state sovereignty', in Thomas J. Biersteker and Cynthia Weber (eds), *State Sovereignty as Social Construct* (Cambridge: Cambridge University Press, 1996), p. 3.

9. Georg Jellinek [1882], *Die Lehre von den Staatenverbindungen* (Goldbach: Keip, 1996), p. 54.

10. Krzysztof Skubiszewski, 'Administration of territory and sovereignty', *Archiv des Völkerrechts*, 23 (1985), pp. 36–7.

11. See, for example, David E. Paul, 'Sovereignty, survival and the Westphalian blind alley in international relations', *Review of International Studies*, 25 (1999), pp. 217–31.

12. Quoted in The International Commission on Intervention and State Sovereignty, *The Responsibility to Protect. Research, Bibliography, Background* (Ottawa: International Development Research Centre, 2001), p. 11.

13. Richard Caplan, *International Governance of War-Torn Territories* (Oxford: Oxford University Press, 2005), p. 8.

14. For a critical assessment, see Michael J. Kelly, 'Pulling at the threads of Westphalia: "involuntary sovereignty waiver"', *UCLA Journal of International Law and Foreign Affairs*, 10 (2005), pp. 361–442.

15. This does not mean that the phenomenon or the reservations it encounters are entirely new. See, for example, Antoine Rougier, 'La theorie de l'intervention humanitaire', *Revue Générale de Droit International Public*, 17 (1910), pp. 468–526, especially his conclusion.

16. Robert H. Jackson, *Quasi-States: Sovereignty, International Relations and the Third World* (Cambridge: Cambridge University Press, 1990), p. 21.

17. Stephen D. Krasner, *Sovereignty: Organized Hypocrisy* (Princeton, NJ: Princeton University Press, 1999), p. 9.

18. On the turn to Grotius more generally, see Edward Keene, *Beyond the Anarchical Society* (Cambridge: Cambridge University Press, 2002); on the application to Iraq, see Rolf Schwarz and Oliver Jütersonke, 'Divisible sovereignty and the reconstruction of Iraq', *Third World Quarterly*, 26 (2005), pp. 649–55.

19. David Schleicher, 'Liberal international law theory and the United Nations mission in Kosovo', *Tulane Journal of International and Comparative Law*, 14 (2005–6), pp. 179–236.

20. John Horton, *Political Obligation* (Basingstoke: Macmillan, 1992), p. 167.

21. Norman Davies, *Heart of Europe. A Short History of Poland* (Oxford: Oxford University Press, 1986), pp. 175–278.

22. Chales E. Magoon, *Reports on the Law of Civil Government in Territories Subject to Military Occupation by the Military Forces of the United States* (Washington, DC: War Department, 1903), pp. 12–13.

23. See the views of Bluntschli and Martens as summarised by Doris A. Graber, *The Development of the Law of Belligerent Occupation 1863–1914* (New York, NY: AMS Press, 1949), pp. 52, 58–9.

24. Frantz Despagnet, *Cours de Droit International Public* (Paris: Larose, 1894), pp. 580–1.

25. Paul Fauchille, *Traité de Droit International Public*, vol. 2 (Paris: Rousseau, 1921), p. 223.

26. Graber, *The Development of the Law of Belligerent Occupation*, p. 66.

27. Raymond Robin [1913], *Des Occupations Militaries en Dehors des Occupations de Guerre* (Washington, DC: Carnegie, 1942), p. 5.

28. Ibid. p. 92.

29. William Edward Hall, *A Treatise on International Law* (Oxford: Oxford University Press, 1924), p. 556.

30. Henry Bonfils, *Manuel de Droit International Public* (Paris: Rousseau, 1894), p. 644. See also G. Rolin-Jaequemyns, 'Chronique du droit international 1871–1874', *Revue de Droit International et de Législation Comparée*, 7 (1875), p. 99; War Department, *Rules of Land Warfare* (Washington, DC: War Department, 1917), p. 105.

31. 'The United States *v.* Rice', *US Reports*, 17 (1819), p. 254.

32. Caplan, *International Governance of War-Torn Territories*, p. 9. On suspended sovereignty more widely, see Alexandros Yannis, 'The concept of suspended sovereignty in international law and its implications in international politics', *European Journal of International Law*, 13 (2002), pp. 1037–52.

33. '*Auditeur Militaire v.* G. Van Dieren', *Annual Digest*, 1 (1919–22), p. 446.

34. 'De Nimal *v.* De Nimal', *Annual Digest*, 1 (1919–22), p. 447.

35. Ernst Fraenkel [1944], 'Military occupation and the rule of law', in Ernst Fraenkel, *Gesammelte Schriften*, vol. 3 (Baden-Baden: Nomos, 1999), pp. 212–13.

36. Ibid. pp. 508–11.

37. F. E. Oppenheimer, 'Governments and authorities in exile', *American Journal of International Law*, 36 (1942), pp. 572–6.

38. Ibid, p. 594.

39. See Robin Edmonds, *The Big Three* (London: Penguin, 1991), pp. 376–7.

40. John H. E. Fried, 'Transfer of civilian manpower from occupied territory', *American Journal of International Law*, 40 (1946), p. 319.

41. Ibid. p. 319.

42. On the Confederation and similar plans, see Piotr S. Wandycz, 'Recent traditions of the west for unity', in J. Lukazewski (ed.), *The Peoples' Democracies after Prague* (Bruges: de Tempel, 1970), pp. 37–93.

43. 'State of the Netherlands *v.* Federal Reserve Bank', *International Law Reports*, 18 (1951), p. 559.

44. Egon Schwelb, 'Legislation for enemy-occupied territory in the British Empire', *Transactions of the Grotius Society*, 30 (1944), pp. 252–3.

45. Arnold D. McNair, 'Municipal effects of belligerent occupation', *Law Quarterly Review*, 57 (1941), p. 68.

46. Schwelb, 'Legislation for enemy-occupied territory in the British Empire', pp. 258–9.

47. Eyal Benvenisti, *The International Law of Occupation* (Princeton, NJ: Princeton University Press, 2004), p. 23.

48. 'State of the Netherlands *v.* Federal Reserve Bank', p. 561.

49. Eric Stein, 'Application of the law of the absent sovereign in territory under belligerent occupation: the Schio massacre', *Michigan Law Review*, 46 (1948), pp. 341–70, especially p. 344.

50. Yehuda Z. Blum, 'The missing reversioner: reflections on the status of Judea and Samaria', *Israel Law Review*, 3 (1968), p. 283.

51. Ibid. p. 293. See also Julius Stone, *Israel and Palestine* (Baltimore, MD: Johns Hopkins University Press, 1981), p. 119.

52. W. Thomas Mallison and Sally V. Mallison, *The Palestine Problem* (Harlow: Longman, 1986), p. 258.

53. Ibid. p. 255.

54. Willliam M. Brinton, 'Israel: what is occupied territory?', *Harvard Journal of Law and Public Policy*, 2 (1979), p. 207.

55. Quoted in Pieter H. F. Bekker, 'The world court's ruling regarding the West Bank barrier and the primacy of international law', *Cornell International Law Journal*, 38 (2005), p. 558.

56. Ibid. pp. 557–8.

57. Iris Canor, 'When *jus ad bellum* meets *jus in bello*', *Leiden Journal of International Law*, 19 (2006), p. 136.

58. Ibid. p. 136.

59. H. W. Halleck, *International Law* (San Francisco, CA: Bancroft, 1861), p. 785.

60. See Sedgwick Green, 'Applicability of American laws to overseas territories controlled by the United States', *Harvard Law Review*, 68 (1954–5), p. 795.

61. Quoted in George Melling, 'The war power and the government of military forces', *Journal of the Institute of Criminal Law and Criminology*, 7 (1916), p. 254.

62. 'Sanchez *v.* United States', *US Reports*, 216 (1909), p. 170.

63. William E. Birkhimer, *Military Government and Martial Law* (Kansas, MO: Hudson, 1914), p. 296.

64. Quoted in David Yancy Thomas [1904], *A History of the Government in Newly Acquired Territory of the United States* (Honolulu, HI: University Press of the Pacific, 2002), p. 317.

65. Quoted in Carman F. Randolph, 'Some observations on the status of Cuba', *Yale Law Journal*, 9 (1898–1900), p. 356.

66. Ibid. p. 361.

67. 'Neely *v.* Henkel' quoted in Melling, 'The war power and the government of military forces', pp. 254–5.

68. Allan Gerson, 'Trustee-occupant: the legal status of Israel's presence in the West Bank', *Harvard Journal of International Law*, 14 (1973), pp. 1–49.

69. Allan Reed Millet, *The Politics of Intervention. The Military Occupation of Cuba, 1906–1909* (Ohio State University Press, OH: 1968), pp. 147–8.

70. Takemae Eiji, *The Allied Occupation of Japan* (New York, NY: Continuum, 2002), p. 230.

71. Nisuke Ando, *Surrender, Occupation and Private Property in International Law* (Oxford: Clarendon Press, 1991), p. 100.

72. Quoted in Takemae, *The Allied Occupation of Japan*, p. 231.

73. Hans Kelsen, 'The international legal status of Germany to be established immediately upon termination of the war', *American Journal of International Law*, 38 (1944), pp. 691–2.

74. Hans Kelsen, 'The legal status of Germany according to the Declaration of Berlin', *American Journal of International Law*, 39 (1945), p. 518.

75. Ibid. p. 519.

76. Ibid. p. 519.

77. Ibid. p. 521.

78. For the legal advice, see Ulrich Meister, 'Stimmen des Auslandes zur Rechtslage Deutschlands', *Zeitschrift für ausländisches öffentliches Recht und Völkerrecht*, 13 (1950), p. 176. See also Quincy Wright, 'The status of Germany and the peace proclamation', *American Journal of International Law*, 46 (1952), p. 305.

79. Kelsen, 'The legal status of Germany according to the Declaration of Berlin', p. 522.

80. Ibid. p. 523.

81. Günter Dürig, quoted in Michael Stolleis, 'Besatzungsherrschft und Wiederaufbau deutscher Staatlichkeit 1945–1949', in Josef Isensee and Paul Kirchhof (eds), *Handbuch des Staatsrechts der Bundesrepublik Deutschland*, vol. 1 (Heidelberg: Müller, 2003), p. 285. For Kelsen's relative isolation, see Christoph Möllers, *Staat als Argument* (Munich: Beck, 2000), pp. 136–7.

82. Josef Kunz, 'The status of occupied Germany under international law', *The Western Political Quarterly*, 3 (1950), p. 559.

83. Ibid. p. 559.
84. F. A. Mann, 'The present legal status of Germany', *International Law Quarterly*, 1 (1947), p. 326.
85. R. V Jennings, 'Government in commission', *British Yearbook of International Law*, 23 (1946), p. 137.
86. Charles Fahy, 'Legal problems of German occupation', *Michigan Law Review*, 47 (1948), p. 12.
87. Quoted in Hajo Holborn, *American Military Government: its Organization and Policies* (Washington, DC: Infantry Journal Press, 1947), p. 206.
88. Ibid. p. 207.
89. Takemae, *The Allied Occupation of Japan*, pp. 224–5.
90. For MacArthur's often misguided assumptions, see John Dower, *Embracing Defeat* (London: Penguin, 1999), pp. 280–345.
91. Quoted in Ando, *Surrender, Occupation and Private Property in International Law*, p. 100.
92. Ibid. p. 101.
93. 'Cobb *v.* United States', *International Legal Reports*, 18 (1951), p. 551.
94. Ibid. p. 551.
95. Ibid. p. 552.
96. Nicholas Evan Sarantakes, *Keystone. The American Occupation of Okinawa and U.S-Japanese Relations* (College Station, TX: Texas A&M University Press, 2000), pp. 56–9.
97. See Daniel Philpott, *Revolutions in Sovereignty* (Princeton, NJ: Princeton University Press, 2001).
98. Yannis, 'The concept of suspended sovereignty in international law and its implications in international politics', p. 1048.
99. Benvenisti, *The International Law of Occupation*, p. 95.
100. Gerson, 'Trustee-occupant', pp. 43, 35.
101. Quoted in ibid. p. 27.
102. Jarat Chopra, 'Building state failure in East Timor', *Development and Change*, 33 (2002), pp. 984–5. For an alternative view, see Matthias Ruffert, 'The administration of Kosovo and East Timor by the International Community', *International and Comparative Law Quarterly*, 50 (2001), p. 630.
103. Even this underestimates the problem from the perspective of a wider Palestine understood as 'one land' with 'two peoples'. See Ilan Pappe, *A History of Modern Palestine* (Cambridge: Cambridge University Press, 2006).
104. Quoted in *The Guardian* (18 February 2008).
105. Helen Thompson, 'The case for external sovereignty', *European Journal of International Relations*, 12 (2006), p. 266.
106. 'First circuit rejects sovereignty immunity claim by Palestinian

Authority', *American Journal of International Law*, 99 (2005), p. 699.

107. S/RES/1483 (2003).
108. S/RES/1511 (2003).
109. S/RES/1546 (2004).
110. Adam Roberts, 'The end of occupation: Iraq 2004', *International and Comparative Law Quarterly*, 54 (2005), p. 42.
111. 'Remarks by President Bush and Prime Minister Blair on transfer of Iraqi sovereignty', Press Release (28 June 2004).

Chapter 7

Justice under Occupation

The emergence of military occupation as a distinct phenomenon was bound up with considerations of justice. Those seeking its deepest historical roots tended to trace it back to the Roman right of *postliminium*, that is, to the 'legal principle or right by virtue of which a person taken captive in war, upon his recapture or his return to his own country, was restored to his former civil status'.[1] As even many of those who cited this origin noted, the comparison of the modern conception of occupation with this Roman right relied upon a 'somewhat distant analogy'.[2] The attraction of the term and the source lay in the authority of Roman law and the analogy with the returning sovereign anxious to assert his former status, though the application of the doctrine to the sovereign as well as the citizen was a later development.[3] The right of *postliminium* was consequently elaborated in terms of what should happen at the end of occupation; that could not be determined without some judgement upon which acts of the occupier, or acts performed under the authority of the occupier, were to be recognised as valid. Justice and the rights which it secures were not regarded as wholly suspended. Unlike the captive Roman, the inhabitants of occupied territory did not become slaves, they were not assumed to have lost their title to property nor were their relations with each other dissolved.[4] Unlike the Roman captive or the sovereignty of the legitimate power, however the latter is construed, their rights are not automatically in abeyance or some state of suspension pending their restoration.

However, their rights have become precarious, subject to interference by the occupier or simply deprived of the sanction that had previously guaranteed them. Both direct suppression and violation of their rights or failure to guarantee rights are destructive of justice. It is, however, the former that has tended to form the focus of discussion. It was this that Carl Schmitt seized upon in order to expose what he saw as the refusal of nineteenth-century jurists to recognise the analogy between military occupation and the state of emergency in a domestic setting. According to Schmitt, these jurists were, despite

175

their own inclinations, unable to provide a 'juridical answer to any of the important practical questions' involved in military occupation.[5] Consequently, their 'positivistic jurisprudence . . . simply shuns them and declares them to be *not juridical*, but political'.[6] This was arguably the fate of doctrines such as war treason and problems of the *levée en masse*. Yet the legal formalism of which Schmitt complained mirrors his own contrast between law and politics. As Judith Shklar has argued

> extreme legal formalism puts politics in brackets . . . to maintain the contrast between legal order and political chaos and to preserve the former from any taint of the latter it is not just necessary to define law out of politics; an entirely extravagant image of politics as essentially a species of war has to be maintained.[7]

Politics as a species of war might seem less extravagant in the context of military occupation, especially where the latter is seen as an 'incident of war'.[8] Yet it remains extravagant for, close though the incidence of war may be, military occupation presupposes the possibility of the occupier governing by virtue of the authority that the occupier has acquired. It will not be possible to constrain that form of government entirely within the ambit of justice, understood as a 'commitment to obeying rules, to respecting rights, to accepting obligations under a system of principles'.[9] It has proved possible to institute some rules and the disputes surrounding them have in part been based upon the assumption that the rules of justice must be analogous to the domestic laws of states. That was clear when the Chief of the German General Staff, Count von Moltke, wrote to Johann Bluntschli in protest about the codification of the laws of war in the Oxford Manuel of 1880, which was a reformulation of the text of the Brussels Conference of 1874. Although Moltke was motivated by a certain veneration of warfare and by the desire to keep as free a hand as possible, his objection to codification was that 'all law supposes an authority to watch over and execute it, and it is this power that is lacking in the observation of international agreements'.[10] Yet Moltke himself, in addition to invoking the 'gradual softening of manners', referred to other mechanisms for imposing rules: 'rigorous discipline, maintained in times of peace and of which the soldier has gotten the habit, and vigilance of administration which provides for the subsistence of the troops in the field'.[11] While Moltke contrasted international agreements with these less specific mechanisms, suggesting that the former were superfluous, other commentators more plausibly found some justification for his protest in the insufficiency of codification alone.[12]

It is, however, codification that has continued to appear to dominate the search for justice in military occupation. That is evident in the major conventions of 1907 and 1949 that form the heart of international humanitarian law, of which the law of occupation forms a subset. It is even more strikingly evident in recourse to the codes reflecting the triumph of human rights as a programme in the wake of the Second World War.[13] Human rights law, in the shape of the International Covenant on Civil and Political Rights, the International Covenant on Economic, Social and Cultural Rights and United Nations Convention on the Rights of the Child, amongst others, has been invoked either as 'guidance' or as directly applicable and binding.[14] The fusion of international humanitarian law and human rights law has even been adopted by the International Court of Justice, albeit not to the satisfaction of all its members.[15]

The courts that ensure justice under condition of occupation, or manifestly fail to do so, are those under the greater or lesser control of the occupier, depending upon whether they are courts directly established by the occupier or indigenous courts operating with the tolerance of the occupier. That, of course, leads to the suspicion that such justice as is present is no more than 'victor's justice', meaning thereby that it is partial and hence no justice at all. It may indeed be the case that justice is not sought at all and, as in the Nazi courts condemned by Gustav Radbruch, 'where justice is not even sought, where equality, which constitutes the core of justice, is consciously denied, there the law is not only an "unlawful law" but rather it lacks entirely the nature of law'.[16] Similarly, where justice or the show of justice is entirely instrumental, incidental to a system of terror, and courts could equally as well be dispensed with, there is no justice at all.[17] Some taint of that was evident in Ngao Ariga's observation on the administration of justice in the Russo-Japanese war of 1904 to 1905, though he made it in the context of an argument against the need to impose the customary draconian penalty in all cases: 'The end of martial law being intimidation rather than the punishing of acts which are immoral or contrary to the public interest, when this end is attained, it is unnecessary to punish every infraction'.[18]

Justice is significant as a virtue in its own right, as a constraint upon the arbitrary and capricious will of the occupier and as a condemnation of a facade of justice that can take on a perverted form to the point where it loses any connection with justice in a meaningful sense of the term. Yet, formal legal order is itself a form of power and a type of legitimacy, as Max Weber argued.[19] Similarly, some form of justice enhances the authority of the occupier. That has not escaped the attention of at least some occupiers, though it is something which they can only imperfectly imitate because the occupier is by definition not the legitimate power and because occupiers inevitably act in ways that violate the legal order, even where it is the one they attempt to impose. It remains the case that the more they can rely upon it the less they must rely upon the force that ultimately explains the fact of occupation. Yet, while some have realised that justice and the rule of law or some approximation of it are not only constraints, the attempt to move too quickly towards the rule of law brings with it its own risks. That was recognised by Ernst Fraenkel:

> From a psychological point of view, the co-existence of two systems of government – a rule of arbitrariness and a rule of law – is probably harder to endure than an outright rule of martial law . . . if legal procedures are presumably respected, extra-legal measures appear arbitrary and the activities of the courts hypocritical.[20]

The charge or suspicion of hypocrisy, or victor's justice, readily arises where occupying powers are tempted to try inhabitants for war crimes or crimes against humanity. Military occupation, of course, is not a necessary condition for such efforts. Those presumed to be guilty of war crimes or crimes against humanity can fall into the hands of the courts of other states or international courts by other means, including extradition or simply entering another jurisdiction without anticipating such prosecutions.[21] Military occupation, however, potentially places the accused at the disposal of the occupier more directly and certainly than other mechanisms. The fact that Germany as a whole was not occupied at the end of the First World War provides evidence of the limits upon victors who are not also occupiers. Unable to seize those they wished to prosecute, the victorious powers were forced to agree to trials by German courts whose judgements and lenient sentences outraged them, leaving the French president, Aristide Briand, denouncing this 'parody of justice'.[22]

The victors' stance was not helped by the fact that there were significant differences between the American view of the nature of the tribunals before which individuals might be tried and of the nature of those individuals, and the views of the other victors. The Americans protested that they knew of 'no international statute or convention making a violation of the laws and customs of war . . . an international crime, affixing a punishment to it, and declaring the court which has jurisdiction over the offence'.[23] They allowed, however, that national 'military courts or commissions' could exercise such jurisdiction for violations of the laws of war affecting their own subjects 'whether such acts were committed within portions of their territory occupied by the enemy or by the enemy within its own jurisdiction'.[24] They were less cooperative over the prospect of the trial of the ex-Emperor of Germany, noting that the others were determined, in disregard of the doctrine of sovereign immunity in international law, 'to try and punish by judicial process the "ex-Kaiser"'.[25] Despite these reservations, President Wilson eventually agreed to a trial, though that meant little given the refusal of the Netherlands, to which the ex-Emperor had fled, to extradite him.[26]

Over a century earlier, in the aftermath of the battle of Waterloo, the victors had also been divided. The Prussians favoured summary execution of Napoleon and leading Bonapartists in the name of justice but were vigorously opposed by the Duke of Wellington. The outcome was that the Prussians deferred to Wellington; as the Prussian General Gneisenau put it 'from esteem for the Duke and – weakness'.[27] The British prime minister, Lord Liverpool, favoured a French trial of Bonapartists if only because he held that the French king would not be 'secure upon his throne till he has dared spill traitors' blood', adding that 'it is not that many examples would be necessary; but the *daring* to make a few will alone manifest any strength in the government'.[28] The French king, whose security still depended on Allied armies of occupation, hesitated, eventually resorting to a few symbolic trials and executions. When, as anticipated, Napoleon handed himself over to the British, they showed no more enthusiasm for a trial and dispatched him to the island of St Helena as a prisoner of state. Although the deliberations of the victors of 1815 took place in a radically different atmosphere from that of the twentieth century, they already exhibited a blend of vengeance and aversion from it, expediency and considerations of justice, and a preference for relying upon indigenous courts where possible.

Napoleon's fate, the failed attempt to impose justice by proxy at Leipzig after the First World War, and the disassociation of justice from any judicial process were all invoked in the debates that led to the establishment of the International Military Tribunal at Nuremberg. Summary execution, at least of leading Nazis, was favoured by key figures from all of the Allied powers. Churchill's view was that as suspected Nazi leaders were seized by Allied troops, the nearest officer of the rank or equivalent rank of Major-General will forthwith convene a Court of Inquiry, not for the purpose of determining the guilt or innocence of the accused but merely to establish the fact of identification. Once identified, the said officer will have the outlaw or outlaws shot to death within six hours and without reference to higher authority.[29]

The British lord chancellor, John Simon, concurred that 'the question of their fate *is a political, not a judicial*, question'.[30] The divided British cabinet subsequently gave way to American pressure for a judicial process.

Ensuring justice through a judicial process appeared, however, to be an uncertain process given the scale of Nazi atrocities, the number of people complicit in them and the potential difficulties of demonstrating guilt in individual cases. The solution, so it seemed to Colonel Murray Bernaeys, was to charge the Nazi leadership with criminal conspiracy thereby condemning them all by demonstrating the existence of the conspiracy. Declaring the core organisations of the Nazi movement to be criminal organisations would likewise ensure that lower ranking Nazis would not escape. Neither strategy appealed to the American legal advisor, Herbert Wechsler, who noted that the charge of criminal conspiracy was a specifically Anglo-Saxon legal concept.[31] In fact, both the significance of the identification of criminal organisations and the specifically Anglo-Saxon nature of conspiracy were modified in the course of the Tribunal's deliberations.[32]

It was not only the charges that seemed to challenge judicial probity. Both the wider nature of the law to be applied and the status of the Tribunal were open to the accusation of being screens for victors' justice. In its final judgement, the Tribunal explicitly sought to refute such accusations, stating that the charter creating it 'was the exercise of the sovereign legislative power by the countries to which the German Reich unconditionally surrendered' but also that the Charter 'is not an arbitrary exercise of power on the part of the victorious Nations, but . . . is the expression of international law existing at the time of its creation; and to that extent is itself a contribution to international law'.[33] In this, as in much else, the Tribunal struggled to combine the idea that, in terms of its own existence and the rules it applied, it was following established precedent with the fact that it was precisely the unprecedented barbarity of the Nazi regime that made the imposition of some form of justice so imperative.[34] The same imperative drove the numerous other tribunals and military government courts to impose judgements 'irrespective of when or where the crime was committed, the belligerency or non-belligerency status of the punishing power or the nationality of the victims'.[35] That stood in marked contrast to the American view at the end of the First World War.[36]

Despite the reservations that surrounded the Nuremberg Tribunal and the difficulty of constraining its status and judgements within traditional understanding of international law and justice, the trials it conducted were not rigged trials, as the disagreements amongst the judges over both judgements and sentences illustrates. The process was fair in terms of requirements of evidence and opportunities for defence. At the minimum, as Shklar put it, even critics tended to agree 'that the Trial was fair and that something deserving punishment had been committed'.[37] There was more reservation about the fairness of the war crimes trials in the Far East, though these too illustrate the connection between the fact of occupation and the attempt to enforce justice. That the United States was entitled to establish trials for this purpose was, as the Supreme Court saw it, 'an exercise of the authority sanctioned by Congress to administer the system of military justice recognised by the law of war'.[38] In the case of appeals by the former minister Hirota Koki and others, the Supreme Court held that

> the tribunal sentencing these petitioners is not a tribunal of the United States . . . The military tribunal sentencing these petitioners has been set up by General MacArthur as the agent of the Allied Powers . . . [and hence] . . . the courts of the United States have no power or authority to review, to affirm, set aside or annul the judgements and sentences imposed.[39]

Whether that meant that the tribunal was wholly independent was disputed. On the tribunal itself, Judge Radhabinod Pal insisted that 'we are to be "a judicial tribunal" and not "a manifestation of power"' but complained in fact that the tribunal had turned out to be the latter rather than the former.[40] An American Supreme Court judge concurred as to the nature of the tribunal. It was, he declared

> an instrument of military power . . . It responded to the will of the Supreme Commander as expressed in the military order by which he constituted it. It . . . did not act as a free and independent tribunal . . . It was solely an instrument of political power.[41]

There was, he concluded, nothing objectionable in that. However, it was not only some of the judges on the Tokyo tribunal who had reservations about the process; General Charles Willoughby, a leading figure in MacArthur's occupation administration, privately denounced the trial as 'the worst hypocrisy in recorded history'.[42] Far more so than the Nuremberg Tribunal, the various tribunals in the Far East were surrounded by acrimony and the charge or suspicion that this was no more than victor's justice. The acrimony did not readily subside.[43] and the dilemma was that some such process was unavoidable. The fact of occupation put the accused within the grip of the occupier. That acts 'deserving punishment had been committed' was undeniable. The national courts of the victors were not regarded as having jurisdiction and the courts of the inhabitants could not be trusted, or burdened, with trials of those regarded as major war criminals. No independent international court existed. The justice of the occupier was the only alternative to no justice.

The perceived alternative to this dilemma has long been the creation of an independent international court, established on a permanent basis, which would ensure justice without creating the suspicion of victor's justice. The eventual emergence of the Statute of the International Criminal Court in 1998 marked a hesitant step in that direction. Lacking ratification by the United States, reliant upon states for investigation and arrest of suspects and restricted by the principle of complementarity (giving priority to adjudication by state courts), its impact upon justice in cases of military occupation is at best uncertain.[44] Resort to ad hoc tribunals continued in the case of the International Criminal Tribunal for the Former Yugoslavia, sitting at The Hague. Although the Tribunal could indict suspects on its own initiative, it too was divorced from power. As one commentator put it, 'What made Nuremberg suspect made it strong; what made The Hague unimpeachable made it weak'.[45]

That weakness was demonstrated in Bosnia-Herzegovina where NATO's Implementation Force was reluctant to seek out suspects indicted by the Hague Tribunal or even to provide security for the investigation of the scenes of war crimes.[46] In Kosovo, the decision to rely on indigenous courts rather than military courts or their equivalents led to problematic cases, especially given that these local courts were dominated by the Albanian majority. Sheer prejudice as well as community pressure and even threats encouraged these courts to exonerate suspects regarded by their community as 'war heroes' while pursuing Serb suspects.[47] In acknowledgement of these difficulties the UN Mission in Kosovo proposed a Kosovo War and Ethnic Crimes Court with the power to assume jurisdiction over cases as it deemed fit. This court, though including indigenous judges, was to be dominated by international judges. The entire project was allowed to wither, apparently because of concerns about costs.[48]

In Iraq, a range of options was considered, including an international tribunal under the authority of the UN Security Council, analogous to the Hague Tribunal. That option was rejected in favour of an Iraqi court, the Iraq Special Tribunal established by the Iraqi Governing Council in December 2003, but sanctioned by the Coalition Provisional Authority.[49] That meant that the Tribunal was in reality the creation of the occupying powers – a fact reinforced by its specific designation as a special tribunal standing apart from the wider Iraqi legal system.[50] Close involvement of American advisors in the trial of Saddam Hussein further reinforced the impression.[51] Much as British leaders had hoped that trial of the King's enemies at the end of the Napoleonic wars would strengthen the role of the monarchy in France, so too the occupiers in Iraq hoped Iraqi judgment upon Hussein and others guilty of war crimes or crimes against humanity would bolster the new Iraqi regime. The latter did indeed prove to be more ready to spill blood than the French king.

Justice under conditions of military occupation cannot entirely escape the suspicion that it is victor's justice, especially where former enemies or perpetrators of war crimes, or both, stand before courts of some form or another. The unveiled justice of the occupier is no guarantee either that it will seem better or worse than the veiled justice exercised via international tribunals or indigenous courts operating with the assistance or by the toleration of the occupier. It guarantees only that power is available to those who seek justice, assuming, that is, that they seek it at all.

Although the justice entailed in the condemnation of traitors or war criminals has been a part of the administration of justice under occupation it is only a part. Justice in these conditions also entails the administration of justice over the inhabitants more generally and over the forces of the occupier. It was in fact the latter that pushed the issue of justice to the forefront as General Scott heard of the abuses committed by his own forces as they entered Mexican territory, and more specifically of the murder of a Mexican civilian by an American soldier, for which the only available punishment at the time was the dismissal of the murderer from the army. Scott's response was to decree the creation of military commissions, modelled on courts martial, with the authority to impose punishments analogous to American practice. The novelty of his order was evident in the response of the Secretary of State, as recorded by Scott, 'a *startle* at the title was the only comment he then, or ever made on the subject'.[52] The Attorney General, he noted, 'was stricken with legal dumbness'.[53] The hesitancy in this attempt to exert justice over the occupier's army was confirmed by the case of an officer, accused of murder, who escaped and was detected only after the end of the war. Since the only law and courts to which his crime was subject were those of Scott's occupation, and that occupation had ended, he was deemed to be beyond the reach of justice.[54]

Scott's order was intended to be provisional, 'until Congress could be stimulated to legislate on the subject' as he wrote, and directed primarily at his own forces, although it also applied to Mexicans.[55] Where possible, conflicts between Mexicans were to be left to Mexican courts and law. Separate councils of war were instituted to deal with offences against the laws of war while courts-martial were also maintained.[56] The plethora of courts and the varying legal codes – army regulations, Mexican law, the law enshrined in Scott's orders, the laws of war – are but two indications of the difficulty of maintaining some form of justice in this uncertain atmosphere. Moreover, although Scott proudly maintained that his system of justice 'conciliated Mexican [and] intimidated the vicious of the several races', other methods were also deployed.[57] Collective punishment and punitive raids also formed part of Scott's justice and some Mexicans, being less than conciliated, denounced a rule of 'tyrannical caprice'.[58]

What was clear was that while the inhabitants of occupied territory were subject to multiple jurisdictions and laws, the forces of the occupier were subject solely to the jurisdiction of occupier. Attempts by indigenous courts during the Civil War to assert jurisdiction over individuals within the occupying force were brusquely rebutted by the United States Supreme Court.[59] It was still possible, towards the end of the century, to raise the question of whether the jurisdiction was restricted to cases arising under the laws of war or extended to crimes against common law, though Bonfils found little difficulty in deciding that it did, at least where the safety of members of the occupying force was concerned.[60] That justice – that is the justice of the occupier – protected the occupier's interests, and that it was a form of power, was one face of justice. The other, equally acknowledged, was that justice remained an interest of the occupied and, so far as possible, that interest was best served by existing law and systems of adjudication. As Birkhimer argued,

> It would be productive of the greatest confusion if a community who had been governed by one law should have that law, with which they

are acquainted, suddenly changed for another of which they are totally ignorant, as well, of the tribunals which are to administer justice among them.[61]

Efforts were often made in cases where indigenous judges had fled to provide justice according to the indigenous law where such cases would otherwise have been left in the hands of indigenous courts, as General Funston's army did in Mexico in 1914 and the Japanese did in occupied Chinese territory in 1894 and 1904–5.[62]

Despite the fears of General von Moltke, the sense that justice could serve the interests of both occupied and occupier facilitated the gradual extension of the presumption that some form of judicial process should prevail wherever possible. That presumption was evident in the agreement in 1899 that there should be provision for a trial 'in espionage as in all other cases'.[63] Similarly, one of the innovations in the Hague Regulations of 1907 was the prohibition 'to declare abolished, suspended or inadmissible in a court of law the rights and actions of the nationals of the hostile party', although most commentators seem to have viewed this as merely declaratory of customary law.[64]

Whether the institution of some form of judicial process actually served an interest in justice depended not just upon codes and courts for these could be deployed so far in the interest of power as to become a substitute for the 'tyrannical caprice' they were meant to constrain. Such caprice could take the form of the minute regulation of life adopted by Imperial German tribunals in Belgium during the First World War, conducted in German and applying German court procedures. The activities of these tribunals were so extensive that prisons had to be supplemented by requisitioned hotels and other buildings in order to house those condemned to imprisonment.[65] Both Soviet and German administration of occupied territory in the Second World War inevitably went further still in the instrumentalisation of the administration of justice, though even here some minimal level of protection or moderation of otherwise severe penalties could be obtained where the occupier deemed it expedient.[66] In the Netherlands, one of the greatest constraints on the instrumentalisation of the judicial system was, as the Nazi Security Service complained, 'the acute shortage of ideologically reliable lawyers who are also professionally competent'.[67] Less constraint came from the Dutch Supreme Court, which declined the opportunity to claim a right to scrutinise the decrees of the occupier on the grounds that neither the Hague Conventions nor Dutch practices suggested that 'there had been the intention or even the idea that in the case of an occupation . . . the Dutch judicial power should have the right of scrutiny'.[68] In reality the Supreme Court's own commitment to legality weakened it when faced with an occupier for whom justice – where justice is understood to presuppose 'an identifiable rule and the disposition to follow it'[69] – was even more secondary in the administration of occupied territory than it was within its own domestic system.

While it is clear that where justice is not even sought the facade of it can only be corrosive, it is also true, in conditions of military occupation, that the proclamation of the rule of law beyond what the occupier can tolerate whilst remaining an occupier can also be corrosive. That, as Fraenkel pointed out, was the outcome of the occupation of the Rhineland. The immediate difficulty lay in the provisions of the Rhineland Agreement whereby 'German courts shall continue to exercise civil and criminal jurisdiction' limited only by the exceptions that the occupying forces and people employed by them 'shall be exclusively subject to military law and jurisdiction of such forces' and that offences against the 'person or property' of the occupying forces 'may be made amenable to the military jurisdiction of the said forces'.[70] German publicists interpreted this as implying that German courts could try people committing offences against the occupying forces, albeit only in accordance with German law and duly enacted decrees of the High Commission and in accordance with the military codes of the occupiers. The High Commission predictably took a different view, asserting its jurisdiction in its Ordinance No. 2. Even this, however, left open the possibility that the military authorities could choose to leave a case in the hands of the German courts, subject to the reservation that they could transfer it to another court at any point.[71] This was the course followed by the American commander in the case of a German accused of murdering an American soldier. He noted his expectation that the 'sentence would doubtless be death' but added that if 'indications cause me to believe that the court is not going to mete out justice, right is reserved to suspend the proceedings and give the case to a military commission'.[72] In practice, the military authorities found little fault in the rulings of the German courts but the equivocation gave the Germans the opportunity to protest against the threat to the independence of the German judiciary and the elevation of caprice over the rule of law.[73]

French publicists and courts effectively sought to expand the jurisdiction of the High Commission and the military authorities, extending the traditional presumption that the military authorities were entitled to exercise jurisdiction over threats to their security to a wider jurisdiction over matters in the interest of their states. This was applied even to French citizens who violated customs regulations established by the High Commission. The French Court of Appeal concluded that since the 'customs regulations were enacted in the Rhenish provinces in the interest of the Allied powers . . . and therefore in the interests of the French state' the military tribunal had jurisdiction.[74] The tension between such interest and the form of law broke through in the case of a German separatist condemned by German courts. According to the American commander, General Allen, the French president of the High Commission, Paul Tirard, declared that 'the matter was not to be considered in a judicial sense, which was of no importance to him, but in its political aspect'.[75] Objections by other members of the Commission led to equivocation and the emergence of a compromise which would lead to the eventual freeing of the separatist and to Allen's recording that 'I detest this policy of sacrificing our ordinances, judicial considerations, and fairness to political exigency'.[76] Even in their own eyes, and with the elastic French interpretation of the remit of jurisdiction in terms of state interest, the occupiers could not maintain their principled commitment to the rule of law. To the Germans, of course, the case amounted to 'an unheard of infringement of the legal powers of the Prussian courts'.[77]

These disputes were inflamed by German resentment against the Treaty of Versailles, which the occupation of the Rhineland embodied on German territory, and by the foolish French strategy of support for separatism in the Rhineland. Yet there was, as Fraenkel concluded, a deeper flaw:

> the concept of 'rule of law' has different meanings in a government based on democratic consent and a government based on military force. It was the failure to recognise this fundamental fact that constituted the greatest weakness of the Rhineland Agreement.[78]

His point was not that justice had to be abandoned to caprice but rather that, initially at least, such justice as could be established would have to be an imposed justice, one which could not presume the consent that played such an essential role in the rule of law in an established democratic state. To treat a regime of occupation '"as if" it were a democratic regime' is to expose the hypocrisy of such a supposition.[79]

There could be no such deception as Allied armies occupied enemy territory towards the end of the Second World War. Especially in Germany, the laws, judges and judicial procedures were unacceptable to the occupier. Earlier, in North Africa, a different problem had arisen, reminiscent of British experience in Mesopotamia and Palestine during the First World War.[80] There, in Cyrenaica, only the Sharia and Rabbinical religious courts still functioned. The Italian judges and lawyers had fled and qualified indigenous personnel were practically non-existent. The British occupation administration struggled to develop a judicial system, issuing a Civil Offences Promulgation in place of the Italian penal code. Particular difficulty was experienced with the system of appeals which followed the traditional practice of making the Chief Administrator of the occupation administration the ultimate source of appeal. Although these officers could turn to legal advisers, they were, as one adviser lamented,

> not always willing to accept the advice of their Legal Advisers . . . and, doubtless with the best of intentions, sometimes intervened to interfere with sentences upon no apparent legal principles, or to stultify the provisions of their own proclamations, or to over-rule The Hague Regulations with which they not seldom displayed a disconcerting unfamiliarity.[81]

That some system of appeal was necessary to serve justice was as evident as the difficulty of establishing one that did not itself turn out to be a source of caprice.[82]

Imposing justice in Italy and Germany, especially in the latter, became bound up with the purge of Fascists and National Socialists, but it also encountered more common obstacles. The sheer extent of the number of cases was aggravated by the dislocation of war and food shortages. In Germany, as one Allied legal officer recalled, the 'struggle for survival was making potential criminals of the whole nation'.[83] Prolonged reliance upon the black market in the light of an official food supply insufficient to prevent malnutrition raised a similar problem in Japan.[84] In Italy, consideration of this even deterred Allied military courts from imposing what their superiors regarded as adequate sentences.[85]

Since, contrary to Birkhimer's expectation, justice could not in many cases be left to courts and procedures with which the inhabitants were familiar, and since even qualified Allied officers were unfamiliar with continental legal procedures, those brought before Allied military courts were confronted with an alien Anglo-Saxon adversarial system. However, in both Italy and Germany there was an intention to establish a form of justice that, especially in contrast to the subversion of anything resembling the rule of law by the defeated regimes, would rebound to the advantage of the occupiers as well as serving their proclaimed principles. Indeed it was claimed that military courts became the major interface between the population and the occupiers and were a 'force for democracy'.[86] The same linkage was asserted by American General Lucius Clay: 'I believed that democratic growth in German was possible and I determined to make military government a rule of law'.[87] Initially, though, establishing military government took priority.

The immediate impact of the occupation was a paralysis of the judicial system as Military Government Law No. 2 closed all German courts. As an American legal officer at the time acknowledged, the military government courts made 'little or no attempt . . . to impress upon the inhabitants of the occupied areas the superiority of the American way of life. Their judgements were harsh, and the justice they dispensed was summary'.[88] Initially, their prime concern was reflected in the types of case they adjudicated, notably illegal possession of war material and violations of military regulations such as curfews and false identification.[89] By July 1945, however, some effort was being made to mitigate these characteristics of the initial phase. As German courts were reopened further confusion arose from a provision of Military Government Law No. 2 prohibiting German courts from dealing with cases involving offences against the orders of the occupation forces. Since the military government had asserted supreme authority, including all legislative power, that left German courts unable to enforce the law, necessitating an amendment providing that they could be specifically authorised to deal with such cases.[90]

That amendment was part of the process whereby greater coherence was given to the 'initial judicial system which was adopted as an emergency measure' and which had tried 385,000 cases before it was replaced in August 1948.[91] Even before then, some restriction had been placed upon the authority of army commanders, with searches normally requiring warrants issued by military government courts in 1947, and a right of habeas corpus being extended to those subject to military courts early in 1948.[92] Under the reformed system, civil jurisdiction was largely returned to the re-established German courts, at least over German nationals. Displaced persons remained under military jurisdiction until much later. Members of the occupation forces and those accompanying them also remained under military jurisdiction, either in the shape of courts-martial or military government courts.[93] Whether exercising jurisdiction over Germans or non-Germans, the administration of justice by the occupying forces remained a self-enclosed system insulated from the domestic judicial systems of the occupiers. In that respect it abided by the prohibition upon extending the jurisdiction of the courts of the occupier over occupied territory, which was seen as a prelude to annexation or even as the assertion of annexation.[94]

It was, therefore, with some hesitation that the Israeli High Court of Justice moved to exercise judicial review over the acts of the Israel armed forces in occupied Palestinian territory, being encouraged in this by the Israeli state's agreement not to dispute its jurisdiction.[95] The Court responded by assuming 'without ruling on the matter, that the jurisdiction exists on the personal level against functionaries in the military government . . . as "persons fulfilling public duties according to law" and who are subject to the review of this court'.[96] Amongst the reasons for this highly unusual extension of jurisdiction was the desire to present the occupation as one embodying the rule of law, thereby enhancing its legitimacy in the eyes of the Israeli population and of the wider world. It has, however, exposed the ambivalence of the administration of justice, calling forth accusations that it is a sham justice that casts a veil of legality over the arbitrary acts of the occupying forces. The Court itself has acknowledged that, as an agent of the state of Israel, it cannot be indifferent to the hostility of inhabitants of occupied territory to Israel. Thus, in a case of Palestinians petitioning against deportation, one of the judges acknowledged considering the argument that given the evidence that the petitioners had

> incited the population in the Territories to violent action and to the destruction of the State of Israel by violent means . . . or that they would engage in such incitement if they were allowed to return to their homes, they are not worthy for any remedy from this court, which serves as one of the authorities of the state.[97]

While the Israeli Court has not in fact rejected a right of petition on this ground, the Court, as a court of the occupying power, is trapped between the need to maintain the autonomy of law from politics, and its own independence and legitimacy, and the imperatives of the Israeli state as an occupying power.[98] That, as even its critics admit, has allowed some scope for petitions from inhabitants of the occupied territories, but only limited scope.[99] The 'landmark cases' in which the Court has found in favour of the petitioners are limited in number, giving rise to the suspicion that these are no more than token concessions behind which lies a judicial system inevitably predisposed to give priority to the security considerations of the occupying forces. Again, even those well disposed to the Court (and to the Israeli judicial administration of the occupied territories more generally) have conceded that faced with an 'intolerable balance' the Court has presided over a system characterised by mass arrests and arbitrary arrests intended as means of intimidation, administrative detention, violation of procedural safeguards and a conviction rate of 95 per cent, inducing those accused to plead guilty in the light of the futility of pleading their innocence.[100]

Initially at least the Court was disinclined to question assertions by the state relating to security considerations. As Justice Landau put it,

> The spheres of intervention of this court in the military considerations of the military government are very narrow, and the judge as an individual will certainly refrain from placing his views on political and security matters in place of the military considerations of those who are entrusted with the defence of the state and with maintaining public order in occupied territory.[101]

That did not exclude the possibility that the Court would challenge such judgements where it was clear that it was not military considerations that drove a particular decision, as was true of the Elon Moreh case concerning the requisition of land for an Israeli settlement. In that case, however, divisions amongst the Israeli authorities, including within the Cabinet, as well as the Court's suspicion that they had attempted to mislead the Court, emboldened its decision.[102] Yet even the less restrictive view of the Court's competence in assessing security issues that subsequently emerged could not remedy the basic underlying constraints.[103] The Court could not engage in open confrontation with the government of Israel without risking a reaction that could prove a threat to its own autonomy within Israel. Nor can it be presumed to have wished to concede too many victories of principle to the inhabitants of the occupied territories.[104]

Despite these constraints, the Court has mitigated the harshness of military occupation by promoting out-of-court settlements and by imposing restrictions, usually of a procedural nature, upon the occupation authorities. The 'shadow' effect, as it has been called, may have been more significant than its formal decisions and was openly acknowledged in a case relating to the demolition of housing as a punishment for terrorist acts: 'on more than one occasion our remarks motivated the security authorities to agree (without waiting for a judicial decision) to mitigate the damage to the living quarters of others which are in the building that is to be demolished'.[105]

None of this could bring the reality of occupation wholly within the rule of law, nor even challenge key political decisions – most notably Israeli settlements in the occupied territories – that clearly violated the international law of occupation. Even mechanisms that benefited petitioners, such as the settlements effected through government lawyers prior to the initiation of formal proceedings, were not free of suspicion. For as a study of such mechanisms concluded: 'instead of enjoying legal *rights*, Palestinians were dependent on discretionary concessions rendered to them on an *ex gratia* basis because of the (contingent) "good will" of the judge (or the government lawyer'.[106] The caprice that justice was to have mitigated surfaced in the judicial system even as it sought to bring caprice under some form of control.

While Israel sought to reconcile military occupation and the rule of law through the extension of the jurisdiction of its High Court, in other recent cases occupiers have sought to establish the rule of law through indigenous courts as a part of a wider process of regime transformation and democratisation, eschewing the utilisation of the administration of justice themselves. Indeed, there was a tendency to give priority to the establishment of democracy. In retrospect at least that seemed a dubious strategy, for, as Paddy Ashdown, a former High Representative in Bosnia, reflected:

> In Bosnia, we thought that democracy was the highest priority and we measured it by the number of elections we could organize . . . In hindsight, we should have put the establishment of the rule of law first, for everything else depends on it: a functioning economy, a free and fair political system, the development of civil society, public confidence in policing and the courts.[107]

In fact, even the rule of law, understood as the precondition of a functioning democratic regime rather than the administration of justice by the occupier, strained the resources of the indigenous courts as the occupiers rushed to establish or re-establish them, and then strained the resources of the occupiers as they sought to deal with the consequences. In Bosnia, where existing courts continued to function, the multiplicity of jurisdictions, the sheer plethora of courts, the existence of multiple sources of legislation and the partisan behaviour of indigenous judges led one international report to conclude that 'Bosnia's legal and judicial systems were themselves principle obstacles to the rule of law'.[108] Attempts to reform it were hampered by the proliferation of international agencies, sometimes operating discontinuous review programmes. The shortage of qualified legal personnel led international agencies to seek the appointment of people who had fled from the territory during the conflict, only for such people to be denounced as traitors for having fled in the first place.[109] The same problem, solution and accusation recurred in Kosovo.

In Kosovo, as in East Timor, the judicial system had served as one of the prime means of discrimination and oppression by the previous regimes, leaving no more than a handful of qualified personnel, if that, from the majority populations. Destruction of the infrastructure, including court buildings and records, especially in East Timor, meant that there was effectively no judicial system to administer.[110] The preference for relying on indigenous legal staff, in part at least for fear of being perceived as imperialists, could only be partially realised and effectively constricted the administration of justice. Insufficient personnel meant both the failure to investigate crimes and prolonged periods of pre-trial detention.[111] In the absence of a functioning judicial system and police force both the Kosovo Force and the International Force in East Timor resorted to a policy of detention without trial, with the former persisting in detaining individuals even against court orders for their release.[112] Neither, however, had the capacity or perceived authority to establish their own courts to try those detained, despite their own concerns about international expectations that such people should be tried.[113]

As international judges were brought in to supplement the simple shortage of qualified legal expertise or to remedy the partiality of indigenous judges, the diversity of their own legal backgrounds, compounded by the brevity of their period in office, resulted in cases where such judges applied their own national law rather than the law supposedly applicable in the territory.[114] The participation of international judges in a system initially intended to be run by indigenous staff, rather than the operation of a separate judicial system in the manner of more traditional military courts, may even have aggravated some features of the inevitable departure of the administration of justice from the rule of law. That is evident in the complaints about the immunity of international judges from the regulatory procedures to which the indigenous judges sitting on the same panel were subject.

Such 'double standards' were denounced in Kosovo even by the Ombudsperson established by the UN Mission's own regulations.[115] Yet such consequences followed inevitably from the initial strategy of reliance upon an indigenous system which either did not exist or, so far as it did, was ill-equipped to administer justice. In retrospect, it seemed to Hansjorg Strohmeyer, a legal adviser in both East Timor and Kosovo, that more direct involvement of the military in the administration of justice for an initial period might be desirable, though there was some hesitation in drawing this conclusion:

> Intuitively, one would hesitate to involve military actors in this sensitive area of civil administration, but in the absence of sufficient and immediately deployable civilian resources, it may be the only appropriate response to avoid the emergence of a law enforcement vacuum.[116]

The law enforcement vacuum in Iraq resulted from lack of preparation, the limited manpower of the occupation forces and the failure of those available to respond to their obligation 'to restore and ensure, as far as possible, public order and civil life'.[117] There was, however, no shortage of qualified judges comparable to that in East Timor and Kosovo. The peripheral role of the court system in the repressive apparatus of the regime of Saddam Hussein also meant that it was less tainted than many had feared.[118] The occupation authorities did establish a Judicial Review Committee, analogous to practice in Kosovo, to vet judges. The rapid deterioration of security persuaded them to create a Central Criminal Court of Iraq in Baghdad to deal with the more serious cases, believing that this would act with a degree of professionalism they could not expect of the rest of the court system.[119] This reliance upon indigenous courts to try cases including accusations of launching attacks upon occupation forces was, as one strident critic of the practice complained, 'unprecedented in U.S. military history'.[120] The continuation of the insurgency along with abuses by occupation forces, most notably in Abu Graib jail, inevitably polarised judgements, setting advocates of a return to military courts against those who demanded the subjection of the occupier to the same rule of law applied to Iraqis.[121] The immunity of the occupation forces was aggravated in Iraq by the widespread use of private security channels outside the chain of military command.[122]

This sharp divergence of assessments was fuelled not just by the exigencies of administering justice amidst an aggressive insurgency against the occupation forces but also by the growing tension between a view of justice that gave priority to the security interests of the occupier and one that drew upon the ever-expanding codification of human rights as a supplement to the international humanitarian law that governed military occupation. That such a development might overstretch the capacity and inclination of occupying forces had been recognised in the debates over the International Covenant on Civil and Political rights in 1950. There, on behalf of the United States, Eleanor Roosevelt had insisted that states should only be required to guarantee such rights 'to all individuals within its territory and subject to its jurisdiction' rather than simply to all 'within its jurisdiction', specifically in order to exempt states from such obligations in cases of military occupation.[123] The fear or the aspiration that a more rigorous catalogue of rights might shackle the occupier remains prominent. Ironically, however, at least where the administration of justice is in the hands of the occupier, the invocation of human rights as a supplement to the requirements of international humanitarian law has not necessarily benefited the inhabitants of occupied territory. Reference to human rights has been used by the Israeli High Court of Justice to consider the human rights of Israeli citizens and settlers alongside the human rights of the occupied Palestinians. Balancing the one set against the other, the rights of Israelis to security and religious worship against, for example, the property rights of Palestinians, has led to the triumph of the former over the latter.[124] As Aeyal Gross has argued, this shift from 'a balance between security and the rights of the local population as envisaged in IHL [international humanitarian law] (vertical balancing) . . . to a horizontal balancing between the rights of different individuals' potentially leads to an exclusion of the political considerations affecting military occupation and to an abstraction from the distinctive status of the inhabitants as protected persons.[125]

Even where occupiers have sought justice, it has never been a justice of the equality of all before the law, of common subjection to the same rules, for the rules and the structural nature of military occupation have assigned a different status to the occupier and the inhabitant. Yet that has not meant that justice, even in Radbruch's sense, has no meaning in this context. From General Scott's creation of military commissions onwards, some occupiers have sought to constrain the caprice, and much else, of their own forces as well as imposing a system of justice upon the occupied, for the benefit of the occupier as much as the occupied. It is far from clear that going further, the aspiration for a rapid transition to a rule of law or the invocation of the full panoply of human rights, has proved to be much more than a veil which serves only to conceal the reality of military occupation. In fact, it has not even done that, for the enhanced expectations have led to the avoidance of responsibility by the occupier and the insecurity of the occupied, or to the manipulation of these rights by the occupier to enhance the power that the administration of justice serves, even where it also seeks equality.

Notes

1. Gordon Ireland, 'The jus postliminii and the coming peace', *Tulane Law Review*, 18 (1944), p. 585. For a broader treatment, see Jacob Elen Conner, *The Development of Belligerent Occupation* (Iowa City, IA: Iowa University, 1912).
2. William Edward Hall, *A Treatise on International Law* (Oxford: Oxford University Press, 1924), p. 577.
3. Seymour Wurfel, 'Military government – the Supreme Court speaks', *North Carolina Law Review*, 40 (1962), pp. 774–6.
4. At one stage, the Romans considered that captivity entailed the end of marriage. See Ireland, 'The jus postliminii and the coming peace', p. 586.
5. Carl Schmitt, *The Nomos of the Earth* (New York, NY: Telos, 2003), p. 207.
6. Ibid. p. 207.
7. Judith N. Shklar, *Legalism* (Cambridge, MA: Harvard University Press, 1964), p. 122.
8. H. W. Halleck, *International Law* (San Francisco, CA: Bancroft, 1861), p. 776.
9. Shklar, *Legalism*, p. 113.
10. Quoted in Percy Bordwell, *The Law of War Between Belligerents* (Chicago, IL: Callaghan, 1908), p. 114.
11. Ibid. p. 114. Only the 'softening of manners' is noted by Martti Koskenniemi, *The Gentle Civilizer of Nations* (Cambridge: Cambridge University Press, 2002), pp. 84–5.
12. Bordwell, *The Law of War Between Belligerents*, p. 115.
13. There is a temptation to see this as the outcome of a progressive or cumulative trend, but see Mark Mazower, 'The strange triumph of human rights, 1933–1950', *The Historical Journal*, 47 (2004), pp. 379–98.
14. See Michael J. Dennis, 'Application of human rights treaties extra-territorially in times of armed conflict and military occupation', *American Journal of International Law*, 99 (2005), p. 119.
15. See the reservation of Judge Higgins quoted in Michael J. Kelly, 'Critical analysis of the International Court of Justice ruling on

Israel's security barrier', *Fordham International Law Journal*, 29 (2005), pp. 187–8.

16. Gustav Radbruch [1946], 'Gesetzliches Unrecht und übergesetzliches Recht', in Gustav Radbruch, *Gesamtausgabe*, vol. 3 (Heidelberg: Müller, 1990), p. 89.

17. See Shklar, *Legalism*.

18. Quoted in J. M. Spaight, *War Rights on Land* (London: Macmillan, 1911), p. 349. See also the observation of Henry Sutherland Edwards that military, as opposed to civil, justice determines punishment in disregard of proportionality to the offence, considering only the deterrent effect, *The Germans in France* (London: Stanford, 1874), p. 284.

19. See Ronen Shamir, '"Landmark cases" and the reproduction of legitimacy: the case of Israel's High Court of Justice', *Law & Society Review*, 24 (1990), pp. 781–2.

20. Ernst Fraenkel [1944], 'Military occupation and the rule of law', in Ernst Fraenkel, *Gesammelte Schriften*, vol. 3 (Baden-Baden: Nomos, 1999), p. 244.

21. The most striking case is that of General Pinochet. See Geoffrey Robertson, *Crimes Against Humanity* (London: Penguin, 2002), pp. 373–426.

22. Quoted in Gary Jonathon Bass, *Stay the Hand of Justice. The Politics of War Crimes Trials* (Princeton, NJ: Princeton University Press, 2000), p. 89.

23. This was entered as part of the American reservations to the 'Commission on the responsibility of the authors of the war and on enforcement of penalties', *American Journal of International Law*, 14 (1920), p. 146.

24. Ibid. p. 146.

25. Ibid. p. 148.

26. Margaret Macmillan, *Peacemakers* (London: John Murray, 2001), p. 174.

27. Bass, *Stay the Hand of Justice*, p. 51.

28. Quoted in ibid. p. 47.

29. Ibid. pp. 185–6.

30. Ibid. p. 188.

31. Joseph E. Persico, *Nuremberg* (London: Penguin, 1995), pp. 17–18. ✳

32. See Earl F. Ziemke, *The U.S. Army in the Occupation of Germany, 1944–1947* (Honolulu, HI: University Press of the Pacific, 2005), p. 395; Robert K. Woetzel, *The Nuremberg Trials in International Law* (London: Stevens & Sons, 1962), pp. 200–17.

33. International Military Tribunal, 'Judgement', *American Journal of International Law*, 41 (1947), p. 216.

34. Shklar, *Legalism*, p. 162. See also Hannah Arendt, *Eichmann in Jerusalem* (Harmondsworth: Penguin, 1975), pp. 256–8.

35. Quoted in Ziemke, *The U.S. Army in the Occupation of Germany*, p. 393. See also Myres S. McDougal and Florentinno P. Felciano, *The International Law of War* (New Haven, CT: New Haven Press, 1994), pp. 714–18.
36. 'Commission on the responsibility of the authors of the war and on enforcement of penalties', p. 147.
37. Shklar, *Legalism*, p. 168.
38. 'In re Yamashita', *US Reports*, 327 (1945), p. 11.
39. 'Hirota *v.* MacArthur', *US Reports*, 338 (1948), p. 198.
40. Ibid. p. 211.
41. Ibid. p. 215.
42. John Dower, *Embracing Defeat* (London: Penguin, 1999), p. 451.
43. As is evident from the title, Frederick Bernays Wiener, 'Comment. The years of MacArthur, volume III: MacArthur unjustifiably accused of meeting out "victor's justice" in war crimes trials', *Military Law Review*, 113 (1986), pp. 203–18.
44. See Leila N. Sadat, 'The establishment of the International Criminal Court', *Michigan State University DCL Journal of International Law*, 8 (1999), pp. 97–118; Philippe Kirsch, 'The role of the International Criminal Court in enforcing international criminal law', *American University International Law Review*, 22 (2007), pp. 539–47.
45. Bass, *Stay the Hand of Justice*, p. 282.
46. Ibid. pp. 251–4.
47. Iain King and Whit Mason, *Peace at Any Price* (Ithaca, NY: Cornell University Press, 2006), pp. 64–5.
48. Amnesty International, 'Kosovo (Serbia): the challenge to fix a failed UN justice mission', EUR 70/001/2008, pp. 12–14.
49. M. Cherif Bassiouni, 'Post-conflict justice in Iraq', *Cornell International Law Journal*, 38 (2005), p. 345.
50. For objections to this status, see ibid. pp. 361–3.
51. The tribunal had been reconstituted as the Supreme Iraqi Criminal Tribunal. On perceptions of the trial, see Leslie Scheuermann, 'Victor's justice? The lessons of Nuremberg applied to the trial of Saddam Hussein', *Tulane Journal of International and Comparative Law*, 15 (2006), pp. 291–310.
52. Quoted in David Glazier, 'Kangaroo court or competent tribunal?', *Virginia Law Review*, 89 (2005), p. 2029.
53. Ibid. p. 2029.
54. Ibid. p. 2029.
55. Louis Fisher invokes this in the context of an argument that authority for military commissions in America is legislative not executive, 'Military commissions: problems of authority and practice', *Boston University International Law Journal*, 24 (2006), pp. 15–53, especially pp. 23–4.

56. Glazier, 'Kangaroo court or competent tribunal?', pp. 2029–33.
57. Quoted in Fisher, 'Military commissions', p. 24.
58. Justin H. Smith, 'American rule in Mexico', *American Historical Review*, 23 (1918), pp. 289–91.
59. William E. Birkhimer, *Military Government and Martial Law* (Kansas City, KS: Hudson, 1914), pp. 157–8.
60. Henri Bonfils, *Droit International Public* (Paris: Rousseau, 1894), p. 648.
61. Birkhimer, *Military Government and Martial Law*, p. 134.
62. Eldridge Colby, 'Occupation under the laws of war II', *Columbia Law Review*, 26 (1926), p. 154; Doris A. Graber, *The Development of the Law of Belligerent Occupation 1863–1914* (New York, NY: AMS Press, 1949), p. 276.
63. David Glazier, 'Ignorance is not bliss', *Rutgers Law Review*, 58 (2005), p. 165.
64. Graber, *The Development of the Law of Belligerent Occupation*, pp. 151–2.
65. James Wilford Garner, *International Law and the World War*, vol. 2 (London: Longmans, 1920), pp. 91, 95–7.
66. See the perspectives of two lawyers who appeared before them: Jurij Fedynskyj, 'Sovietization of an occupied area through the medium of the courts', *American Slavic and East European Review*, 12 (1953), pp. 44–56 and Nikolas Laskovsky, 'Practicing law in the occupied Ukraine', *American Slavic and East European Review*, 11 (1952), pp. 123–37.
67. Quoted in Gerhard Hirschfeld, *Nazi Rule and Dutch Collaboration* (Oxford: Berg, 1988), pp. 156–7.
68. Ibid. p. 160.
69. Shklar, *Legalism*, p. 119.
70. Fraenkel, 'Military occupation and the rule of law', p. 319.
71. Ibid. pp. 259–60, 326.
72. Henry T. Allen, *My Rhineland Journal* (Boston, MA: Houghton and Mifflin, 1923), p. 108.
73. Fraenkel, 'Military occupation and the rule of law', p. 261.
74. Ibid. p. 294.
75. Allen, *My Rhineland Journal*, p. 284.
76. Ibid. p. 286.
77. Quoted in Fraenkel, 'Military occupation and the rule of law', p. 264.
78. Ibid. p. 314.
79. Ibid. p. 314.
80. On the latter, see Chapter 1 of this book.
81. G. Tracey Watts, 'The British military occupation of Cyrenaica, 1942–1949', *Transactions of the Grotius Society*, 37 (1951), p. 76.

82. See also the argument for the prohibition of the normal appeals procedure as Allied occupation forces permitted the re-establishment of Italian civil courts in Trieste: 'Military occupation of Trieste', *Stanford Law Review*, 4 (1951), pp. 112–24.

83. Worth B. McCauley, 'American courts in Germany: 600,000 cases later', *American Bar Association Journal*, 40 (1954), p. 1043.

84. Dower, *Embracing Defeat*, pp. 89–97.

85. Ian Campbell, 'Some legal problems arising out of the establishment of the Allied military courts in Italy', *International Law Quarterly*, 1 (1947), p. 201.

86. See Eli E. Nobleman, 'American military government courts in Germany', *Annals of the American Academy of Political and Social Science*, 267 (1950), pp. 95–6.

87. Lucius D. Clay, *Decision in Germany* (London: Heinemann, 1950), p. 245.

88. Nobleman, American military government courts in Germany', p. 88.

89. McCauley, 'American courts in Germany', p. 1042

90. Karl Loewenstein, 'Reconstruction of the administration of justice in American-occupied Germany', *Harvard Law Review*, 61 (1948), p. 423.

91. Clay, *Decision in Germany*, p. 247.

92. Ibid. p. 249.

93. For a denunciation of the jurisdiction of military government courts over American civilians, see Robert Donihi, 'Occupation justice', *South Texas Law Journal*, 1 (1955), pp. 333–58.

94. For the link between the extension of the jurisdiction of domestic courts and annexation, see Irenée Lameire, *Théorie et Practique de la Conquête dans l'Ancien Droit* (Paris: Rousseau, 1902).

95. The Attorney General at the time later claimed that the state 'agreed expressly to jurisdiction'. Meir Shamgar, 'Legal concepts and problems of the Israeli military government – the initial stage', in Meir Shamgar (ed.), *Military Government in the Territories Administered by Israel 1967–1980* (Jerusalem: Hebrew University, 1982), p. 43.

96. Quoted in David Kretzmer, *The Occupation of Justice* (Albany, NY: State University of New York Press, 2002), p. 20.

97. Ibid. p. 192.

98. Shamir, '"Landmark cases" and the reproduction of legitimacy', p. 782.

99. See Raja Shehadah, *Occupier's Law. Israel and the West Bank* (Washington, DC: Institute of Palestine Studies, 1988), pp. 95–100.

100. Steve Fireman, 'The impossible balance: the goals of human rights and security in the Israeli administered territories', *Capital University Law Review*, 20 (1991), pp. 421–54.

101. Quoted in Kretzmer, *The Occupation of Justice*, pp. 119–20.
102. Ibid. pp. 86–9.
103. On the less restrictive interpretation, see ibid. p. 120.
104. Yoav Dotan, 'Judicial rhetoric, government lawyers, and human rights', *Law & Society Review*, 33 (1999), pp. 346–8.
105. Quoted in Kretzmer, *The Occupation of Justice*, p. 189.
106. Dotan, 'Judicial rhetoric, government lawyers, and human rights', p. 355.
107. Quoted in Asli Ü. Bâli, 'Justice under occupation: rule of law and the ethics of nation building in Iraq', *Yale Journal of International Law*, 30 (2005), p. 455.
108. International Crisis Group, 'Courting disaster: the misrule of law in Bosnia and Herzegovina', Balkans Report 127 (25 March 2003), p. 5.
109. Ibid. p. 20.
110. Hansjorg Strohmeyer, 'Collapse and reconstruction of a judicial system', *American Journal of International Law*, 95 (2001), p. 50.
111. King and Mason, *Peace at Any Price*, pp. 63–4; OSCE, 'Kosovo. Review of the criminal justice system (April 2003–October 2004)', pp. 14–33.
112. Richard Caplan, *International Governance in War-Torn Territories* (Oxford: Oxford University Press, 2005), pp. 64–5.
113. Strohmeyer, 'Collapse and reconstruction of a judicial system', p. 51; Bruce Oswald, 'The law on military occupation: answering the challenges of detention during contemporary peace operations', *Melbourne Journal of International Law*, 8 (2007), pp. 312–13.
114. Amnesty International, 'Kosovo (Serbia)', p. 22.
115. Ibid. p. 34. On the institution of an ombudsperson, see Caplan, *International Governance*, pp. 200–4.
116. Strohmeyer, 'Collapse and reconstruction of a judicial system', p. 61.
117. Article 43, Hague Regulations, 1907.
118. Hilary Synnott, *Bad Days in Basra* (London: Tauris, 2008), pp. 194–5; John C. Williamson, 'Establishing the rule of law in post-war Iraq', *Georgia Journal of International and Comparative Law*, 33 (2004), p. 231. For a different view, see Craig Trebilock, 'Legal cultures clash in Iraq', *The Army Lawyer*, 48 (November 2003), pp. 48–50.
119. Williamson, 'Establishing the rule of law in post-war Iraq', pp. 238–9.
120. Michael J. Frank, 'U.S. military courts and the war in Iraq', *Vanderbilt Journal of Transnational Law*, 39 (2006), p. 776.
121. For the former view, see ibid. pp. 645–778; for the latter view, see Bassiouni, 'Post-conflict justice in Iraq', pp. 467–9.
122. See Mark Bina, 'Private military contractor liability and accountability

after Abu Graib', *The John Marshall Law Review*, 38 (2005), pp. 1237–63.

123. Dennis, 'Application of human rights treaties extraterritorially', pp. 122–4.

124. Aeyal M. Gross, 'Human proportions: are human rights the emperor's new clothes of the international law of occupation?' *European Journal of International Law*, 18 (2007), pp. 1–35.

125. Ibid. p. 16.

Chapter 8

Occupation and Regime Transformation

It is frequently asserted that the greatest challenge to the concept of military occupation, as understood in the law of occupation, is the issue of regime transformation. It is held that Article 43 of the Hague Regulations amounts to a prohibition of regime transformation appropriate to an age in which military occupiers were largely indifferent to the nature of the regime in occupied territory, including 'misrule' by the ousted regime, being concerned instead with the strategic value of occupied territory.[1] It is further claimed that such indifference has given way to an age in which regime change is a primary intention of occupiers. They justify their actions in the name of liberation from oppressive rule, humanitarian concerns and the self-determination of the inhabitants of occupied territory – although whether the humanitarian concerns frequently invoked in such cases are accepted is another matter. At the same time, the international law of occupation has moved from a concern with the rights of states and governments towards a concern with the rights of individuals and peoples, privileging the principle of self-determination. The outcome of these two trends is an apparently inescapable dilemma, for 'it is inherently contradictory to impose a government on a population and justify it as part of a process of self-determination'.[2]

Responses to this dilemma have varied according to which of the two trends is given priority and the broader theoretical positions and sympathies of commentators. One type of argument, often explicitly following Carl Schmitt's vision of an epochal transition in international law, or rather the collapse of the traditional international order of the sixteenth to the nineteenth centuries and the emergence of a new period of legal indeterminacy, focuses on the first trend.[3] Thus, Nehal Bhuta draws on Schmitt's distinction between commissarial dictatorship, intended to restore the constitution after a period of crisis, and sovereign dictatorship, intended to institute a new constitutional order.[4] In the case of the occupation of Iraq in 2003, Bhuta presents the United States' occupation regime as a 'sovereign dictatorship' whose transformative occupation exceeds the legal order and authorizes its pro-visional assumption of control, in the name of 'a new and better order'. It derives its legitimacy, in other words, from *the promise of the order to come*, a horizon of expectation that is invoked to relativize the legal rules which bind it to the present. The occupying power as sovereign dictator essentially undertakes a gamble, in which the illegality of the present will become moot or even cured by the concrete legitimacy of the future order: *ex factis jus oritur* . . .[5]

The purpose of this comparison, however, is to deny the legitimacy of the American attempt at the transformation of Iraq. As Jean L. Cohen has noted, 'it rejects any attempt to give a legal/conceptual impri-matur to the project of transformative occupation'.[6] In Schmitt's account, military occupation as a concept is firmly tied to a social and constitutional order, that of the nineteenth century, whose principles have been abandoned. For Schmitt the era of military occupation was an interlude between two phases of just war theory:

> In medieval theory, the just war meant that the victor had the right to enslave the subjects of his opponent and to seize his land; today, with more highly organized forms of mass domination it means above all: determining the constitution and regime of the defeated.[7]

An alternative to this response, though one whose outcome is little different, is summed up in the title of an article on the subject: 'Why regime change is (almost always) a bad idea'.[8] Following the lead of United Nations' General Secretary Kofi Annan, the principle of regime change is conceded in exceptional circumstances of humani-tarian crisis, only for a host of reasons to be invoked for why such change is likely to fail. The ability of small numbers of the inhabitants of occupied territory to mount major challenges to the process, the limited resources of occupiers, the need to present the enterprise to the occupier's citizens as being in the national interest, while simulta-neously needing to present it as a humanitarian act devoid of national interest to outsiders, and other obstacles, all point to the prospect of failure and counsel constraint.[9]

Not all, however, counsel restraint. At the time of the occupation of Iraq, John Yoo, in testimony before a subcommittee of the United States' Senate, invoked an equally wide-ranging set of justifications for regime change, while explicitly avoiding the issue of whether the invasion of Iraq was justified.[10] While many invoke the development of occupation law in the nineteenth century through to the Hague Conferences as a model of constraint Yoo, with some plausibility, pointed to the elasticity of formulations from the Lieber Code onwards.[11] That argument faltered as Yoo claimed that even were the Hague Regulations to be construed in a more restrictive manner it did not matter for Iraq was not a party to the Hague Conferences.[12] Yoo displayed more confidence in asserting that under the Fourth Geneva Convention the United States was entitled to engage in regime transformation for two sets of reasons. First, it was entitled in order to ensure the security of the occupying forces, and more broadly in order to ensure the security of the United States. Second, it was entitled, indeed required, to transform the regime in order to guarantee the rights enumerated in the Convention.[13] Amongst the various objections raised to such arguments is the complaint that even though the Convention provides extensive guarantees, because 'occupation law by its nature contemplates rule by the occupying power, political participation is not a protected right. Designing and monitoring elections, therefore, could not be justified by Convention obligations'.[14] On the one hand, that is true, but on the other hand, it merely restates the dilemma created by the two trends in the practice and law of occupation.

Another attempt to escape the dilemma in some ways points towards an even more expansive agenda than suggested by Yoo's search for a justification of American policy in Iraq, though it is one shared by explicit critics of the invasion of Iraq. Thus, in November 2003, with specific reference to Iraq, Michael Walzer speculated that

> a misguided military intervention or a preventive war fought before its time might nonetheless end with the displacement of a brutal regime and the construction of a decent one. Or a war unjust on both sides might result in a settlement, negotiated or imposed, that is fair to both and makes for a stable peace between them . . . If this argument is right, then we need criteria for *jus post bellum* that are distinct from (though not wholly independent of) those that we use to judge the war and its conduct.[15]

This *jus post bellum*, Walzer explained, 'concerns war's endings'.[16] Whether, as some claim, this would constitute a 'new major category of war',[17] is doubtful. In large part it overlaps with the law of occupation which, through its presumption that the occupier exercises effective authority, tends to presume that active conduct of warfare has ceased; though there was also acknowledgement that insurgency that fell short of displacing that authority did not abrogate the condition of occupation.[18] It does move the focus by seeing some element of transformation as an integral part of ending war and by emphasising that this is about more than the cessation of conflict. To that extent it could be construed as being compatible with notions about the termination of military occupation at the end of a period of transformation. It also shifts the focus in terms of a presumption that, as Walzer put it, 'once we have acted in ways that have significant consequences for other people . . . we cannot just walk away'.[19]

Although few commentators advocate simple and immediate withdrawal, hesitancy about regime transformation and suspicion about its perceived lack of legitimacy have induced a presumption that occupiers should depart in favour of duly constituted indigenous authorities as soon as possible; a presumption facilitated by the demand that 'sweeping reforms' should be reserved until the occupier has departed.[20] The tension between the desire to see a rapid withdrawal of occupation forces and the desire to see a reform that would remove the vices that induced the occupation in the first place is hardly new. It was clearly expressed by Consul General Evelyn Baring in respect of the British occupation of Egypt that began in 1882:

> Two alternative policies were open to the British Government. These were, first, the policy of speedy evacuation; and, secondly, the policy of reform. It was not sufficiently understood that the adoption of one of these policies was wholly destructive of the other.[21]

In Egypt, unwilling to end the occupation speedily the British were compelled to engage in some measure of reform while being uncertain of their own status. As early as 1884, Baring, by then Lord Cromer, expressed unease about what he described as a 'hybrid form of government to which no name can be given and for which there is no precedent' and which could 'be justified [only] if we are able to keep before our eyes the possibility of evacuation'.[22] In fact, Britain asserted a protectorate over Egypt in 1914, opining that after 'thirty years of reform' this was the best way to 'accelerate progress towards self-government'.[23] Egypt provides an early illustration of the concerns which still lie behind resistance to abandoning the 'conservationist principle' that is held to be embodied in Article 43 of the Hague Regulations, namely that this will 'dangerously blur the line between occupation and annexation' or that '"transformative occupations"' are 'more akin to a modern form of indirect colonialism than the selfless liberation they often pose as'.[24] As Adam Roberts has noted, annexation has indeed been accompanied by the 'rhetoric of transformation', for example, in Italy's annexation of Tripoli and

Cyrenaica in November 1911 following its proclamation of the need for transformation the preceding month.[25]

Since the Second World War, however, the prospect of regime transformation under conditions of military occupation leading to the assertion of annexation, let alone the recognition of such annexation by other states, has become an increasingly remote possibility, though examples are not unknown. The most prominent instance was East Timor where, following Indonesian invasion in 1975, a People's Assembly under the control of the occupation authorities petitioned for incorporation into Indonesia, which duly followed in July 1976. A policy of integration, including the imposition of the official Indonesian language and population resettlement, followed. Even there, however, most states failed to formally recognise annexation, even if many acquiesced in it.[26] Other examples of annexation or attempted annexation in this period are the Chinese annexation of Tibet (1950), Indian annexation of Goa (1962), Moroccan annexation of the Western Sahara and Iraq's attempted annexation of Kuwait (1990). Roberts notes that in most of these cases 'the original status of the annexed territory was itself less than one of full sovereignty'.[27] Nor, it might be added, was the need for reform or the 'rhetoric of transformation' prominent in the justifications of such annexations.

Despite the invocation of the spectre of annexation, it is rather the prospect that greater or lesser regime transformation will perpetuate dependence upon the occupier, either in the sense of direct strategic or economic dependence or in the shape of ideological conformity to the visions and practices of the occupier, which lies behind defence of the conservationist principle. This dependence exposes the supposed practitioners of 'selfless liberation' as practitioners of a 'modern form of indirect colonialism'. Indeed the relationship between conquest and regime transformation is more complex than suggested by the fear that regime transformation could tip over into annexation. Such a transition is indeed a possibility. Yet it is also arguable that the possibility of conquest – that is occupation followed by annexation, preferably accepted in a treaty ending a war – facilitated the emergence of the concept of occupation, including the presumption in favour of maintaining the laws in force in the territory. An occupier desirous of effecting a change of regime could afford to wait because regime transformation would be an automatic consequence of such annexation. Annexation, of course, would also automatically enhance the former occupier's security interests. By the same token, the presumption that military occupation would not lead to annexation increased the temptation to secure its interests by regime transformation, at the same time as regime transformation at the behest of the occupier came to be seen as incompatible with the right to self-determination. That, in turn, made the compliance of some at least of those subject to occupation all the more desirable. Such considerations were evident to those who reflected on the British occupation of Egypt: 'The justification of our presence in Egypt remains based, not upon the defensible right of conquest, or on force, but upon our own belief in the element of consent'. The difficulty was 'that element, in 1919, did not in any articulate form exist. It was dramatically challenged by the Egyptian outburst of March 1919'.[28]

In fact, these considerations were evident as the concept of occupation began to emerge amidst the wreckage of the French revolutionary and Napoleonic wars. Regime transformation was built into those wars because they were understood as wars between radically different political systems and peoples rather than limited wars over territory between sovereigns. Especially in the Napoleonic Empire, but earlier as well, the sheer scale of French military victories had an impact on occupation and regime transformation. On the one hand, the peace treaties entailed the return of large tracts of territory to defeated powers, consolidating the idea of temporary military occupation. On the other hand, the indeterminacy of French strategic goals and the range of actual or potential enemies encouraged the transformation of regimes in neighbouring territories to provide a buffer in the next war.[29]

On the surface, at least, French practice was ruthless. As one historian has written, the annexed territories 'regardless of their history and traditions, were melted down into standard-issue French *départements*' and subject to 'the entire panoply of Revolutionary reforms' and even the satellite kingdoms were subject to 'profound transformations'.[30] In some respect this was true; but the success of these transformations was dependent upon the cooperation of local elites and the strength of local traditions. French centralisation could provoke opposition where the apparently weaker states of the *ancien régime* had avoided it by the expedient of avoiding challenging established social forces.[31] Sometimes the obstacles were noted by Napoleon's officials and their allies. As a report on conditions in the Kingdom of Westphalia acknowledged,

the feudalism that exists in your state of Westphalia is not the weak and almost extinct feudalism that existed in France in 1789 . . . Here feudalism is part of the social order . . . All reform must be slow and measured: this is one of those matters where time is required for success.[32]

In Italy, officials fulminated against their inability to enforce the prohibition of religious holidays, while the anticlerical Minister of Justice in Naples neglected to circulate the parts of the Code Napoleon that provided for the civil marriage of priests.[33] Regime transformation was not, however, a simple matter of a struggle between an ideologically driven occupier and recalcitrant inhabitants of occupied territory. The sale of church lands in the Rhineland was driven by financial considerations, namely the extraction of revenue for Napoleon's wars;[34] but these sales created vested interests. Indeed, it has been suggested that one of the reasons for adopting Article 43 of the Hague Regulations was fear of creating vested interest in the continuation of occupation.[35] Innovations could also be welcomed because of the leverage that they offered *vis-à-vis* the occupier. In the Rhineland, the inhabitants adapted to new consultative and judicial institutions in order to defend local interest against the French state. This lead the historian Michael Rowe to conclude that the 'Rhineland was not "colonised" by the French Empire; rather, Rhinelanders "colonised" certain French institutions'.[36] Not all of these reforms were rejected by those who subsequently administered the Rhineland in the name of the Allied armies that defeated Napoleon.[37]

In the case of these occupations, the equivocal status of the territories, especially those annexed, rather than the satellite kingdoms, encouraged a form of regime transformation that went far further than the mere replacement of rulers and governments. These occupations also show that regime transformation, especially when understood in a wider sense, is not only a matter of an occupier imposing his will and vision upon a recalcitrant population but a matter involving the interests and visions of those subject to occupation. That impression is confirmed by the reconstruction of the American south that began in the Civil War.

Here, too, there was uncertainty about the status of the southern states, even after the surrender of Confederate armies. To this must be added the conflict between President Lincoln and his successor Andrew Johnson on the one hand and Congress on the other hand, as the two presidents sought rapid reincorporation of the rebel states into the Union. Even with what emerged as the conditions of abolition of slavery, repudiation of the Confederate war debt and disavowal of secession, Congress balked at the manifestly unrepresentative nature of the new, supposedly loyal, governments of southern states, prolonging military rule in the process. Moreover, faced with the Attorney General's opinions of May and June 1867 that military governors must restrict themselves to maintaining order, Congress legislated to empower them to guide reconstruction and expressly instructed military officers to ignore the opinions of 'any civil officer of the United States'.[38] Long before this, military officers had been taking decisions about what reconstruction and a Union without slavery might mean. Indeed they had done so in their capacity as military governors during the war itself. Lacking any consistent direction from above they acted according to their perceptions about what was expedient and just in respect of the crucial issue of the ownership of land and hence the form of labour which would be open to the liberated slaves. Options sanctioned by Union commanders ranged from the operation of cotton plantations at the initiative of former slaves, as accepted by General Grant at Davis Bend, through to the distribution of land in forty-acre packets by General Sherman in parts of South Carolina and Georgia, and General Banks' enforcement of the plantation system in Louisiana – that looked to some suspiciously like a continuation of slavery.[39] The eventual outcome was seen by many former slaves as a betrayal that favoured former plantation owners.[40] However one assesses the controversial issues of the reconstruction period in the South, it is clear that once the decision had been taken to end the system of slavery some process of far reaching reconstruction, in which the ownership of land and system of labour were crucial, was inescapable. Given the uncertainty as to what it should be, the competing considerations of the principle of emancipation and the need to reconcile former rebels to the Union, and the sheer complexity of the problem, it is not surprising that the revolutionary implications of the Lieber Code's rejection of slavery found no acknowledgement elsewhere in the Code. Reconstruction also demonstrated that, in the words of William Birkhimer:

> military government ceases at the pleasure of him who instituted it upon such conditions as he elects to impose, and that its termination is not in point of time coincident, either necessarily or generally, with the cessation of hostilities between the contending parties.[41]

To that extent, the emphasis asserted by advocates of a *jus post bellum* was already understood as a part of military government.

Both the Napoleonic war and the American Civil War had regime transformation built into their rationale and hence into the military occupations that came with them. That is not true of all military occupations. As one textbook states, with some underestimation: 'occupants do not commonly govern in accordance with the division and allocation of the competence established by the constitution of the occupied country'.[42] Its authors add, however, that even if one accepts the suspension of the constitution of the occupied country 'in respect of the occupant's relationship with inhabitants, there seems little necessity to assume that even among the inhabitants *inter se*, the Constitution should in its entirety be held suspended in its applicability'.[43]

There is indeed no such necessity inherent in the fact of military occupation. There are, however, two contingent considerations that have disposed occupiers to engage in regime transformation and the imposition of constitutions. Firstly, military occupiers have acted on the assumption that the internal structure of states matters. They have not accepted the claims of the dominant element of contemporary neo-realism according to which only the distribution of capabilities within the international structure is decisive.[44] That was true both of the French revolutionaries and Napoleon, as well as their opponents. Secondly, by virtue of the impact of occupation and the release of contending forces amongst the inhabitants of occupied territory, the occupier has often become a participant in a constitutional struggle, whether willingly or not. The more virulent that struggle, the less plausible is the restrictive injunction of Article 43 of the Hague Regulations. Where both factors are involved, commitment to regime transformation becomes the precondition of the end of occupation for both the occupiers and the occupied. The invocation of ideas of sovereign dictatorship here errs not in the exaggeration of the degree of transformation but in the presumption that the nature of the new regime is solely at the disposition of the occupier. Frequently, avoidance of regime change is not an available choice. To condemn this in the name of self-determination is at the same time to condemn the inhabitants of occupied territory to the perpetuation of occupation, to an internecine struggle in the event of rapid withdrawal or to the prospect of re-occupation. Occupiers, of course, have themselves contributed to such outcomes, frustrating regime change, especially but not only where they have been guided by the desire to exploit occupied territory for their own strategic or commercial interest; though to condemn any and all such interests serves only to encourage occupiers to attempt to conceal them.

All of these factors and considerations were present during the

Russian occupation of Bulgaria and Eastern Rumelia in 1878 to 1879. The Russian occupation was constrained by the restriction of the period of occupation to nine months at the Congress of Berlin in place of the two-year occupation agreed under the earlier Treaty of San Stefano.[45] Russian urgency in promoting the adoption of a constitution was driven by fear that disorder after Russian withdrawal could serve as a pretext for intervention by the Ottoman Empire, which had been ousted during the Russo-Turkish war of 1877–8. Yet, although Russia put forward a proposed constitution it exercised some restraint during the deliberations of the Bulgarian constituent assembly, partly because the Russians were themselves divided, as were the Bulgarians, over whether to favour a strong executive or a strong legislature in the new regime. In both Russian and Bulgarian deliberations it was the latter option that predominated. Amongst the Russians the calculation that popular support rather than the dynastic interest of the newly installed monarch of Bulgaria would enhance Russian influence was a significant factor.[46] In Eastern Rumelia an international commission presided over the new regime, with the different nationalities of the commission devising elements of the new system according to their respective traditions. Although the settlement facilitated the withdrawal of Russian occupation forces and the appointment of Russian officers to the Bulgarian army, the constitutional arrangements were unstable in Bulgaria and unworkable in Eastern Rumelia. Moreover, Russian opposition to the union of the two states fostered growing anti-Russian sentiment rather than the popular support for Russian influence that the former occupier had hoped for.[47]

The treatment of Bulgaria under a regime of occupation was regarded as unusual by some publicists. According to Spaight, the Russians 'were quite unable to comply with the Brussels rule which enjoined respect for local laws and institutions, for local laws and institutions there were none'.[48] Yet neither the Russians nor the other European powers showed any great hesitancy about imposing constitutions, arguing instead about whether this should done under Russian auspices, as in Bulgaria, or under the auspices of an international commission, as in Eastern Rumelia.[49] The United States' occupation of Haiti was even less successful and much more protracted, lasting from 1915 until 1934. Here, commercial interests and strategic considerations, notably exaggerated fears of German influence, induced an occupation under the public veil of humanitarian considerations.[50] By the end of the First World War, those strategic considerations had ceased to be a significant factor yet the United States was locked into an occupation from which it believed it could withdraw only at the cost of acknowledging a humiliating defeat by Haitian insurgents.[51] However, suppression of the insurgency did not bring the end of occupation any closer. The imposition of a constitution in 1918, including the removal of the prohibition of foreign ownership of land that had been part of all preceding Haitian constitutions, and the facade of a Haitian government, made no substantial difference. The dilemma from the American perspective was summed up by the High Commissioner General, John Russell, in 1921:

> The absurdity of dual control or of two nations administering the affairs of a country is too obvious to need comment. Two men can ride a horse but one must ride behind. If the United States is to ride behind in its conduct of Haitian Affairs it had better withdraw entirely and let the country revert to a condition of chaos when, after a time, the United States would be forced again to occupy Haiti or permit some foreign nation to do so.[52]

Russell's position, as he himself noted, bore a striking resemblance to that of Lord Cromer in Egypt.[53] Reform in Haiti, however, proved even more difficult than in Egypt. Even when the Americans began to look to the development of Haitian institutions and the economy as a way to facilitate their exit the results were meagre. The racism of many among the occupation forces further alienated an already hostile Haitian elite. Economic development faltered and by the mid 1920s General Russell was resorting to Malthusian predictions of Haiti's economic future.[54] American commentators and politicians despaired of any further benefit, either to the United States or the Haitians, from prolonging the occupation yet further. As one of them put it, if 'we are unable to develop the Haitian's power of self-government sufficiently in twenty-one years of occupation there is little likelihood of our ever being able to do so'.[55] Regime transformation in Haiti had not in fact been a consistent policy but rather emerged in a fitful manner as a way to escape from an occupation undertaken for different reasons. Beyond the client government, the Americans had failed either to find local allies amongst the existing elite or to promote a new elite as a substitute.[56] The failure of reform was encouraged by a view of the Haitians as incorrigibly corrupt and idle, at the same time as the occupation authorities proclaimed their commitment to modernisation.[57]

Dramatic changes to the structure and composition of indigenous elites, and indeed the presumed mentality of much of the population, was a central element of regime transformation in the occupations of Germany and Japan at the end of the Second World War. In Germany the commitment to democratisation and denazification clearly excluded cooperation with sections of the German elite. As Carl Schorske noted at the time, that was reinforced in the British and American zones by the fact that

> occupation policy has been based on the nature of Nazism as a thing of the mind, an evil idea which would have to be rooted out through the elimination of the bearers of the idea and the re-education of the German people as a whole.[58]

This amounted to the assumption of the collective guilt of the German people, which was reflected in the initial policy of non-fraternisation. Even while the military encouraged the selective use of German civil servants it also proclaimed that the 'German civil service, while maintaining the character of a body of trained officials, has now lost its reputation for impartial application of the law and has become an instrument of the Nazi regime'.[59] Even in the Soviet zone, where Marxist accounts of the nature of Nazism naturally predominated, the German communists also operated with a collective guilt thesis, asserting that 'the German people also carry a decisive portion of the guilt and co-responsibility for the war and its results'.[60] Indeed they included their own members amongst the ranks of the guilty.

In the case of Japan, there was also a presumption that Japanese attitudes, deeply rooted in a feudal past, were the source of the problem.[61] That was reinforced by the racial overtones of the war in the Pacific, leading to the acknowledgement to those being prepared to exercise military government that 'under the heat of wartime emotions the Japanese were commonly seen as treacherous, brutal, sadistic, and fanatical "monkey men"'.[62] While this characterisation had to be revised, especially after the decision to rely upon indirect administration of occupied territory, the presumption of widespread complicity, and hence the need for equally wide-ranging re-education, was evident in the instructions to those responsible for conducting a purge in Japan: 'in the absence of evidence . . . to the contrary, you will assume that any persons who have held responsibility since 1937 in industry, finance, commerce and agriculture have been active exponents of militant nationalism and aggression'.[63]

In Japan, as in Germany, this was not just a case of seeking to impose justice upon those who had committed crimes but was seen as part of the process of regime transformation, and indeed as a key element of it. In the Potsdam Declaration of 2 August 1945 the process included not only the destruction of 'the National Socialist Party and its affiliated and supervised organizations' and the 'complete disarmament and demilitarization of Germany' but also the provisions that all organisations 'which serve to keep alive the military tradition in Germany, shall be completely and finally abolished', that 'German education shall be so controlled as completely to eliminate Nazi and militaristic doctrines' and that 'the German economy shall be decentralized for the purpose of eliminating the present excessive concentration of economic power as exemplified in particular by cartels, syndicates, trusts and other monopolistic arrangements'.[64]

Although the Potsdam Declaration relating to Japan was less wide-ranging and specific, in the light of the continuation of the war with Japan, and subsequent documents relating to the occupation of Japan which envisaged the continuation of a Japanese government, the 'US Initial Post Surrender Policy for Japan' of September 1945 required that 'Japan will be completely disarmed and demilitarized' and that 'the influence of militarism will be totally eliminated from her political, economic and social life'. It also sanctioned changes in the Japanese government, 'modifying its feudal and authoritarian tendencies', and favoured 'a program for the dissolution of the large industrial and banking combinations which have exercised control of a great part of Japan's trade and industry'.[65] The classified directive from the Joint Chiefs of Staff, JCS 1380/15, even instructed General MacArthur to 'encourage and show favour to policies which permit a wide distribution of income and ownership of the means of production'.[66]

At the time and subsequently it has been the clash between this extensive commitment to regime transformation and the conservationist principle of Article 43 of the Hague Regulations that has attracted attention, above all in legal commentary. Advocates of subsequent regime transformation have cited the proclamations and practices of the Allied powers as precedent and proof of the obsolescence of the Hague Regulations. Opponents, while typically declining to condemn those proclamations and practices in the context of the Second World War, have denied that they should be construed as a precedent, invoking the explicit reaffirmation of the Hague Regulations in the Geneva Conventions of 1949 and the subsequent Security Council assertion of the relevance of the Hague and Geneva Conventions in the case of the occupation of Iraq.[67]

However, occupation officials and the inhabitants of occupied territory at the time, and commentators subsequently, have been agitated as much, if not more, by the extent of the transformation brought about under military occupation rather than the mere fact of transformation. Often they have condemned not the excess of transformation but its limitations. That was already evident when Carl Schorske added to his observation on the conception of Nazism as a 'thing of the mind':

> This conception of Nazism involves the introduction of no change in the fundamental structure of society. Property relations are unchanged. Administration has been largely entrusted to putatively non-political, middle class technicians. Thus the continuity of the social structure of Imperial, Weimar, and National Socialist Germany is maintained in the Western zones.[68]

In retrospect, the blanket assertion of the continuity of social structure is implausible. Yet the suggestion that an occupier openly committed to radical change could be in some respects an agent reinforcing continuity, could falter in its determination to effect change, or could find itself in opposition to elements of the indigenous population desirous of more radical change, is less easy to dismiss. Even in the Soviet zone of occupation in Germany, the convoluted course of Joseph Stalin could leave German communists frustrated at Soviet restraint on their radical ambitions. It was this frustration that led Walter Ulbricht to protest in April 1948 that the Soviet Union would have to make up its mind about what it wanted, adding, 'If we establish a dictatorship of the proletariat everything will be clear and simple . . . But then we cannot be asked to play at democracy and conduct parliamentary elections'.[69] Earlier, Germans in the Soviet zone had protested against lack of Soviet support for denazification, only for the Soviet Military Administration to subsequently blame the Germans for lack of vigour in implementing Soviet denazification directives.[70]

Whereas the Soviet Union could publicly gloss over the problems they encountered in denazification and proclaim the process to have been successfully completed in March 1948, doubts about denazification in the West could not be suppressed. As in other cases, the limitations often appeared to be at least as, if not more, striking, to contemporaries than to subsequent commentators. While noting that denazification was being criticised either because it was presumed to have been ineffective or because it was presumed to have been too extreme, John Herz left little doubt of his assessment under the title 'The fiasco of denazification in Germany' in 1948:[71]

> Nothing could be more revealing than the strange modification of meaning that the term 'denazification' itself has undergone. While at first signifying the elimination of Nazis from public life, it has now in German everyday language come to mean the removal of the Nazi stigma from the individual concerned.[72]

The implementation of the purges in Japan proceeded by category, including certain military ranks and party leaders and members, extending to members of the Japanese Cabinets. An 'education' purge followed in May 1946 and then a less rigorous economic purge.[73] Ironically, the same machinery used to implement these purges was deployed in order to implement the 'red' purge of 1949, which targeted communists or those presumed to be sympathetic to them, or simply those too critical of the occupation regime or of Japanese business management.[74] The 'red' purge formed a major element in what came to be seen as the 'reverse course' and a betrayal of the initial occupation objective of democratisation. Much here depends upon how radical the initial ambition is presumed to have been.[75] It is also true that the initial wave of purges in the earlier history of the occupation facilitated significant transformation in sections of the Japanese elites; in, for example, the leadership of conservative parties.[76] The impact on the Japanese civil service, however, was notably less marked. This was partly because the weakening of its traditional competitor, the military elite, automatically benefited it and partly because the occupation authorities approached reform of the civil service in the spirit of apolitical bureaucratic reform.[77]

As Schorske had noted, the lure of the 'putatively non-political, middle class technicians' was prominent in Germany too. Indeed, both British and American occupation officials attempted to promote apolitical administration and to separate it from political processes where this made no sense in terms of German traditions or in terms of German understanding of the obstacles to democracy in their own history. The British attempted to promote apolitical local government;[78] both the British and Americans tried to insist upon rigid separation between civil service and political parties.[79] The same motive lay behind American opposition to any measure of corporatism on the assumption that this would constitute a threat to democracy and on the assumption that economic structures were inherently apolitical; Germans understood them to be inherently political and saw the threat to democracy in their lack of regulation.[80] In none of these cases were the occupiers successful.

There were significant constraints upon the process of regime transformation in Germany and Japan. However, they did not come from any inhibition about exceeding the remit of Article 43 of the Hague Regulations. They came from the limited resources military government could deploy and above all from the contradictory pressures and forces that their own victory released. They could choose, in varying degrees, which to seek to crush and which to favour. They could promote greater or lesser radical reform, though with limited ability to estimate the efficacy of such reform. They could not, and had no inclination to, conserve the existing order in the sense implied by Article 43.

This was also true of the occupations of East Timor, Bosnia, Kosovo and Iraq. In the case of the first three, secession from the territory of the former power was more or less inevitable, despite the hesitancy to openly acknowledge this at the outset in the case of Kosovo. The imposition of a constitution, at least in a sense of using the authority of the occupier to sanction a constitution, was effectively unavoidable. Nor did the basic presumption that such constitutions should be democratic, envisaging the legitimation of power through elections, meet with substantial opposition from the inhabitants of the occupied territories. That was true also in Iraq. Indeed, challenges to the occupier's authority were launched in the name of such legitimacy. As Noah Feldman noted, the Ayatollah Ali-Sistani's fatwa in 2003, opposing the constituent assembly planned by the Coalition Provisional Authority, was based on 'pure democratic theory, with nary a reference to Islamic legal texts'.[81] Even leaving aside the tension between the principle of democratic legitimacy and constituent bodies of dubious democratic legitimacy imposed by the occupier, conflict between indigenous bodies and the occupier is more likely to arise over other aspects of the transformation process. That was already evident in the occupation of Japan. There the Americans had been prompted to engage in their most dramatic action, the drafting of a constitution by the occupation authorities, precisely because the initial Japanese proposals were based on the understanding of

> liberalizing political changes as essentially a function of increased power for the legislature. This inevitably led to an almost complete neglect of other forms of liberalizing change highly prized, by Americans in particular, to wit the constitutional protection of civil and human rights and the role of the judiciary as a means of assuring these.[82]

Ironically, non-governmental organisations and other groups have an even greater prospect of promoting such principles – even at the expense of the democratically expressed preferences of the occupied – in forms of occupation with more pronounced involvement of the United Nations than where a power such as the United States predominates, as in the case of Iraq.[83]

Thus, regime transformation has readily become more than imposed constitutionalism in a narrow sense, turning into a form of explicit cultural transformation reaching into such matters as the educational system and family law.[84] It was, of course, precisely such institutions and practices that the Hague Regulations presumed to be viable and functioning parts of an occupied community, requiring only protection from arbitrary or self-interested intervention by military occupiers and preservation through the authority that the occupier alone possessed. That may indeed be so, as General Scott rightly held in the case of the Catholic religion in occupied Mexico. It may also be the case that such institutions or practices have become the foci of conflict amongst the inhabitants of occupied territory. Here the occupier is an implicit party to the conflict even where it would prefer not to be. As critics of the occupation of Kosovo wrote:

> The international community – and UNMIK in particular – did not have as a priority the question of culture . . . it sidelined as irrelevant an issue of enormous sensitivity in the context of a conflict in which the symbols of cultural identity were often more powerful than weapons.[85]

Inactivity merely helped to determine how the conflict was conducted.

Under the dislocation brought about by military occupation – especially if preceded or accompanied by internal strife amongst the inhabitants, destruction of the machinery of state by the occupier or predatory policies of former authorities or occupiers – much the same may be said of the distribution of wealth and the structure of the economic system that generates it. Even where this is not the case, occupiers have sought to break up concentrations of economic power and redistribute resources. In Japan that meant the break up of the economic combines, the *Zaibatsu* companies, and the redistribution of farm land. Both were construed not just as economic measures but as significant contributions to the process of democratisation. That practice even found its echo in a redrafted article of the American manual on land warfare: 'an occupant is authorized to expropriate either public or private property solely for the benefit of the local population'.[86] Where, for example, there is systematic uncertainty over title to property, as in Kosovo or East Timor, the presumption behind the Hague Regulations is unfounded.[87] There, too, the occupier becomes an actor in the struggle for resources.

Especially in terms of economic resources and title to land, the prime motive of occupiers has sometimes been the exploitation of such resources for the prosecution of a war, as it frequently was in the case of revolutionary and Napoleonic France and in the world wars of the twentieth century.[88] It was precisely this that the Hague Regulations sought to restrain. Occupiers have also sought to restructure economic laws and relationships, including title to land, in part at least for their longer term security or economic benefit: as the United States did in Haiti through constitutional revision, or in Iraq through CPA Order 39, eliminating obstacles to foreign investment in most cases, or as Israel did in its policy of establishing settlements in the West Bank and Gaza.[89] Such policies may be intended to facilitate an end of occupation, even if they fail to have the envisaged effects, as they did in Haiti. They may also be an expression of an inability to end an occupation that threatens to tip over into a revival of a policy of conquest. That remains the risk in occupied Palestinian territory where the 'settlements also represented a return to ethnic conflict over the whole land'.[90]

This final dilemma may provide the best guide to the issue of regime transformation. Setting imposed constitutionalism against the principle of self-determination presumes that 'among the inhabitants *inter se*' not only that some constitutional order persists but that sufficient constitutional order persists to permit an end of occupation. The Hague Regulations presumed that this would normally be compatible with respect for existing laws. Even at the time of the Hague Regulations, however, it was recognised that this would not always be the case. Where the constitutional order has been so disrupted, either by the actions of the occupier or by virtue of internal strife, that it can no longer function as it previously did, then the occupier has become a participant in the determination of a new constitutional order, and indeed a privileged participant by virtue of the authority and force at its disposal. The assertion of the principle of self-determination against participation of the occupier in this process presumes the existence of a constitutional order that has to be recreated for the principle of self-determination to be meaningful. Regime transformation may be the only alternative to the perpetuation of occupation, conquest or descent into anarchy. Occupiers, of course, may prefer those alternatives.

Notes

1. See Gregory H. Fox, *Humanitarian Occupation* (Cambridge: Cambridge University Press, 2008), p. 249.
2. Andrea Carcano, 'End of the occupation in 2004? The status of the multinational force in Iraq after the transfer of sovereignty to the interim Iraqi government', *Journal of Conflict and Security Law*, 11 (2006), p. 54.
3. For an early assertion of the transition, see Carl Schmitt [1941], 'Staat als ein konketer, an eine geschichtliche Epoche gebundener Begriff', in Carl Schmitt, *Verfassungsrechtliche Aufsätze* (Berlin: Duncker & Humblot, 1958), pp. 375–85.
4. See Chapter 2 of this text for an objection to the analogy.
5. Nehal Bhuta, 'The antinomies of transformative occupation', *European Journal of International Law*, 16 (2005), p. 737.
6. Jean L. Cohen, 'The role of international law in post-conflict constitution making', *New York Law School Law Review*, 51 (2006/07), p. 517.
7. Carl Schmitt, *Glossarium. Aufzeichnungen der Jahre 1947–1951* (Berlin: Duncker & Humblot, 1991), p. 269.
8. W. Michael Reisman, 'Why regime change is (almost always) a bad idea', *American Journal of International Law*, 98 (2004), pp. 516–25.
9. Ibid. pp. 521–4.
10. John Yoo, 'Iraq reconstruction and the law of occupation', *University College Davis Journal of International Law and Policy*, 11 (2004), pp. 7–21. Strictly, Kofi Annan's statement invoked by Reisman concerned the legitimacy of intervention rather than the legitimacy of regime change, 'Why regime change is (almost always) a bad idea', p. 521.
11. Yoo, 'Iraq reconstruction and the law of occupation', pp. 14–16.
12. Ibid. p. 16.
13. Ibid. pp. 17–22.
14. Fox, *Humanitarian Occupation*, p. 240.
15. Michael Walzer, *Arguing about War* (New Haven, CT: Yale University Press, 2004), p. 163.
16. Ibid. pp 18–22. For a survey identifying Michael Schmuck as the first to use the term, in 1994, see Richard P. DiMeglio, 'The evolution of the just war tradition: defining jus post bellum', *Military Law Review*, 186 (2005), pp. 116–63.
17. Louis V. Iasiello, '*Jus post bellum*: the moral responsibility of victors in war', *Naval War College Review*, 57, 3/4 (2004), p. 51.
18. The category of *jus post bellum* is also wider in that it deals with situations that do not necessarily involve any kind of occupations. Some caution about its potential elasticity is expressed by one of it main proponents, Brian Orend, 'Justice after war', *Ethics and International Affairs*, 16, 2 (2002), pp. 54–5.

19. Walzer, *Arguing about War*, p. 20.
20. Cohen, 'The role of international law in post-conflict constitution making', p. 525.
21. Quoted in David M. Edelstein, *Occupational Hazards. Success and Failure in Military Occupation* (Ithaca, NY: Cornell University Press, 2008), p. 111.
22. Quoted in Hannah Arendt, *The Origins of Totalitarianism* (London: George Allen & Unwin, 1967), p. 213.
23. Quoted in Malcolm McIlwraith, 'The declaration of a protectorate in Egypt and its legal effects', *Journal of the Society of Comparative Legislation*, 17 (1917), p. 239.
24. Fox, *Humanitarian Occupation*, p. 251; Cohen, 'The role of international law in post-conflict constitution making', p. 500.
25. Adam Roberts, 'Transformative military occupation', *American Journal of International Law*, 100 (2006), p. 583.
26. Eyal Benvenisti, *The International Law of Occupation* (Princeton, NJ: Princeton University Press, 2004), pp. 153–9.
27. Roberts, 'Transformative military occupation', p. 584. See also Benvenisti, *The International Law of Occupation*, pp. 150–3; Tanisha M. Fazal, *State Death* (Princeton, NJ: Princeton University Press, 2007), pp. 20–3, 213–28.
28. Harold Nicolson quoted in Arendt, *The Origins of Totalitarianism*, pp. 126–7.
29. On the impact of the changing nature of warfare, see David A. Bell, *The First Total War. Napoleon's Europe and the Birth of Modern Warfare* (London: Bloomsbury, 2007).
30. Ibid. p. 242. It could be argued that when peace treaties have sanctioned these annexations these territories fall outside the remit of military occupation. There is, however, a case for including them based on the perceived provisional character of the Napoleonic settlements. The fact that in 1813 Napoleon plainly distrusted the new 'Frenchmen' points in the same direction. See Michael Rowe, *From Reich to State. The Rhineland in the Revolutionary Age, 1780–1830* (Cambridge: Cambridge University Press, 2003), p. 219.
31. See Michael Broers, 'Centre and periphery in Napoleonic Italy', in Michael Ropew (ed.), *Collaboration and Resistance in Napoleonic Europe* (Houndmills: Palgrave Macmillan, 2003), pp. 55–73.
32. Quoted in Stuart Woolf, *Napoleon's Integration of Europe* (London: Routledge, 1991), p. 119.
33. Michael Broers, *Europe under Napoleon 1799–1815* (London: Arnold, 1996), pp. 112–13.
34. Rowe, *From Reich to State*, p. 194.
35. Alan Gerson, 'War, conquered territory, and military occupation in the contemporary legal system', *Harvard International Law Journal*, 18

(1977), p. 537. For a more recent illustration, see 'Iraq's new business class fears US exit', *Financial Times* (5 June 2008).

36. Rowe, *From Reich to State*, p. 115.

37. Ibid. pp. 225–30.

38. John Harrison, 'The lawfulness of the Reconstruction Acts', *University of Chicago Law Review*, 68 (2001), p. 407.

39. Eric Foner, *A Short History of Reconstruction 1863–1877* (New York, NY: Harper & Row, 1990), pp. 25–7. 32.

40. For an assessment, see ibid. pp. 55–81.

41. William E. Birkhimer, *Military Government and Martial Law* (Kansas City, KS: Hudson, 1914), p. 368.

42. Myres S. McDougal and Florentino P. Feliciano, *The International Law of War* (New Haven, CT: New Haven Press, 1994), p. 767.

43. Ibid. p. 758.

44. They have adopted the 'second image' not the 'third image' of international relations. For the classic statement of these images, see Kenneth N. Waltz, *Man, the State and War* (New York, NY: Columbia University Press, 1959).

45. On the negotiations, see B. H. Sumner, *Russia and the Balkans 1870–1880* (Oxford: Clarendon Press, 1937), pp. 525–6.

46. Charles and Barbara Jelavich, *The Establishment of the Balkan National States*, 1804–1920 (Seattle, WA: University of Washington Press, 1977), pp. 159–60.

47. Ibid. pp. 162–5.

48. J. M. Spaight, *War Rights on Land* (London: Macmillan, 1911), p. 357.

49. Sumner, *Russia and the Balkans*, pp. 525–7.

50. Hans Schmidt, *The United States Occupation of Haiti 1915–1934* (New Brunswick, NJ: Rutgers University Press, 1995), pp. 42–67.

51. Ibid. pp. 108–9.

52. Ibid. p. 124.

53. Ibid. p. 126.

54. Ibid. p. 177.

55. Paul H. Douglas, 'The American occupation of Haiti II', *Political Science Quarterly*, 42 (1927), p. 394.

56. The problem of limited opportunities for the formation of new elites under prolonged occupation is also noted by Robert L. Tignor, *Modernization and British Colonial Rule in Egypt, 1881–1914* (Princeton, NJ: Princeton University Press, 1966), p. 384.

57. Again, there is a significant analogy with Egypt; see Roger Owen, *Lord Cromer. Victorian Imperialist, Edwardian Proconsul* (Oxford: Oxford University Press, 2004), p. 395.

58. Carl E. Schorske, 'The dilemma in Germany', *Virginia Quarterly Review*, 24 (1948), p. 30.

59. Quoted in Rebecca Boehling, *A Question of Priorities. Democratic Reform and Economic Recovery in Postwar Germany* (New York, NY: Berghahn, 1996), p. 50.

60. Quoted in Timothy R. Vogt, *Denazification in Soviet-Occupied Germany* (Cambridge, MA: Harvard University Press, 2000), p. 35.

61. This ran alongside a different interpretation according to which the years 1932 to 1945 constituted an aberration in Japan's political development. For an assertion of the importance of the aberration thesis, see Robert E. Ward, 'Conclusion', in Robert E. Ward and Sakamoto Yoshikazu (eds), *Democratizing Japan* (Honolulu, HI: University of Hawaii Press, 1987), p. 424.

62. Quoted in John Dower, *Embracing Defeat* (London: Penguin, 1999), p. 214.

63. Quoted in Theodore Cohen, *Remaking Japan. The American Occupation as New Deal* (New York, NY: The Free Press, 1987), p. 157.

64. Quoted in Hajo Holborn, *American Military Government: Its Organization and Policies* (Washington, DC: Infantry Journal Press, 1947), pp. 197–9.

65. Ibid. pp. 210–11, 213.

66. Quoted in Cohen, *Remaking Japan*, p. 12. According to Cohen officers within the occupation administration 'quoted the relevant fragment of JCS 1380/15 like scripture'; ibid. p. 11.

67. See Fox, *Humanitarian Occupation*, pp. 255–9; Gregory H. Fox, 'The occupation of Iraq', *Georgetown Journal of International Law*, 36 (2005), pp. 289–94.

68. Schorske, 'The dilemma in Germany', p. 30. See also the pessimistic observation of Franz Neumann: 'it is becoming increasingly evident that our occupation is likely to fail in its objectives. It will not achieve de-militarization; it has failed in the destruction of Nazism; and it is doubtful that a viable democracy can arise from the conditions prepared between 1945 and 1946'; 'Military government and the revival of democracy', *Columbia Journal of International Affairs*, 2 (1948), p. 4.

69. Quoted in Jochen Laufer, 'Die Verfassungsgebung in der SBZ 1946-1949', *Aus Politik und Zeitgeschichte*, 32–3 (1998), p. 39. Stalin's reservations were evident in his famous remark that 'Communism fits Germany like a saddle fits a cow'; quoted in Anne McElvoy, *The Saddled Cow. East Germany's Life and Legacy* (London: Faber, 1992), p. 2.

70. Vogt, *Denazification in Soviet-Occupied Germany*, pp. 40, 84. See also his claims that Soviet denazification was a 'failed experiment' that showed similarity to the process in the western zones and that it was not part of a coherent programme of Stalinization; pp. 2–9.

71. John H. Herz, 'The fiasco of denazification in Germany', *Political Science Quarterly*, 63 (1948), pp. 569–94. See also a senior official in the denazification programme, Joseph F. Napoli, 'Denazification from an American's viewpoint', *Annals of the American Academy of Political and Social Science*, 264 (1949), pp. 115–23.

72. Herz, 'The fiasco of denazification in Germany', p. 590.

73. Takemae Eiji, *The Allied Occupation of Japan* (New York, NY: Continuum, 2002), pp. 266–70.

74. Ibid. pp. 480–5.

75. See Justin Williams, *Japan's Political Revolution under MacArthur* (Athens, GA: University of Georgia Press, 1979), p. 214.

76. Uchida Kenzo, 'Japan's postwar conservative parties', in Ward and Yoshikazu (eds), *Democratizing Japan*, pp. 326–7, 333.

77. On the latter, see T. J. Pempel, 'The tar baby target: "reform" of the Japanese bureaucracy', in Ward and Yoshikazu (eds), *Democratizing Japan*, pp. 157–87.

78. Barbara Marshall, 'British democratization policy in German', in Ian D. Turner, *Reconstruction in Post-War Germany* (Oxford: Berg, 1989), pp. 197–8.

79. Ibid. pp. 205–8; Boehling, *A Question of Priorities*, pp. 246–7.

80. Diethelm Prowe, 'Economic democracy in post-World War II Germany', *Journal of Modern History*, 57 (1985), pp. 479–80.

81. Noah Feldman, *What We Owe Iraq* (Princeton, NJ: Princeton University Press, 2004), p. 40.

82. Ward, 'Conclusion', p. 422. For striking testimony that drafting a constitution had not been their original intention, see Williams, *Japan's Political Revolution under MacArthur*, pp. 102–3.

83. Noah Feldman, 'Imposed constitutionalism', *Connecticut Law Review*, 37 (2005), pp. 860–3, 867–9.

84. In the case of Japan, see, for example, Toshio Nishi, *Unconditional Democracy. Education and Politics in Occupied Japan 1945–1952* (Stanford, CA: Hoover Institution Press, 1982); Kurt Steiner, 'The occupation and the reform of the Japanese civil code', in Ward and Yoshikazu (eds), *Democratizing Japan*, pp. 188–220.

85. Ian King and Whit Mason, *Peace at Any Price* (Ithaca, NY: Cornell University Press, 2006), p. 80.

86. Quoted in Nisuke Ando, *Surrender, Occupation, and Private Property in International Law* (Oxford: Clarendon Press, 1991), pp. 106–7.

87. For the uncertainty, see Richard Caplan, *International Governance of War-Torn Territory* (Oxford: Oxford University Press, 2005), pp. 149–50.

88. On the latter, see Peter Liberman, *Does Conquest Pay? The Exploitation of Occupied Industrial Societies* (Princeton, NJ: Princeton University Press, 1996).

89. For an interesting attempt to defend this CPA Order 39, see Robert D. Tadlock, 'Occupation law and foreign investment in Iraq', *University of San Francisco Law Review*, 39 (2004), pp. 227–60. For Israeli settlements, see Gershom Gorenberg, *Occupied Territories. The Untold Story of Israel's Settlements* (London: Tauris, 2006).
90. Ibid. p. 360.

Conclusion

Historically military occupation is of relatively recent origin. The brute facts which create it are clearly not. The use of force, or threat thereof, to establish the presence of the armed forces of one state or community in the territory of another is coterminous with recorded history, but this is not what constitutes or defines military occupation. The stark contrast between the assumption of the immediate displacement of sovereignty by virtue of the possession of territory, the policy of conquest, and that of military occupation, as drawn by nineteenth century commentators, may be overdrawn. Nevertheless, despite the uncertainties about title of territory, sovereignty and mere conquest before the French Revolution, faintly reflected in passing comments by international lawyers, it is true that a distinct concept of military occupation, as articulated in memoirs, commentaries, court judgments, military codes and international treaties, only emerged in the nineteenth century.[1]

This conceptual refinement culminated in the Hague Regulations of 1907, especially in the brief Article 43 that has exerted great influence upon subsequent debate about military occupation. The definition of military occupation as occurring under the condition of the 'authority of the legitimate power having in fact passed into the hands of the occupant' is both a perceptive summary of the incipient understanding of military occupation before the Hague Regulations and remains a normative limit upon the claims of the occupier. The injunction that the occupier 'shall take all the measures in his power to restore and ensure, as far as possible, public order and civil life' similarly remains the prime obligation of occupiers, alongside the obligation of occupiers to ensure the security of their own forces, though here some qualification is necessary. Article 43 presumed that public order and civil life were more or less adequately reflected in the 'laws in force in the country'. Whether or not laws adequate in principle to public order and civil life exist and whether or not they can be said to have been 'in force' is both a normative and empirical question. It would be difficult, indeed impossible, to find any serious contemporary commentator who would contest the Lieber Code's rejection of the institution of slavery or Allied rejection of National Socialist anti-Semitic legislation. Beyond that limited consensus dissension reigns, with many clinging to a restrictive reading of the conservation principle. Indeed, some commentators look to ever tighter and more refined codes in order to condemn what are, in the light of such codes, the excesses and caprice of the occupier. The historical record suggests, however, that Eyal Benvenisti was right to decline the attempt to 'formulate a code of conduct for the scrupulous occupant, or any other set of strict definitions and minutely drafted rules' on the grounds that 'codes and strict definition would fail to accommodate the contingencies that occupants face during their rule, as much as they would fail to instruct any other government'.[2]

Important though the debate over the conservation principle is, not least because of the problems of ending military occupation once occupiers have embarked upon a policy of regime transformation, it has tended to dominate discussion to the exclusion of more fundamental issues, namely the nature of military occupation as a political phenomenon and a form of government. Military occupiers have been consistently inadequately prepared for military government, even on those occasions where they have recognised the problem in advance and made great efforts to prepare for it, such as the Allied occupations of Germany and Japan at the end of the Second World War. The subsequent denial or evasion of the fact that military occupiers are engaged in the business of occupation has merely compounded this problem. As in any other form of government, the structure of military government and how it interacts with the society over which it presides matters. Occasionally, this has received some recognition, as in the consideration of the relative merits of 'operational' and 'territorial' forms of occupation during the Second World War.[3] Too often, however, the structure and organisation of occupation has been a matter of improvisation, at which occupiers have been more or less adept. In almost all cases, occupiers have been surprised by the enormity of the task, frequently perceiving its extent as unprecedented. They have been constrained by a shortage of resources and often by the poor quality of personnel available for the task of government. They have suffered from internal fragmentation, especially but not solely where civilian governors have also been involved. This has been true regardless of whether their intent and purpose has been manifestly vicious and perverse or arguably decent.

The structure of military government also matters because it can be used to flatten indigenous institutions, to substantially undermine the very potential of the society subject to occupation to exist as a political entity. It can become part of a scenario which is worse than Hobbes' war of all against all, for in Hobbes' state of nature each man has only to fear each other man as his potential murderer. Military occupation can generate not only that fear but also the fear of organised, armed and predatory groups, namely the occupation forces, and sometimes those who act in the name of resistance to them.

Although it is often the vicious practices of occupiers that attract attention, and lead to calls for codes and agreements in the hope of constraining occupiers, seeing military occupation as a political phenomenon also helps to recognise the importance of the understanding of occupation by those subject to it. This was, in fact, well understood by the men who drew up the codes and agreements leading up to the Hague Regulations. Failure to recognise the circumstance of the 'authority of the legitimate power having in fact passed into the hands of the occupant' could have disastrous consequences for the inhabitants. The bare fact is important but still leaves scope for disagreement over both substantive and symbolic issues about what an occupying force might legitimately do and what it might not legitimately do. That is evident, for example, in Japanese acquiescence in the American imposition of a constitution after the Second World War but their successful resistance to American efforts to determine the leadership of the Liberal Party in 1948.[4] There was surprise and even alarm in many quarters about the nature of the American draft but in the context of that occupation no serious resistance to the fact that constitutional change was necessary.

The bare fact of the authority of the occupier presents one highly contentious problem, namely the corresponding obligation of the inhabitants to obey the occupier. Both the necessity of the obligation and the problems it presented were clear to the men who drew up the nineteenth-century codes. They, however, despite their reservations, were in no doubt that occupiers would assume such an obligation. Occupiers still do, though less explicitly and less confidently. Swayed by the conviction of their lack of legitimacy they have become less confidant of their authority: when circumstances and the remit of their mandates prompt them to intervene, they do so with a vigour at least equal to that of their predecessors in some respects, only to hesitate and evade responsibility in others. Doubt about the extent of the occupier's authority is coterminous with the history of the concept of military occupation. It is nevertheless true that understanding the exercise of authority without legitimate power has become more difficult, as has understanding the nature of military occupation at all.

Understanding military occupation, both by those who merely observe the phenomenon and for those engaged in it or subject to it, is made difficult by the disinclination, if not outright refusal, to recognise some of its other consequences. Military occupation pushes sovereignty to the point at which its existence and meaning are precarious. All that is left is a hollow shell whose significance lies in a negative fact: the occupier is not sovereign. The desperation to deny this lies behind the frenetic efforts of ousted elites to demonstrate the efficacy of their legitimacy, and behind calls for the occupier to return sovereignty to the people, as if it were something in the occupier's possession. The precariousness of justice may be less dire but one presumption of justice, namely subordination to a common rule, is inevitably broken. Justice is in some degree always the victor's justice; but this need not amount to saying that it is no justice at all. Indeed, there are circumstances where the victor's justice is the only alternative to no justice.

It is precisely these difficulties and dilemmas, as well as the recurrence of the savagery captured by Francisco de Goya, that lie behind Paul Bremer's characterisation of occupation as an 'ugly word, not one that Americans feel comfortable with'.[5] Even without the recurrence of savagery, the presumption is that military occupation, and especially military government, is inherently dishonourable or a reversion to archaic practices and principles. The danger of that presumption is that it leads to the evasion of even the label of military occupation, the evasion of the responsibilities of military occupation, including the assumption of authority, and a failure to prepare for those responsibilities. When Bremer described occupation as an 'ugly word' he added 'but it is a fact';[6] it became a fact of international political life as an alternative to what was seen as conquest and annexation. Despite the attempts to evade the label or the consequences of military occupation, both practical and theoretical, short of a return to the alternative of conquest and annexation, it will continue to be a recurrent fact.

Notes

1. For an early expression of the provisional conditions established under military occupation, see Emer de Vattel [1758]: 'Immovable possessions, lands, towns, provinces &c. become the property of the enemy who

makes himself master of them: but it is only the by the treaty of peace, or the entire submission and extinction of the state to which those towns and provinces belonged, that the acquisition is completed, and property becomes stable and perfect'. *The Law of Nations* (Indianapolis, IN: Liberty Fund, 2008), p. 596.
2. Eyal Benvenisti, *The International Law of Occupation* (Princeton, NJ: Princeton University Press, 2004), p. 216.
3. War Department, *Military Government and Civil Affairs*, FM 27-5 (22 December 1943), p. 24.
4. Ray A. Moore, 'Reflections on the occupation of Japan', *Journal of Asian Studies*, 38 (1979), pp. 727–8.
5. Quoted in Ivo H. Daalder and James M. Lindsay, *America Unbound* (Washington, DC: Brookings Institution Press, 2003), p. 154.
6. Ibid. p. 154.

Select Bibliography

Allen, Henry T., *My Rhineland Journal* (Boston, MA: Houghton and Mifflin, 1923).

Ando, Nisuke, *Surrender, Occupation and Private Property in International Law* (Oxford: Clarendon Press, 1991).

Arendt, Hannah, *The Origins of Totalitarianism* (London: George Allen & Unwin, 1967).

Arendt, Hannah, *Eichmann in Jerusalem* (Harmondsworth: Penguin, 1975).

Arendt, Hannah, 'What is authority?' in Hannah Arendt, *Between Past and Future* (Harmondsworth: Penguin, 1977), pp. 91–141.

Ariga, Nagao, *La Guerre Russo-Japonaise* (Paris: Pedone, 1908).

Bâli, Asli Ü., 'Justice under occupation: rule of law and the ethics of nation building in Iraq', *Yale Journal of International Law*, 30 (2005), pp. 431–72.

Bass, Gary Jonathon, *Stay the Hand of Justice. The Politics of War Crimes Trials* (Princeton, NJ: Princeton University Press, 2000).

Bassiouni, M. Cherif, 'Post-conflict justice in Iraq', *Cornell International Law Journal*, 38 (2005), pp. 327–90.

Baty, Thomas, 'The relations of invaders to insurgents', *Yale Law Journal*, 36 (1927), pp. 966–84.

Baxter, R. R., 'The duty of obedience to the belligerent occupant', *British Yearbook of International Law*, 27 (1950), pp. 235–66.

Beauvais, Joel C. 'Benevolent despotism', *New York University Journal of International Law and Politics*, 33 (2001), pp. 1101–78.

Bekker, Pieter H. F., 'The World Court's ruling regarding the West Bank barrier and the primacy of international law', *Cornell International Law Journal*, 38 (2005), pp. 553–68.

Bell, David A., *The First Total War. Napoleon's Europe and the Birth of Modern Warfare* (London: Bloomsbury, 2007).

Ben-Naftali, Orna, A. M. Gross and K. Michaeli, 'Illegal occupation: framing the occupied Palestinian territory', *Berkeley Journal of International Law*, 23 (2005), pp. 551–614.

Benda, Harry J., J. K. Irikura and K. Kishi (eds), *Japanese Military Administration in Indonesia: Selected Documents* (New Haven, CT: Yale University, 1965).

Bentwich, Norman, *England in Palestine* (London: Kegan Paul, 1932).

Benvenisti, Eyal (2004), *The International Law of Occupation* (Princeton, NJ: Princeton University Press, 2004).

Best, Werner, 'Grundfragen einer deutschen Grossraum-Verwaltung', in *Festgabe für Heinrich Himmler* (Darmstadt: Wittich, 1941), pp. 33–60.

Bhuta, Nehal, 'The antinomies of transformative occupation', *The European Journal of International Law*, 16 (2005), pp. 721–40.

Birkhimer, William E., *Military Government and Martial Law* (Kansas City, KS: Hudson, 1914).

Bisschop, W. R., 'German war legislation in the occupied territory of Belgium', *Transactions of the Grotius Society*, 4 (1918), pp. 110–68.

Blanning, T. C. W., *The French Revolution in Germany* (Oxford: Oxford University Press, 1983).

Blum, Yehuda Z., 'The missing reversioner: reflections on the status of Judea and Samaria', *Israel Law Review*, 3 (1968), pp. 279–301.

Bluntschli, Johann C., *Das moderne Völkerrecht der civilisirten Staten* (Nördlingen: Beck, 1878).

Boehling, Rebecca, *A Question of Priorities. Democratic Reform and Economic Recovery in Postwar Germany* (New York, NY: Berghahn, 1996).

Bonfils, Henry, *Manuel de Droit International Public* (Paris: Rousseau, 1894).

Boothby, Derek, 'The political challenge of administering Eastern Slavonia', *Global Governance*, 10 (2004), pp. 37–51.

Bordwell, Percy, *The Law of War Between Belligerents* (Chicago, IL: Callaghan, 1908).

Braibanti, Ralph, 'Administration of military government in Japan at the prefectural level', *American Political Science Review*, 43 (1949), pp. 250–74.

Braibanti, Ralph, 'The role of administration in the occupation of Japan', *Annals of the American Academy of Political and Social Science*, 267 (1950), pp. 154–63.

Bremer, L. Paul, *My Year in Iraq* (New York, NY: Threshold, 2006).

Broszat, Martin, *Nationalsozialistische Polenpolitik 1939–1945* (Stuttgart: DVA, 1961).

Bruun, Geoffrey, *Europe and the French Imperium 1799–1814* (New York, NY: Harper & Row, 1938).

Burrin, Philippe, *France under the Germans* (New York, NY: New Press, 1996).

Calvo, Charles, *Le Droit International*, 5 vols (Paris: Guillaumin, 1887–8).

Caplan, Richard, 'International authority and state building: the case of Bosnia and Herzegovina', *Global Governance*, 53 (2004), pp. 53–65.

Caplan, Richard, *International Governance of War-Torn Territories* (Oxford: Oxford University Press, 2005).

Carcano, Andrea, 'End of the occupation in 2004? The status of the multinational force in Iraq after the transfer of sovereignty to the interim Iraqi government', *Journal of Conflict and Security Law*, 11 (2006), pp. 41–66.

Carlton, Eric, *Occupation. The Policies and Practices of Military Conquerors* (London: Routledge, 1992).

Cavaré, L., 'Quelques notions générales sur l'occupation pacifique', *Revue Générale du Droit International Public*, 31 (1924), pp. 339–71.

Chesterman, Simon, *You, the People* (Oxford: Oxford University Press, 2004).

Chopra, Jarat, 'Building state failure in East Timor', *Development and Change*, 33 (2002), pp. 979–1000.

Cicero, Marcus Tulius, *De Re Publica, De Legibus* (London: Heinemann, 1928).

Clarke, F. C. H. (trans.), *The Franco-German War, 1870–71*, part 2, vol. 3 (London: HMSO, 1884).

Clay, Lucius D., *Decision in Germany* (London: Heinemann, 1950).

Cohen, Jean L., 'The role of international law in post-conflict constitution making', *New York Law School Law Review*, 51 (2006/07), pp. 499–532.

Cohen, Theodore, *Remaking Japan. The American Occupation as New Deal* (New York, NY: The Free Press, 1987).

Colby, Elbridge, 'Occupation under the laws of war', *Columbia Law Review*, 25 (1925), pp. 904–22 and 26 (1926), pp. 146–70.

Conner, Jacob Elen, *The Development of Belligerent Occupation* (Iowa City, IA: Iowa University, 1912).

Correspondence Respecting the Brussels Conference on the Rules of Military Warfare (London: House of Commons, 1875).

Cybichowski, Siegmund, 'Die völkerrechtliche Okkupationsrecht', *Zeitschrift für Völkerrecht*, 18 (1934), pp. 295–332.

Daalder, Ivo H. and James M. Lindsay, *America Unbound* (Washington, DC: Brookings Institution Press, 2003).

Dallin, Alexander, *German Rule in Russia 1941–1945* (London: Macmillan, 1981).

de Visscher, Charles, 'L'occupation de guerre', *Law Quarterly Review*, 34 (1918), pp. 72–81.

Dennis, Michael J., 'Application of human rights treaties extraterritorially in times of armed conflict and military occupation', *American Journal of International Law*, 99 (2005), pp. 119–41.

Despagnet, Frantz, *Cours de Droit International Public* (Paris: Larose, 1894).

Diamond, Larry, *Squandered Victory* (New York, NY: Henry Holt, 2005).

Djilas, Milovan, *Conversations with Stalin* (New York, NY: Harcourt, 1962).

DiMeglio, Richard P., 'The evolution of the just war tradition: defining jus post bellum', *Military Law Review*, 186 (2005), pp. 116–63.

Dodge, Toby, *Inventing Iraq* (New York, NY: Columbia University Press, 2003).

Donihi, Robert, 'Occupation justice', *South Texas Law Journal*, 1 (1955), pp. 333–58.

Donnison, F. S. V., *British Military Administration in the Far East 1943–1946* (London, HMSO, 1956).

Donnison, F. S. V., *Civil Affairs and Military Government. North-West Europe 1944–1946* (London: HMSO, 1961).

Donnison, F. S. V., *Civil Affairs and Military Government. Central Organization and Planning* (London: HMSO, 1966).

Dotan, Yoav, 'Judicial rhetoric, government lawyers, and human rights', *Law & Society Review*, 33 (1999), pp. 319–63.

Douglas, Paul H., 'The American occupation of Haiti', *Political Science Quarterly*, 42 (1927), pp. 228–58, 368–96.

Dower, John W., *Embracing Defeat. Japan in the Aftermath of World War II* (London: Penguin, 1999).

Durch, William J. (ed.), *Twenty-First-Century Peace Operations* (Washington, DC: United States Institute of Peace, 2006).

Edelstein, David M., *Occupational Hazards. Success and Failure in Military Occupation* (Ithaca, NY: Cornell University Press, 2008)

Edmonds, James E., *The Occupation of the Rhineland 1918–1920* (London: HMSO, 1987).

Edwards, Henry Sutherland, *The Germans in France* (London: Stanford, 1874).

Fahy, Charles, 'Legal problems of German occupation', *Michigan Law Review*, 47 (1948), pp. 11–22.

Fauchille, Paul, *Traité de Droit International Public*, vol. 2 (Paris: Rousseau, 1921).

Fazal, Tanisha M., *State Death* (Princeton, NJ: Princeton University Press, 2007).

Feilchenfeld, Ernst H., *The International Economic Law of Belligerent Occupation* (Washington, DC: Carnegie, 1942).

Feldman, Noah, *What We Owe Iraq* (Princeton, NJ: Princeton University Press, 2004).

Feldman, Noah, 'Imposed Constitutionalism', *Connecticut Law Review*, 37 (2005), pp. 857–89.

Fiore, Pasquale *Le Droit International Codifié* (Paris: Pedone, 1911).

Fireman, Steve, 'The impossible balance: the goals of human rights and security in the Israeli administered territories', *Capital University Law Review*, 20 (1991), pp. 421–54.

Fischer, Fritz, *Germany's Aims in the First World War* (London: Chatto & Windus, 1967).

235

Fisher, Louis, 'Military commissions: problems of authority and practice', *Boston University International Law Journal*, 24 (2006), pp. 15–53.

Foner, Eric, *A Short History of Reconstruction 1863–1877* (New York, NY: Harper & Row, 1990).

Fox, Gregory H., 'The occupation of Iraq', *Georgetown Journal of International Law*, 36 (2005), pp. 195–297.

Fox, Gregory H., *Humanitarian Occupation* (Cambridge: Cambridge University Press, 2008).

Fraenkel, Ernst, 'Military occupation and the rule of law', in Ernst Fraenkel, *Gesammelte Schriften*, vol. 3 (Baden-Baden: Nomos, 1999), pp. 139–347.

Fraenkel, Ernst, 'Structure of the united army military government in Korea', in Ernst Fraenkel, *Gesammelte Schriften*, vol. 3 (Baden-Baden: Nomos, 1999), pp. 426–39.

Fried, John H. E., 'Transfer of civilian manpower from occupied territory', *American Journal of International Law*, 40 (1946), pp. 303–31.

Friedrich, Klaus-Peter 'Collaboration in a "land without a Quisling"', *Slavic Review*, 64 (2005), pp. 711–46.

Funck-Brentano, T. and Albert Sorel, *Précis de Droit des Gens* (Paris: Plon, 1900).

Gabriel, Ralph H., 'American experience with military government', *American Political Science Review*, 37 (1943), pp. 417–38.

Garner, James Wilford, *International Law and the World War*, vol. 2 (London: Longmans, 1920).

Gerson, Allan 'Trustee-occupant: the legal status of Israel's presence in the West Bank', *Harvard International Law Journal*, 14 (1973), pp. 1–49.

Gerson, Allan, 'War, conquered territory and military occupation in the contemporary international legal system', *Harvard International Law Journal*, 18 (1977), pp. 525–56.

Gimbel, John, *A German Community under American Occupation* (Stanford, CA: Stanford University Press, 1961).

Glazier, David, 'Kangaroo court or competent tribunal?', *Virginia Law Review*, 89 (2003), pp. 2005–93.

Glazier, David, 'Ignorance is not bliss', *Rutgers Law Review*, 58 (2005), pp. 121–94.

Gorenberg, Gershom, *Occupied Territories. The Untold Story of Israel's Settlements* (London: Tauris, 2006).

Graber, Doris Apel, *The Development of the Law of Belligerent Occupation 1863–1914* (New York, NY: AMS, 1949).

Gross, Aeyal M., 'Human proportions: are human rights the emperor's new clothes of the international law of occupation?' *European Journal of International Law*, 18 (2007), pp. 1–35.

Gross, Jan Tomasz, *Polish Society under German Occupation* (Princeton, NJ: Princeton University Press, 1979).

Grotius, Hugo, *The Rights of War and Peace*, 3 vols (Indianapolis, IN: Liberty Fund, 2005).

Gurwood, J. (ed.), *The Speeches of the Duke of Wellington in Parliament*, vol. 2 (London: Murray, 1854).

Halchin, Elaine 'The Coalition Provisional Authority (CPA)', CRS Report RL32370 (6 June 2005).

Hall, William Edward, *A Treatise on International Law* (Oxford: Oxford University Press, 1924).

Halleck, H. W., *International Law* (San Francisco, CA: Bancroft, 1861).

Harris, C. R. S., *Allied Military Administration of Italy 1943–1945* (London: HMSO, 1957).

Harrison, John, 'The lawfulness of the Reconstruction Acts', *University of Chicago Law Review*, 68 (2001), pp. 375–462.

Heffter, August Wilhelm, *Das Europäische Völkerrecht der Gegenwart*, ed. Heinz Geffecken (Berlin: Müller, 1888).

Henning, Eric and Glen Rangwala, *Iraq in Fragments* (London: Hurst, 2006).

Herz, John H., 'The fiasco of denazification in Germany', *Political Science Quarterly*, 63 (1948), pp. 569–94.

Herz, John H., *Political Realism and Political Idealism* (Chicago, IL: University of Chicago Press, 1951),

Herz, John H., *International Politics in the Atomic Age* (New York, NY: Columbia University Press, 1959).

Hirschfeld, Gerhard, *Nazi Rule and Dutch Collaboration* (Oxford: Berg, 1988).

Holborn, Hajo, *American Military Government: its Organization and Policies* (Washington, DC: Infantry Journal Press, 1947).

Horton, John, *Political Obligation* (Houndmills: Basingstoke, 1992).

International Commission on Intervention and State Sovereignty, *The Responsibility to Protect. Research, Bibliography, Background* (Ottawa: International Development Research Centre, 2001).

Independent International Commission on Kosovo, *The Kosovo Report* (Oxford: Oxford University Press, 2000).

International Commission on Intervention and State Responsibility, *The Responsibility to Protect* (Ottawa: International Development Research Centre, 2001).

International Crisis Group, 'Kosovo: let's learn from Bosnia', Balkans Report 66 (17 May 1999).

International Crisis Group, 'The new Kosovo protectorate', Balkans Report 69 (20 June 1999).

International Crisis Group, 'Waiting for UNMIK: local administration in Kosovo', Balkans Report 79 (18 October 1999).

International Crisis Group, 'Bosnia: reshaping the international machinery', Balkans Report 121 (29 November 2001).

International Crisis Group, 'Courting disaster: the misrule of law in Bosnia and Herzegovina', Balkans Report 127 (25 March 2003).

International Crisis Group, 'Collapse in Kosovo', Europe Report 155 (22 April 2004).

International Crisis Group, 'Iraq: can local governance save central government', Middle East Report 33 (27 October 2004).

International Crisis Group, 'An army for Kosovo?', Europe Report 174 (28 July 2006).

International Crisis Group, 'Ensuring Bosnia's future', Europe Report 180 (15 February 2007).

International Military Tribunal, *Trial of the Major War Criminals*, vol. 15 (Nuremberg: International Military Tribunal, 1948).

Ireland, Gordon, 'The *jus postliminii* and the coming peace', *Tulane Law Review*, 18 (1944), pp. 584–96.

Jäckel, Eberhard, *Frankreich in Hitlers Europa* (Stuttgart: DVA, 1966).

Jackson, Mike, *Soldier* (London: Bantam, 2007).

Jackson, Robert H., *Quasi-States: Sovereignty, International Relations and the Third World* (Cambridge: Cambridge University Press, 1990).

Jelavich, Charles and Barbara Jelavich, *The Establishment of the Balkan National States, 1804–1920* (Seattle, WA: University of Washington Press, 1977).

Jellinek, Georg, *Allgemeine Staatslehre* (Berlin: Julius Springer, 1929).

Jellinek, Georg, *Die Lehre von den Staatenverbindungen* (Goldbach: Keip, 1996).

Jennings, R. Y., 'Government in commission', *British Yearbook of International Law*, 23 (1946), pp. 112–41.

Jones, David Martin, *Conscience and Allegiance in Seventeenth Century England. The Political Significance of Oaths and Engagements* (Rochester, NY: University of Rochester Press, 1999).

Kelly, Michael J., T. McCormack, P. Muggleton and B. Oswald, 'Legal aspects of Australia's involvement in the International Force for East Timor', *International Review of the Red Cross*, 83, 841 (2001), pp. 101–39.

Kelly, Michael J., 'Critical analysis of the International Court of Justice ruling on Israel's security barrier', *Fordham International Law Journal*, 29 (2005), pp. 181–228.

Kelsen, Hans, 'The international legal status of Germany to be established immediately upon termination of the war', *American Journal of International Law*, 38 (1944), pp. 689–94.

Kelsen, Hans, 'The legal status of Germany according to the Declaration of Berlin', *American Journal of International Law*, 39 (1945), pp. 518–26.

King, Ian and Whit Mason, *Peace at any Price* (Ithaca, NY: Cornell University Press, 2006).

Klüber, Jean Louis, *Droit des Gens Moderne de l'Europe* (Stuttgart: Gotta, 1819).

Koskenniemi, Martti, *The Gentle Civilizer of Nations* (Cambridge: Cambridge University Press, 2002).

Knaus, Gerald and Felix Martin, 'Travails of the European Raj', *Journal of Democracy*, 14 (2003), pp. 60–74.

Krasner, Stephen D., *Sovereignty: Organized Hypocrisy* (Princeton, NJ: Princeton University Press, 1999).

Kratoska, Paul H., *The Japanese Occupation of Malaya* (London: Hurst, 1998).

Kretzmer, David, *The Occupation of Justice* (Albany, NY: State University of New York Press, 2002).

Kunz, Josef L., 'The status of occupied Germany under international law', *Western Political Quarterly*, 3 (1950), pp. 538–65.

Labs, Walter, 'Die Verwaltung des besetzten Ostgebiete', *Reich-Volksordnung-Lebensraum*, 5 (1943), pp. 132–66.

Lameire, Irénée, *Théorie et Practique de la Conquête dans l'Ancien Droit* (Paris: Rousseau, 1902).

Laufer, Jochen, 'Die Verfassungsgebung in der SBZ 1946–1949', *Aus Politik und Zeitgeschichte*, 32–3 (1998), pp. 29–41.

Lawson, Carl and Guy Seidman, *The Constitution of Empire* (New Haven, CT: Yale University Press, 2004).

Lemkin, Raphael, *Axis Rule in Occupied Europe* (Washington, DC: Carnegie, 1944).

Liberman, Peter, *Does Conquest Pay? The Exploitation of Occupied Industrial Societies* (Princeton, NJ: Princeton University Press, 1996).

Liulevicius, Vejas Gabriel, *War Land on the Eastern Front* (Cambridge: Cambridge University Press, 2000).

Locke, John, *Two Treatises of Government* (New York, NY: Mentor, 1965).

Loening, Edgar, 'L'administration du Gouvernement-Générale de l'Alsace', *Revue de Droit International et de Législation Comparée*, 4 (1872), pp. 622–50 and 5 (1873), pp. 69–136.

Loening, Edgar, 'Das Subjekt der Staatsgewalt im besetzten feindlichen Gebiete', *Niemeyers Zeitschrift für internationales Recht*, 28 (1920), pp. 287–305.

Loewenstein, Karl, 'Reconstruction of the administration of justice in American-occupied Germany', *Harvard Law Review*, 61 (1948), pp. 419–67.

Loock, Hans-Dietrich, 'Zur "Grossgermanischen Politik" des Dritten Reiches', *Vierteljahreshefte für Zeitgeschichte*, 8 (1960), pp. 37–63.

Lower, Wendy, *Nazi Empire-Building and the Holocaust in the Ukraine* (Chapel Hill, NC: University of North Carolina Press, 2005).

Macmillan, Margaret, *Peacemakers* (London: John Murray, 2001).

Madajczyk, Czeslaw, 'Die Besatzungssyteme der Achsenmächte', *Studia Historicae Oeconomicae*, 14 (1980), pp. 105–22.

Magoon, Charles E., *Report on the Law of Civil Government in Territory Subject to Military Occupation by the Forces of the United States* (Washington, DC: War Department, 1903).

Mallison, W. Thomas and Sally V. Mallison, *The Palestine Problem* (Harlow: Longman, 1986).

Mann, F. A., 'The present legal status of Germany', *International Law Quarterly*, 1 (1947), pp. 314–35.

Marx, Karl, 'The Civil War in France', in Karl Marx, *The First International and After* (Harmondsworth: Penguin, 1974), pp. 187–268.

Maslowski, Peter, *Treason Must be Made Odious* (Milwood, NY: Kto, 1978).

McDougal, Myres S. and Florentino P. Feliciano, *The International Law of War* (New Haven, CT: New Haven Press, 1994).

McElvoy, Anne, *The Saddled Cow. East Germany's Life and Legacy* (London: Faber, 1992).

McNair, Arnold D., 'Municipal effects of belligerent occupation', *The Law Quarterly Review*, 57 (1941), pp. 33–73.

Meister, Ulrich, 'Stimmen des Auslandes zur Rechtslage Deutschlands', *Zeitschrift für ausländisches öffentliches Recht und Völkerrecht*, 13 (1950), pp. 173–85.

Melling, George, 'The war power and the government of military forces', *Journal of the Institute of Criminal Law and Criminology*, 7 (1916), pp. 248–68.

Mérignhac, A., *Traité de Droit Public International*, vol. 3 (Paris: Libraire Générale de Droit et de Jurisprudence, 1912).

Meurer, Christian, 'Die völkerrechtliche Stellung der vom Feind besetzten Gebiete', *Archiv des öffentlichen Rechts*, 33 (1915), pp. 353–435.

Millet, Allan Reed, *The Politics of Intervention. The Military Occupation of Cuba, 1906–1909* (Columbus, OH: Ohio State University Press, 1968).

Mini, Fabio, 'Liberation and occupation: a commander's perspective', *Israel Yearbook on Human Rights*, 35 (2005), pp. 71–100.

Morgan, J. H., *War Book of the German General Staff* (Mechanicsburg, PA: Stackpole, 2005).

Morphet, Sally, 'Current international civil administration', *International Peacekeeping*, 9 (2002), pp. 140–62.

Nabulsi, Karma, *Traditions of War* (Oxford: Oxford University Press, 1999).

Naimark, Norman M., *The Russians in Germany* (Cambridge, MA: Harvard University Press, 1995).

Nestler, Ludwig (ed.), *Europa unter Hakenkreuz. Die faschistische Okkupationspolitik in Frankreich (1940–1944)* (Berlin: DVW, 1990).

Neumann, Franz, *Behemoth* (London: Gollancz, 1942).

Newell, William H. (ed.), *Japan in Asia* (Singapore: Singapore University Press, 1981).

Nishi, Toshio, *Unconditional Democracy. Education and Politics in Occupied Japan 1945–1952* (Stanford, CA: Hoover Institution Press, 1982).

Noakes, J. and G. Pridham (eds), *Nazism 1919–1945*, vol. 3 (Exeter: Exeter University, 1988).

Nobleman, Eli E., 'American military government courts in Germany', *Annals of the American Academy of Political and Social Science*, 267 (1950), pp. 87–97.

Oh, Bonnie B. C. (ed.), *Korea Under the American Military Government, 1945–1948* (Westport, CT: Praeger, 2002).

Oppenheim, L. 'On war treason', *Law Quarterly Review* 33 (1917), pp. 266–86.

Oppenheim, L., 'The legal relation between an occupying power and the inhabitants', *Law Quarterly Review*, 33 (1917), pp. 363–70.

Oppenheim, L., *International Law*, 7th edn, ed. H. Lauterpacht (London: Longmans, 1952).

Oppenheimer, F. E., 'Governments and authorities in exile', *American Journal of International Law*, 36 (1942), pp. 568–95.

Oppenheimer, Franz, *The State* (New Brunswick, NJ: Transaction, 1999).

Orlow, Dietrich, *The History of the Nazi Party*, vol. 2 (Newton Abbot: David & Charles, 1973).

Osiander, Andreas, *The States System of Europe, 1640–1990* (Oxford: Clarendon Press, 1994).

Oswald, Bruce, 'The law on military occupation: answering the challenges of detention during contemporary peace operations', *Melbourne Journal of International Law*, 8 (2007), pp. 311–26.

Palumbo, Michael, *Imperial Israel* (London: Bloomsbury, 1990).

Pappe, Ilan, *A History of Modern Palestine* (Cambridge: Cambridge University Press, 2006).

Patterson, Melissa, 'Who's got the title? or the remnants of debellatio in post-invasion Iraq', *Harvard International Law Journal*, 47 (2006), pp. 467–88.

Pawley, Margaret, *The Watch on the Rhine* (London: Tauris, 2007).

Pena, Christopher G., *General Butler. Beast or Patriot* (Bloomington, IN: 1st Books, 2003).

Persico, Joseph E., *Nuremberg* (London: Penguin, 1995).

Phillimore, Robert, *Commentaries upon International Law*, vol. 3, part 2 (London: Butterworths, 1885).

Phillips, David L., *Losing Iraq* (Boulder, CO: Westview, 2005).

Philpott, Daniel, *Revolutions in Sovereignty* (Princeton, NJ: Princeton University Press, 2001).

Pictet, Jean S., *Commentary. Fourth Geneva Convention* (Geneva: ICRC, 1958).

Pictet, Jean S., *Commentary: Third Geneva Convention* (Geneva: ICRC, 1960).

Playfair, Emma (ed.), *International Law and the Administration of Occupied Territories* (Oxford: Clarendon Press, 1992).

Prowe, Diethelm, 'Economic democracy in post-World War II Germany', *Journal of Modern History*, 57 (1985), pp. 451–82.

Radbruch, Gustav, 'Gesetzliches Unrecht und übergesetzliches Recht', in Gustav Radbruch, *Gesamtausgabe*, vol. 3 (Heidelberg: Müller, [1946] 1990), p. 89.

Randolph, Carman F., 'Some observations on the status of Cuba', *Yale Law Journal*, 9 (1900), pp. 353–64.

Rathmell, Andrew, 'Planning post-conflict reconstruction in Iraq', *International Afffairs*, 81 (2005), pp. 1013–38.

Ratner, Stephen R., 'Foreign occupation and international territorial administration: the challenges of convergence', *European Journal of International Law*, 16 (2005), pp. 695–719.

Reisman, W. Michael, 'Why regime change is (almost always) a bad idea', *American Journal of International Law*, 98 (2004), pp. 516–25.

Review of the Civil Administration of Mesopotamia, Cmd. 1061 (London: HMSO, 1920).

Reynolds, B. T., 'A review of the occupation of the Rhineland', *Journal of the Royal Institute of International Affairs*, 7 (1928), pp. 198–211.

Roberts, Adam, 'What is a military occupation?', *British Yearbook of International Law* 55 (1984), pp. 249–305.

Roberts, Adam, 'Prolonged military occupation', *American Journal of International Law*, 84 (1990), pp. 44–103.

Roberts, Adam, 'The end of occupation: Iraq 2004', *International and Comparative Law Quarterly*, 54 (2005), pp. 27–48.

Roberts, Adam, 'Transformative military occupation', *American Journal of International Law*, 100 (2006), pp. 580–622.

Robin, Raymond, *Des Occupations Militaries en Dehors des Occupation de Guerre* (Washington, DC: Carnegie, 1942).

Ropew, Michael (ed.), *Collaboration and Resistance in Napoleonic Europe* (Houndmills: Palgrave Macmillan, 2003).

Rougier, Antoine, 'La theorie de l'intervention humanitaire', *Revue Générale de Droit International Public*, 17 (1910), pp. 468–526.

Rowe, Michael, *From Reich to State. The Rhineland in the Revolutionary Age, 1780–1830* (Cambridge: Cambridge University Press, 2003).

Ruffert, Matthias, 'The administration of Kosovo and East Timor by the International Community', *International and Comparative Law Quarterly*, 50 (2001), pp. 613–31.

Sarantakes, Nicholas Evan, *Keystone. The American Occupation of Okinawa and U.S-Japanese Relations* (College Station, TX: Texas A&M University Press, 2000).

Sassòli, Marco, 'Legislation and maintenance of public order and civil life by occupying powers', *European Journal of International Law*, 16 (2005), pp. 661–94.

Saunders, Myra K., 'California legal history', *Law Library Journal*, 88 (1996), pp. 488–522.

Scheuermann, Leslie, 'Victor's justice? The lessons of Nuremberg applied to the trial of Saddam Hussein', *Tulane Journal of International and Comparative Law*, 15 (2006), pp. 291–310.

Schleicher, David, 'Liberal international law theory and the United Nations mission in Kosovo', *Tulane Journal of International and Comparative Law*, 14 (2005), pp. 179–236.

Schmidt, Hans, *The United States Occupation of Haiti 1915–1934* (New Brunswick, NJ: Rutgers University Press, 1995).

Schmitt, Carl, *The Nomos of the Earth* (New York, NY: Telos, 2003).

Schnaubelt, Christopher M., 'After the fight: interagency operations', *Parameters*, 20 (2005–6), pp. 47–61.

Schorske, Carl E., 'The dilemma in Germany', *Virginia Quarterly Review*, 24 (1948), pp. 29–42.

Schwartz, Thomas Alan, *America's Germany. John J. McCloy and the Federal Republic of Germany* (Cambridge, MA: Harvard University Press, 1991).

Schwarz, Rolf and Oliver Jütersonke, 'Divisible sovereignty and the reconstruction of Iraq', *Third World Quarterly*, 26 (2005), pp. 649–65.

Schwenk, Edmund, 'Legislative power of the military occupant under Article 43, Hague Regulations', *Yale Law Journal*, 54 (1944–5), pp. 393–416.

Shamgar, Meir (ed.), *Military Government in the Territories Administered by Israel 1967–1980* (Jerusalem: Hebrew University Press, 1982).

Shamgar, Meir, 'The observance of international law in the administered territories', *Israel Yearbook on Human Rights*, 1 (1972), pp. 262–77.

Shamir, Ronen, '"Landmark cases" and the reproduction of legitimacy: the case of Israel's High Court of Justice', *Law & Society Review*, 24 (1990), pp. 781–806.

Shehadah, Raja, *Occupier's Law. Israel and the West Bank* (Washington, DC: Institute of Palestine Studies, 1988).

Shklar, Judith N., *Legalism* (Cambridge, MA: Harvard University Press, 1964).

Skubiszewski, Krzysztof, 'Administration of territory and sovereignty', *Archiv des Völkerrechts*, 23 (1985), pp. 31–41.

Smith, Justin H., 'American rule in Mexico', *American Historical Review*, 23 (1918), pp. 287–302.

Spaight, J. M., *War Rights on Land* (London: Macmillan, 1911).

Stewart, Rory, *My Time Governing in Iraq* (London: Picador, 2006).

Stirk, Peter, *Carl Schmitt, Crown Jurist of the Third Reich* (Lampeter: Mellen, 2005).

Stone, Julius, *Israel and Palestine* (Baltimore, MD: Johns Hopkins University Press, 1981).

Strohmeyer, Hansjorg, 'Collapse and reconstruction of a judicial system', *American Journal of International Law*, 95 (2001), pp. 46–63.

Strupp, Karl, 'Das Waffenstillstandabkommen zwischen Deutschland und der Entente vom 11 November 1918 im Lichte des Völkerrechts', *Zeitschrift für Völkerrecht*, 11 (1920), pp. 252–81.

Sumner, B. H., *Russia and the Balkans 1870–1880* (Oxford: Clarendon Press, 1937).

Surridge, Keith Terrance, *Managing the South African War 1899–1902* (Woodbridge: Boydell Press, 1998).

Synnott, Hilary, *Bad Days in Basra* (London: Tauris, 2008).

Tadlock, Robert D., 'Occupation law and foreign investment in Iraq', *University of San Francisco Law Review*, 39 (2004), pp. 227–60.

Takemae, Eiji, *Remaking Japan* (New York, NY: Continuum, 2002).

Tarling, Nicholas, *A Sudden Rampage* (London: Hurst, 2001).

The Proceedings of the Hague Peace Conferences. The Conference of 1899 (New York, NY: Oxford University Press, 1920).

Thomas, David Yancy, *A History of the Government in Newly Acquired Territory of the United States* (Honolulu, HI: University Press of the Pacific, 2002).

Tignor, Robert L., *Modernization and British Colonial Rule in Egypt, 1881–1914* (Princeton, NJ: Princeton University Press, 1966).

Tone, John Lawrence, *The Fatal Knot* (Chapel Hill, NC: University of North Carolina Press, 1994).

Tripp, Charles, 'The United States and state-building in Iraq', *Review of International Studies*, 30 (2004), pp. 545–58.

Turner, Ian D. (ed.), *Reconstruction in Post-War Germany* (Oxford: Berg, 1989).

UK Ministry of Defence, *The Manual of the Law of Armed Conflict* (Oxford: Oxford University Press, 2004).

Umbreit, Hans, 'Towards continental domination', in Militärgeschichtliche Forschungsamt (ed.), *Germany and the Second World War*, vol. 5, part 2 (Oxford: Clarendon Press, 2000), pp. 5–292.

Verzil, J. H. W., *International Law in Historical Perspective*, part IX-A (Alphen aan den Rijn: Sijthoff & Noordhoff, 1978).

Vincent, R. J., *Nonintervention and International Order* (Princeton, NJ: Princeton University Press, 1974).

Vité, Sylvain, 'L'applicabilité du droit international de l'occupation militaire aux activités des organisations internationales', *International Review of the Red Cross*, 853 (2004), pp. 9–35.

Vogt, Timothy R., *Denazification in Soviet-Occupied Germany* (Cambridge, MA: Harvard University Press, 2000).

von Heeren, Arnold Hermann Ludwig, *A Manual of the History of the Political System of Europe* (London: Bohn, 1873).

von Köhler, Ludwig, *The Administration of the Occupied Territories*, vol. 1, Belgium (Washington, DC: Carnegie, 1942).

Waltz, Kenneth N., *Man, the State and War* (New York, NY: Columbia University Press, 1959).

Walzer, Michael, *Just and Unjust Wars* (Harmondsworth: Penguin, 1980).

Walzer, Michael, *Arguing About War* (New Haven, CT: Yale University Press, 2004).

Ward, Robert E. and Sakamoto Yoshikazu (eds), *Democratizing Japan* (Honolulu, HI: University of Hawaii Press, 1987).

Warmbrunn, Werner, *The Dutch under German Occupation 1940–1945* (Stanford, CA: Stanford University Press, 1963).

Warmbrunn, Werner, *The German Occupation of Belgium 1940–1944* (New York, NY: Lang, 1993).

War Department, *Military Government and Civil Affairs*, FM 27-5 (22 December 1943).

War Department, *Rules of Land Warfare* (Washington, DC: War Department, 1917).

War Office, *Manual of Military Law* (London, HMSO, 1914).

Watts, G. Tracey, 'The British military occupation of Cyrenaica, 1942–1949', *Transactions of the Grotius Society*, 37 (1951), pp. 69–81.

Wellesley, A. R. (ed.), *Supplementary Despatches, Correspondence and Memoranda of Field Marshall Arthur Duke of Wellington*, vol. 9 (London: Murray, 1862).

Westlake, John, *International Law. Part II. War* (Cambridge: Cambridge University Press, 1907).

Wheaton, Henry, *Elements of International Law* (Oxford: Clarendon Press, 1936).

Wilde, Ralph, 'From Danzig to East Timor and beyond', *American Journal of International Law*, 95 (2001), pp. 583–606.

Williams, Justin, *Japan's Political Revolution under MacArthur* (Athens, GA: University of Georgia Press, 1979).

Williamson, John C., 'Establishing the rule of law in post-war Iraq', *Georgia Journal of International and Comparative Law*, 33 (2004), pp. 229–44.

Winthrop, William, *Military Law and Precedents* (Washington, DC: War Department, 1920).

Woetzel, Robert K., *The Nuremberg Trials in International Law* (London: Stevens & Sons, 1962).

Wolfe, Robert (ed.), *Americans as Proconsuls* (Carbondale, IL: Southern Illinois University Press, 1984).

Woolf, Stuart, *Napoleon's Integration of Europe* (London: Routledge, 1991).

Wouters, Nico, 'Municipal government during the occupation (1940–5)', *European History Quarterly*, 36 (2006), pp. 221–46.

Wurfel, Seymour, 'Military government – the Supreme Court speaks', *North Carolina Law Review*, 40 (1962), pp. 717–87.

Yannis, Alexandros, 'The concept of suspended sovereignty in international law and its implications in international politics', *European Journal of International Law*, 13 (2002), pp. 1037–52.

Yoo, John, 'Iraq reconstruction and the law of occupation', *University College Davis Journal of International Law and Policy*, 11 (2004), pp. 7–21.

Zaum, Dominick, 'The authority of international administrations in international society', *Review of International Studies*, 32 (2006), pp. 455–73.

Ziemke, Earl F., *The U.S. Army in the Occupation of Germany 1944–1946* (Honolulu, HI: University Press of the Pacific, 1975).

Index